COOKING
WILD

MORE THAN

150 RECIPES FOR EATING

CLOSE TO NATURE

CHEF JOHN ASH

and James O. Fraioli

PHOTOGRAPHY BY
Tucker + Hossler

Running Press
PHILADELPHIA · LONDON

Published by Running Press,
A Member of the Perseus Books Group

All rights reserved under the Pan-American and
International Copyright Conventions

Printed in China

Books published by Running Press are available at special
discounts for bulk purchases in the United States by cor-
porations, institutions, and other organizations. For more
information, please contact the Special Markets Department at the Perseus Books Group, 2300 Chestnut Street,
Suite 200, Philadelphia, PA 19103, or call (800) 810-4145,
ext. 5000, or e-mail special.markets@perseusbooks.com.

ISBN 978-0-7624-5794-6

Library of Congress Control Number: 2015954457
E-book ISBN 978-0-7624-5828-8

9 8 7 6 5 4 3 2 1
Digit on the right indicates the number of this printing

Designed by Frances J. Soo Ping Chow
Edited by Kristen Green Wiewora
Food Stylist: Valerie Aikman-Smith
Photography Credit: p. 31 © Thinkstockphotos
Typography: Brandon, Chronicle TX, Duke,
Harman, and Whiskey Font

Running Press Book Publishers
2300 Chestnut Street
Philadelphia, PA 19103-4371

Visit us on the web!
www.offthemenublog.com

A DISCLAIMER

CONTENTS

Acknowledgments

The authors would like to personally thank the following individuals for their generous support and assistance with this book:

•••••••••••••••

Kristen Green Wiewora and the editorial team at Running Press; **Andrea Hurst & Associates, Literary Management**; mushroom forager **Dean Robbins**; food writer **Jeff Cox**; Broken Arrow Ranch owner **Chris Hughes**; commercial fisherman **Jason Chin**; Lumière restaurant owner **Michael Leviton**; and **Tucker + Hossler** for their extraordinary food photography.

INTRODUCTION

⋯⋯⋯●⋯⋯⋯

*Wild is about Nature going about its own business
without much human intervention.*
—Poet and environmentalist Gary Snyder

My grandmother taught me how to forage wild plants such as lamb's-quarter (also known as goosefoot or pigweed), wild asparagus, purslane, and huckleberries, and to catch trout with my hands. Books by two notable wild foragers gave me more education: Billy Joe Tatum's *Wild Foods Field Guide and Cookbook* and Euell Gibbons's three books *Stalking the Wild Asparagus*, *Stalking the Blue-Eyed Scallop*, and *Stalking the Healthful Herbs*. Another book that has been a useful resource for me over the years is the *L. L. Bean Game & Fish Cookbook* by Angus Cameron and Judith Jones. *The Forager's Harvest and Nature's Garden*, both by Samuel Thayer, should also be part of your library since they do such a good job of describing wild edible plants.

There are many reasons to seek out wild foods. An important one is the difference between foods found in the wild and their cultivated versions.

PLANTS

Humans may have started farming plants twelve thousand or more years ago. Gradually we discovered that we could make plants more attractive and edible through variety selection and cross-pollination. Unfortunately, in our zeal to produce the "best" fruits and vegetables, we've concentrated on just a few varieties and have lost many others and the gene pools that they represent. Agricultural practices such as monocropping, which places a premium on volume and ease of production, have also affected the kinds of fruits and vegetables we produce. And of course many kinds of produce have been engineered for ease of shipping and appearance rather than taste.

It's important today to identify and preserve wild foods, for they represent a biodiversity that can help us maintain our food supply and feed our rapidly growing population. Michael Pollan's cautionary story about potatoes in *The Botany of Desire* is a good example. In Ireland in the 1840s, a blight attacked the potato crop, causing the starvation of over one million people. Potatoes were the main food crop at that time, and the blight that attacked them was the result of planting a single potato variety, the Irish lumper. It was suited for Ireland's poor, soggy soil, but it was not disease resistant. In contrast, potato varieties in the Andes, where potatoes were first domesticated, numbered in the thousands. Because many varieties were grown at the same time, crops were able to survive a wide range of environmental stresses and avoid catastrophic failure. In fact, it was because of disease-resistant varieties found in the diverse Andean gene pool that Ireland was able to rebound from this disaster.

MEAT AND POULTRY

In the early days of this country, most of the protein on our dining room tables came from wild sources. We were a nation of hunters, subsisting on deer, wild turkeys and ducks, rabbits, and other creatures. In the mid-1800s, buffalo covered the plains of the Midwest and were the primary meat for both the native and the expanding settler populations. This all changed by the early 1900s when domesticated animals became the norm. As with produce, specific traits were selected and husbandry practices were followed that allowed animals to grow faster and larger and be ready for market sooner, all in the interest of making the biggest possible profit. But this change in animal husbandry depended on unnatural diets—such as grain instead of grass for beef—and often the physically harmful confinement of animals, not to mention the intensive use of antibiotics. The emphasis today on natural diets and allowing animals to range more freely results in healthier animals and arguably better-tasting meat and poultry.

SEAFOOD

Seafood is the last of the truly wild organisms on earth. As the Seafood Watch initiative of the Monterey Bay Aquarium shows us, many fish populations are under severe stress from overfishing, and the oceans themselves are in peril. Already, 50 percent of our seafood is farmed. In a generation or two, truly wild seafood may be a luxury food for the most part.

The answer is not for us to all become wild foragers. Rather we need to learn about the natural history of our foods and how we can choose produce and sources of protein that have been harmed least by commercial agriculture. Doing so will not just let us eat more healthfully and protect our planet but also allow us to live more closely to nature and its creatures. As early as 1990, Wendell Berry was writing about the importance of eating locally, which is today one of the mainstays of the sustainable-food movement. Here is a quote from his essay "The Pleasures of Eating": "Learn the origins of the food you buy, and buy the food that is produced closest to your home. The idea that every locality should be, as much as possible, the source of its own food makes several kinds of sense. The locally produced food supply is the most secure, the freshest, and the easiest for local consumers to know about and to influence."

Supporting your local farmers by signing up for a Community-Supported Agriculture food basket and patronizing farmers' markets, grocery stores, and restaurants that sell and prepare locally grown food are great ways to eat locally. Growing your own vegetables and fruits, especially if you choose heirloom and native varieties, is another way. And knowing which wild foods grow in your area and can be sustainably foraged is another. This book is dedicated to raising awareness of wild foods and how to find and prepare them, so that we never lose sight of and appreciation for our native-food heritage and the importance of preserving it.

WILD PLANTS AND HERBS

CATTAILS

A MEMBER OF THE GRASS FAMILY, THE COMMON CATTAIL (*TYPHA LATIFOLIA*) IS found in watery places throughout North America and most of the world. Survivalists will tell you there is no more useful plant than the cattail, for it provides both food and medicine. The corms, spikes, and roots of this generous plant can be eaten as food, while the roots can be turned into poultices, and the leaves can be burned and the ash used as an antiseptic. In Euell Gibbons's *Stalking the Wild Asparagus*, his chapter on cattails is titled "Supermarket of the Swamp" for good reason.

Cattail roots, or corms, can be dug up in early spring to peel and eat raw or cooked. Cattails have both female spikes, which bloom in the spring (and later turn into brown cattail heads), and male spikes, which form pollen. To harvest them, just peel back the leaves and look for them in the center of the plant. These spikes can be cooked in a variety of ways (boiling, braising, sautéing) or eaten raw.

Later in the season, the male spike will develop yellow pollen; to harvest this, simply shake the spike over a container. You can harvest so much pollen from cattails that you can use it in place of wheat flour (like wheat flour, it contains gluten) to make pancakes or cornbread; you can also use it to supplement wheat flour in recipes for baked goods and as a thickener for sauces. From fall through winter, you can harvest the root starch by digging up the roots. They should be rinsed, peeled, and then broken up under water, which will make the starch separate from the fibers. Lift off the fibers, pour off the excess water, and dry the starch mixture in the sun.

CATTAIL POLLEN PANCAKES

This recipe comes from food writer Jeff Cox. It uses one cup of cattail pollen, which is easily harvested from male cattail spikes that emerge from within the cattail's early leaves in spring. In fact, you can collect several cups of the pollen in about half an hour from a thick stand of the plants. Jeff says to first make sure that the water the cattails are growing in is clean; then look for the spikes and shake off the pollen into a paper bag. He describes these pancakes as both tasty and beautiful, thanks to the cattail's very fine pollen that turns the pancakes a lovely bright yellow orange.

Makes 6 to 8 pancakes

1 cup all-purpose or pastry flour

1 cup cattail pollen

2 teaspoons baking powder

½ teaspoon sea salt

¼ cup (½ stick) unsalted butter,
    plus more for serving

¼ cup vegetable oil, plus more for greasing

1 large egg

¼ cup honey

2 cups milk, buttermilk, or kefir

Warmed maple syrup or honey,
    for serving

In a large bowl, whisk together the flour, cattail pollen, baking powder, and salt.

In a small saucepan, melt the ¼ cup butter with the vegetable oil over low heat and stir.

Add the egg, honey, and the butter mixture to the dry ingredients, then add the milk and stir until combined. Don't beat until smooth. Some lumps are okay. If the batter seems too thick, add milk as needed.

Heat a lightly oiled large skillet over medium-low to medium heat. Drop ¼-cup portions of the batter into skillet and cook, turning once, until golden brown on both sides, about 2 minutes on each side. Serve the pancakes with butter and warmed maple syrup or honey.

CATTAIL AND LENTIL DAL

The word dal refers both to a hulled pulse, such as the lentil, and the finished dish made with the pulse.
Dal is one of the most important food preparations in India. Because much of India
is vegetarian, lentils are a vital source of protein.

Serves 4

1½ cups vegetable or chicken stock

1 cup brown lentils, picked over and rinsed

1 cup well-stirred coconut milk

2 tablespoons unsalted butter

2 tablespoons vegetable oil

1¼ cups thinly sliced cattail shoots

2 tablespoons finely chopped shallot

1 tablespoon lemon zest

1 tablespoon Madras curry powder,
  or more to taste

Large pinch of sea salt

Freshly ground black pepper

Chopped fresh cilantro leaves

In a medium saucepan, combine the stock and lentils and bring to a boil over medium-high heat. Reduce the heat to a simmer. Cover and cook, stirring occasionally, until the lentils are just tender, 20 to 30 minutes. Add coconut milk and more stock as necessary to keep them a little soupy.

In a medium skillet, melt the butter with the oil over medium heat and stir. Add the cattail shoots and shallot and cook, stirring frequently, until soft and fragrant, 3 to 5 minutes. Stir in the lemon zest and curry powder; cook and stir for another minute or so. Stir in the salt, season with pepper to taste, add cilantro leaves, as desired, and remove from the heat. Adjust seasonings to taste. Serve hot.

CHILTEPÍN CHILES

THE CHILTEPÍN CHILE (*CAPSICUM ANNUUM VAR. GLABRIUSCULUM*) IS KNOWN AS "THE mother of all peppers." Pronounced "ch-ill-teh-pin," it's called *chile tepín* in Spanish and is commonly known as bird's eye chile, because birds like to eat them. Birds can do this because they lack the chemoreceptors that make the heat-producing capsaicin compound in chiles so irritating to us humans; thus, birds are adept at dispersing chiltepín seeds.

The chiltepín (the origin of the name is probably Aztec) is thought to be the only wild chile plant that grows in the United States, and in fact, it might be the original wild chile from which all others evolved. It is found mainly in Texas, Arizona, and northern Mexico—in fewer than fifteen known localities—and is protected in the Coronado National Forest, Big Bend National Park, and Organ Pipe Cactus National Monument.

The chiltepín has very small round fruits that are larger than a peppercorn but smaller than a pea. These fruits are bright red or green in color and grow on bushes that reach about four feet tall and grow in rugged terrain. This makes finding them a challenge, which is good, as sustainable harvesting is important for keeping this chile in the food chain. Harvesting this chile is a tradition in the early fall for some Native American communities.

The chiltepín is extremely hot, which means it ranks way up there on the Scoville scale: about fifty thousand to one-hundred thousand Scoville units, or an eight on a scale of one to ten. This chile, which has a smoky, pungent flavor, is eaten both fresh and dried. It's used as a flavoring for cheese and a base for sauces; it's also made into a condiment with the addition of tomatoes, wild oregano, garlic, and salt. In Mexico, especially in Sonora, chiltepín chiles are often mixed with beef or venison to make *carne machaca* (see the following recipe). If you are a gardener, you can get seeds from Native Seed Search in Tucson, Arizona, which is a wonderful resource for information and for wild plants and seeds native to the Southwest (www.nativeseeds.org).

MACHACADO DE RANCHERO

(Beef Jerky, Ranch Style)

There are many variations of this iconic Sonoran dish. Some braise fresh beef or venison with lots of tomatoes, chiles, onions, and garlic, and when it's done, shred the meat for tacos and enchiladas and to serve with eggs. This recipe is an old one, given to me by Gloria Diaz, a restaurant employee from many years ago, that uses dried beef, which you can sometimes find at Latino markets.

Serves 6

6 ripe plum tomatoes

2 fresh poblano chiles

2 teaspoons cumin seeds

1 teaspoon fennel seeds

4 allspice berries

2 teaspoons crushed dried chiltepín chiles, or more to taste

1½ pounds plain beef jerky

¼ cup pure rendered lard or vegetable shortening

2 cups chopped white onions

2 tablespoons finely chopped garlic

1 to 2 tablespoons masa harina

1 to 2 tablespoons beef stock or water, if needed

Sea salt

Preheat the broiler.

On a rimmed baking sheet, spread the tomatoes and poblano chiles in a single layer. Broil, turning frequently until lightly blackened on all sides. While still hot, transfer to a large resealable plastic bag or paper sack and seal. Allow the tomatoes and poblanos to cool for about 15 minutes. The steam will help loosen the charred skin. Peel off as much of the blackened skin as you can. Don't worry if a little remains. Add the peeled vegetables to a food processor, along with any juices.

In a small, dry skillet, toast the cumin, fennel, and allspice over medium heat, stirring, until fragrant but not burned, about 2 minutes. Grind finely in a mortar with a pestle or in a spice grinder, and add to the tomato mixture along with the chiltepín chiles. Process until the mixture is just combined; remove to a bowl and set aside.

With a meat pounder or the bottom of a heavy pot, pound the beef until the meat is flattened and the fibers and connective tissues are broken down. You'll know it is breaking down because the meat will soften and feel tender. Add to the food processor and pulse until coarsely chopped.

In a deep, heavy saucepan, melt the lard over medium heat. Add the meat and cook until golden brown, about 10 minutes. Add the onions, garlic, masa harina, and the reserved tomato mixture and bring to a simmer. If needed, add a bit of the stock to make a thick sauce. Simmer until the onions are soft, about 10 minutes, and season to taste with salt. Serve hot.

AGUA CHILTEPÍN

(Chile Water)

This simple recipe from Sinaloa uses ripened fresh chiltepín chiles to make a spicy condiment often found on restaurant tables in Mexico. The red chiltepín variety offers the most pungency. Dried Mexican oregano is available at Mexican markets.

Makes about ½ cup

2 ripened fresh red chiltepín chiles, crushed, or more to taste

1 small garlic clove, finely chopped

½ tomato

Pinch of dried Mexican oregano

Sea salt

Boiling chicken stock or water, as needed

In a small bowl, stir together the chiles, garlic, tomato, oregano, and salt to taste. Add the boiling chicken stock to just cover the ingredients and reach the desired consistency, then mash everything together with a large spoon.

CHILTEPÍN FLAN

Some Mexican flans are flavored with chiles, adding their spicy heat to a sweet dessert.
You could add a little chile to the egg mixture, as I've done here, or
simply sprinkle the chile flakes on top of the finished flan.

Serves 6

1 cup granulated sugar

1 (14-ounce) can sweetened condensed milk

1½ cups whole milk, at room temperature

3 large eggs, at room temperature

2 dried chiltepín chiles, finely crushed,
  or more to taste

2 teaspoons vanilla extract

¼ teaspoon salt

Adjust the oven rack to the middle position and preheat the oven to 325°F. Place a clean kitchen towel in a roasting pan and set a 9-inch round baking pan on top of the towel. Bring a teakettle of water to a boil.

In a medium, heavy saucepan, combine the sugar and ¼ cup water. Cook over medium-high heat without stirring until the sugar is dissolved. Wet a clean pastry brush and brush down any sugar crystals from the sides of the pan to keep the sugar from crystallizing. Boil, swirling the pan occasionally, until the sugar turns deep amber, 10 to 12 minutes. Immediately pour the caramel into the baking pan and swirl to coat the bottom. Allow it to set and harden.

Add the condensed milk, milk, eggs, chiles, vanilla extract, and salt to a blender and blend until thoroughly combined, about 1 minute. Alternatively, in a large bowl, whisk together the ingredients by hand. Pour the flan mixture over the set caramel in the baking pan.

Place the baking pan in the roasting pan and transfer to the oven. Carefully pour the hot water into the roasting pan to halfway up the sides of the baking pan. Bake until the flan is set but still a bit wobbly in the center, about 1 hour.

Remove the baking pan from the roasting pan and let cool on a wire rack for about 15 minutes. Refrigerate for at least 2 hours to chill completely. To serve, run a knife along the flan edges and invert onto a large serving plate. Cut into portions.

DANDELIONS

THE DANDELION (*TARAXACUM OFFICINALE*) IS PROBABLY THE MOST RECOGNIZED PLANT in North America. The name comes from the French *dent de lion*, or "lion's tooth," because of the saw-toothed edges of the leaves. Early settlers looked forward to dandelions because they were usually the first greens of spring, and because they provide a useful tonic for the digestive system and the liver. (Dandelions and other wild spring greens were thought to thin the blood made heavy and sluggish by winter inactivity.) My grandmother ate all parts of the dandelion for her rheumatism. The milky sap of a mature plant is believed to be useful for treating warts. But this "weed" is also highly nutritious, with twice the calcium of spinach and many more antioxidants.

The common complaint about dandelion greens is that they are very bitter. However, as we have learned to enjoy bitter greens in North America, their place on our table has grown. Dandelions are popular around the world, and there are hundreds of traditional dishes that utilize them. Although despised by gardeners, the dandelion has potential health benefits that should encourage you to try them occasionally. All parts of the dandelion are edible, including the flowers and roots. Just remember that the leaves are best when young, in the early spring, at which time they aren't so bitter. Like arugula, they add a sharp, spicy taste to salads and stir-fries. The roots can be rinsed and chopped to steam or stir-fry, and they can also be roasted to make an interesting caffeine-free coffee substitute. The flowers are used to make wine and are pretty added to salads.

WARM DANDELION SALAD

This is an old-fashioned wilted salad made with bacon and bacon fat that utilizes the notorious weed. Be sure to use only young and tender dandelion leaves, as older leaves can be tough and very bitter. For variety, you could add chopped oil-cured olives or capers to the salad.

Serves 4 to 6

6 cups tender dandelion leaves, stemmed

2 large hard-cooked eggs

¼ cup freshly squeezed lemon juice

1 tablespoon honey, or more to taste

2 teaspoons Dijon mustard

⅓ cup olive oil

Salt and freshly ground black pepper

Chicken or vegetable stock, as needed

2 teaspoons finely chopped fresh chives

4 ounces thick-cut bacon, diced

2 tablespoons white wine vinegar or champagne vinegar

Dandelion flower head or petals for garnish (optional)

Pat or spin the dandelion leaves dry, then refrigerate them.

Remove the yolks from the eggs and mash the yolks in a bowl with the lemon juice, honey, and mustard. Gradually whisk in the oil until a smooth dressing is formed. Season to taste with salt and pepper; thin, if necessary, with a little stock, and stir in the chives. Set aside until ready to serve.

Finely dice the egg whites and set aside. In a medium sauté pan, brown the bacon over medium heat until crisp. Transfer to paper towels to drain. Discard all but 2 teaspoons of the bacon fat.

When ready to serve, reheat the bacon fat over medium heat and add the vinegar. Deglaze the pan, scraping the bottom to incorporate any browned bits. Quickly toss the greens with the mustard dressing, then add to the pan to very briefly coat with the vinegar mixture. Divide among plates and top with the diced egg whites. Crumble the reserved bacon over the salads and garnish with the flowers if you wish. Serve immediately.

CREAMED DANDELION GREENS

In this twist on classic creamed spinach, the bitterness of dandelion greens
is balanced by the cream and cheese.

Serves 4 to 6

1 tablespoon olive oil, plus more as needed

1½ cups (12 ounces) tender dandelion leaves, stemmed

2 tablespoons unsalted butter

½ cup chopped leek (white part only)

1 teaspoon finely chopped garlic

3 tablespoons dry white vermouth

⅔ cup heavy whipping cream

Salt and freshly ground black pepper

¼ cup freshly grated Parmigiano-Reggiano cheese

In a large skillet, heat the oil over medium heat and sauté the dandelion greens until just wilted. (Sauté in batches if necessary, using a little more oil.) Transfer to a cutting board (reserve the pan), let cool, and coarsely chop the greens.

In the same pan, melt the butter over medium heat and sauté the leek until translucent but not browned, about 5 minutes. Add the garlic and sauté for another minute or two. Add the vermouth and cook until it's nearly evaporated. Stir in the cream and season with salt and pepper to taste; simmer until thickened, about 3 minutes. Stir in the greens and cheese; heat through. Serve hot.

EDIBLE WILDFLOWERS

LOOK FORWARD TO SPRING WHEN APPLE BLOSSOMS BLOOM, DANDELIONS SPROUT, AND violets peek out along the edges of the forest. Many spring wildflowers are not only beautiful as garnishes, but they taste good and pack lots of nutrition.

Remember that not all wildflowers are safe to eat. In her book *Edible Flowers* (which I contributed to), Cathy Wilkinson Barash offers some important tips about edible flowers. She cautions: "Eat flowers only when you are positive they are edible. Not all flowers are edible, some are poisonous. Do not eat flowers from florists, nurseries or garden centers as they may have been sprayed or otherwise adulterated. If you have hay fever, asthma or allergies, do not eat flowers."

Here's a good list of edible wildflowers:

Alfalfa
Apple blossoms
Bear's garlic
Borage
Broadleaf plantain
Burdock
Cattail
Celandine
Chickweed
Chicory
Coltsfoot
Common daisy
Creeping Charlie
  (also known as ground ivy)
Dandelion

Dead nettle
Echinacea
Elderflower
Garlic mustard
Goldenrod
Henbit
Herb Robert
Honeysuckle
Horsetail
Joe-pye weed
Johnny-jump-up
Milk thistle
Mullein
Nasturtium
Oxeye daisy

Prickly pear cactus
Queen Anne's lace
Redbud tree buds
Red clover
Rue
St. John's wort
Sweet woodruff
Violet
Wild rose
Wood sorrel
Yarrow
Yellow dock
Yellow rocket
Yucca

WILDFLOWER VINEGAR

This is really easy to make. All you need is a jar, some vinegar, one or more of your favorite flowers, and a vanilla bean. In a month or so, you'll have a seductive scented vinegar to use in vinaigrettes and other sauces. This recipe uses wild roses.

Makes 1 quart

2 cups loosely packed wild roses
(20 to 25 heads)

4 cups white wine vinegar or champagne
vinegar (do not use distilled vinegar)

½ vanilla bean, halved lengthwise

Rinse the flowers and remove any insects. Put the flowers in a sterilized jar and fill with the vinegar. Store covered in a cool, dark place for at least 1 month before using. Strain out the flowers and vanilla bean. Will keep for a year or more in a cool, dark place.

CRYSTALLIZED WILDFLOWERS

Flowers are best eaten immediately after picking. Another lovely way of using flowers is to crystallize them. They make delightful decorations for cakes, tarts, and custards.

For this, you'll need a small, clean, fine-bristled brush. Note that raw egg white is used to make these flowers; pregnant women or anyone with a compromised immune system should not eat these flowers. Use pasteurized egg whites if you can find them.

1 large egg white

Edible flowers (such as borage flowers,
chive flowers, violets, roses, pineapple sage,
nasturtiums, rosemary, lavender,
and dianthus)

Superfine sugar, for dusting

Line a wire rack with parchment or waxed paper.

In a small bowl, whisk the egg white with ½ teaspoon cold water until just foamy. Holding a flower by the stem or stem end in one hand, and your paintbrush in the other hand, gently brush the flower all over with the egg white mixture (be certain to lightly coat every part of each flower or the uncoated part will wilt and wither). Carefully sprinkle the sugar evenly over all sides of the flower. Place on the prepared rack and repeat with the remaining flowers.

Set the flowers aside in a cool, dry place for 12 to 36 hours, or until dried. Store the flowers in a single layer in an airtight container. They will keep for several months.

FIDDLEHEAD FERNS

FIDDLEHEADS ARE AN EARLY SPRING DELICACY WITH A VERY SHORT SEASON. SO called because they resemble the curved head of a violin, fiddleheads are the young coiled fronds of the fiddlehead fern (*Matteuccia struthiopteris*), also called ostrich fern or shuttlecock fern. Fiddlehead ferns have a papery brown covering and a smooth stem, with a U-shaped indentation on the inside of the stem. Be sure you're harvesting fiddleheads, as not all ferns are edible.

Fiddlehead ferns grow in moist sites like riverbanks in late spring and early summer. They have an intriguing green flavor something like a combination of asparagus, artichokes, and okra. Their distinct taste and firm texture make them a good addition to stir-fries, and they can be cooked and served with cheese or tomato sauce. They should be eaten cooked, not raw, either boiled or steamed before preparing with any other method.

Cooking Fiddleheads

Rinse the fiddleheads in a container of water, rubbing them to remove the brown coating. Refrigerate them in a resealable plastic bag if not cooking them immediately; they can be kept for up to 2 weeks. Fiddleheads must be cooked before eating and before using in recipes that cook them further by additional methods, such as braising or sautéing; precooking them removes some of their bitterness. To cook them, boil in lightly salted water to cover until tender, 2 to 3 minutes; or steam them for 3 or 4 minutes if you prefer crispier fiddleheads with a more pronounced flavor. If not using immediately, let them cool and then refrigerate in a resealable plastic bag.

I think fiddleheads are best served simply with olive oil or melted butter and a splash of lemon juice or vinegar. Cooked and chilled, they are a wonderful addition to salads.

PICKLED FIDDLEHEADS

Try these pickled fiddleheads as an accompaniment to smoked meats and cheeses.
Or use one in place of an olive for a woodsman's martini!

Makes six 1-pint jars

2½ pounds fiddlehead ferns

6 peeled whole garlic cloves

2 tablespoons mustard or dill seeds

4 cups white vinegar

½ cup salt

¼ cup granulated sugar

Trim and rinse the fiddleheads in a container of water, rubbing to remove the brown coating. Sterilize the canning jars, bands, and lids in boiling water. Remove the hot jars one at a time and carefully pack the fiddleheads in each jar, up to ½ inch from the top. Place a garlic clove and 1 teaspoon of the mustard seeds in each jar. In a saucepan, bring the vinegar, salt, sugar, and 4 cups water to a boil, and pour over the fiddleheads.

Wipe the jar rims with a clean towel and cover with lids. Screw on the bands snugly but not too tight and place in simmering water in a canner. The jars should be covered by at least 2 inches of simmering water. Simmer for 10 minutes, following the manufacturer's directions, making sure jars are properly sealed when cool. Will keep for up to 1 year.

SAUTÉED FIDDLEHEAD FERNS

This simple recipe can be eaten as is, but I really like it as a topping for meats
or fish or combined with pasta or rice.

Serves 4

1 pound fiddlehead ferns

Sea salt

2 tablespoons olive oil

½ cup finely diced pancetta

1 tablespoon unsalted butter

1 garlic clove, thinly sliced

Large pinch of red pepper flakes,
plus more to taste

Freshly squeezed lemon juice

Trim and rinse the fiddleheads in a container of water, rubbing to remove the brown coating. In a deep pot, bring 3 quarts of water to a boil and add salt (using enough so the water tastes like the sea). Add the fiddleheads and cook for 2 minutes, then drain, rinse with cold water, and set aside.

In a large skillet, heat the oil over medium heat. Add the pancetta and cook until nicely browned and crispy, about 5 minutes. Using a slotted spoon, transfer to paper towels to drain; reserve the pan.

Pour off all but 1 tablespoon of fat from the pan. Add the butter and garlic; cook until fragrant, about 30 seconds. Add the reserved fiddleheads and sauté until they start to brown, about 3 minutes. Add the red pepper flakes and cooked pancetta. Season to taste with salt, lemon juice, and more red pepper flakes, if desired.

LAMB'S-QUARTER

ALSO KNOWN AS WHITE GOOSEFOOT OR PIGWEED, LAMB'S-QUARTER WAS ONE OF the first plants I remember foraging for as a kid. The plant is part of the *Chenopodium* genus and is related to quinoa, beets, and spinach. Lamb's-quarter has been described as a superfood, high in vitamins A, C, and K, as well as riboflavin, calcium, manganese, and potassium. The best known and most common variety is *C. album*. Lamb's-quarter is found in every part of North America, including the desert and other arid locales. It's easy to identify. In addition to its "goose foot" shape, the plant has a distinctive white powder in the center of the new growth that will rub off on your fingertips. The seeds have the ability to remain dormant for long periods of time, waiting for a bit of moisture to quickly complete their life cycle. The leaves have a flavor very much like spinach, and they can be used in any way that spinach is used. Tender leaves also make wonderful salad greens and are great on sandwiches. Like many other leafy greens, however, they can pick up heavy metals from the soil, so avoid harvesting them around possibly contaminated areas, like construction sites or along busy highways. They grow so abundantly that you should have no trouble finding a clean site.

Rinse lamb's-quarter well; dry in a salad spinner and store in a resealable plastic bag in the refrigerator.

LAMB'S-QUARTER FRITTERS

This is a recipe from Olivia Rathbone, the kitchen manager at the Occidental Arts & Ecology Center in west Sonoma County, California. She says these fritters can be made with any nonbitter wild green, such as amaranth, and she recommends serving them by themselves or with a marinara dipping sauce.

Makes about twenty 1-inch fritters; serves 6

8 to 10 tightly packed cups lamb's-quarter (young shoots or leaves)

6-inch piece day-old baguette, or 2 slices of country bread

2 tablespoons olive oil

1 cup freshly grated Parmigiano-Reggiano cheese

½ cup (1 stick) unsalted butter, melted

3 large eggs

3 garlic cloves, finely crushed through a garlic press

2 teaspoons finely chopped fresh oregano

1 teaspoon finely chopped fresh sage

Pinch of red pepper flakes

Salt and freshly ground black pepper

Fill a large bowl with ice water. Bring a large pot of water to a boil, add the lamb's-quarter and cook for 15 seconds. Using a pair of kitchen tongs, transfer the lamb's-quarter to the ice-water bath to stop the cooking and set the color. Squeeze most of the water out of the lamb's-quarter, chop finely, and set aside. You should have about 2 cups of chopped cooked greens.

Preheat the oven to 400°F.

Slice or tear the bread into pieces and spread on a baking sheet. Drizzle with the oil and sprinkle with salt to taste. Toast in the oven until crisp and dry, about 7 minutes. Let cool. Pulverize in a food processor to make fine breadcrumbs.

In a large bowl, stir together the chopped greens, breadcrumbs, cheese, butter, eggs, garlic, oregano, sage, red pepper flakes, and salt and pepper to taste. With your hands, shape the mixture into 1-inch balls or patties and arrange them on a baking sheet.

(At this point, the fritters can be frozen on a baking sheet and stored in the freezer in a resealable plastic bag.)

Reduce the oven temperature to 350°F and bake until golden brown, about 8 to 12 minutes (bake frozen fitters for 15 to 20 minutes in a preheated oven).

Occidental Arts & Ecology Center

The OAEC is an amazing and beautiful place and should be on everyone's bucket list for a visit or retreat. The organization describes itself as "an eighty-acre research, demonstration, education, advocacy, and community-organizing center that develops strategies for regional-scale community resilience and the restoration of biological and cultural diversity."

OAEC trains and supports "whole communities," including schools, public agencies, Native American tribes, urban social-justice organizations, and watershed groups, in designing and cultivating resilience to mounting ecological, social, and economic challenges.

OAEC also has one of the most abundant gardens I've ever seen, focused on both species and seed saving and the cultivation of forgotten plants of the Americas.

LAMB'S-QUARTER FRITTATA

Fritattas are a great way to showcase fresh greens. You can also substitute or supplement other leafy greens, such as spinach and chard, in this recipe.

Serves 4

6 large eggs

¼ cup freshly grated Parmigiano-Reggiano or Asiago cheese

2 tablespoons heavy whipping cream or milk

2 tablespoons unsalted butter, divided

½ cup (1½ ounces) diced cremini mushrooms

3 strips of thick-cut bacon, finely chopped

½ cup finely chopped green onions (white and green parts)

Kosher salt and freshly ground pepper

3 packed cups lamb's-quarter, stemmed

Preheat the broiler.

In a medium bowl, whisk together the eggs and cream; set aside.

In an ovenproof 12-inch skillet (preferably nonstick), melt 1 tablespoon of the butter over medium heat and sauté the mushrooms until all the moisture has evaporated and the mushrooms are lightly browned; transfer to a plate and set aside. Add the bacon to the pan with the remaining 1 tablespoon butter and sauté until bacon is nearly crisp. Add the green onions and sauté for 1 minute longer; and salt and pepper to taste.

Add the lamb's-quarter and cook until wilted, about 2 minutes. Add the reserved mushrooms and spread the contents evenly across the pan. Pour in the reserved egg mixture and spread it across the pan with a spatula. Cook for a few minutes gently stirring the mixture with the spatula until the egg mixture has begun to set. Transfer the skillet to the oven and broil until the top is lightly browned, 3 to 4 minutes. Serve warm or at room temperature.

MESQUITE

MESQUITE WOOD IS USED FOR FURNITURE AND IS HIGHLY PRIZED AS A FUEL source for grilling. Mesquite honey is a delicious novelty, but the seedpods of this tree were the single most important wild food for native desert peoples prior to World War II, according to ethnobotanist Dr. Gary Paul Nabhan. He notes that, unfortunately, the force of civilization discouraged such wild foods and they dropped out of native diets.

You can find mesquite growing throughout the southwestern United States, as well as from Kansas to Texas and in California and Hawaii. At least six species of mesquite were harvested by American natives, but *Prosopis velutina*, was evidently the most preferred. The young pods were eaten raw or cooked, and the mature ones were ground for flour. An alcoholic beverage was made from the dried pods.

Foragers of mesquite pods will tell you to taste a pod before you do anything with it. If you locate a good tree, the pods will have a sweet, smoky taste that's reminiscent of molasses or chocolate. Every tree isn't always sweet or of good flavor, however. Good trees outnumber the bad, but you must taste the pods to know. As with most plants in nature, terrior—where and how a plant is grown—is important to mesquite trees. Choose dry, brown pods still on the tree that release easily when tugged. Test the pods you've chosen by snapping one in half. They should snap easily. Do not harvest pods that have dropped on the ground, as they can harbor mold or bugs or both.

Whether you grind your own (there are several videos on the Internet to show you how) or buy it online, mesquite flour (also called mesquite meal) is very healthy. In addition to being gluten-free, it is higher in protein than all-purpose flour, and it benefits diabetics by helping to regulate blood sugar.

Mesquite flour is used primarily in baking but, because it lacks gluten, it is typically used in concert with wheat flour in contemporary recipes. Try substituting 25 percent mesquite flour for regular flour.

MESQUITE CHOCOLATE CHIP COOKIES

This recipe is adapted from *Super Natural Cooking* (Ten Speed Press) by Heidi Swanson. The mesquite flour adds a rich, slightly smoky taste to this classic cookie and complements the chocolate flavor.

Makes about 30 cookies

2½ cups all-purpose flour

1 cup mesquite flour

1 teaspoon baking powder

1 teaspoon baking soda

1 teaspoon fine sea salt

2 cups granulated sugar

1 cup (2 sticks) unsalted butter, at room temperature

3 large eggs, at room temperature

2 teaspoons vanilla extract

2 cups rolled oats

1 package (12 ounces) chocolate chips

1 tablespoon lemon zest

Preheat the oven to 375°F. Line two baking sheets with parchment paper.

In a medium bowl, whisk together the flours, baking powder, baking soda, and salt. In another medium bowl, combine the sugar and butter. Using an electric mixer, beat until creamy. Stop a couple of times to scrape down the sides of the bowl. Beat in the eggs one at a time until completely incorporated, and then mix in ¼ cup water and the vanilla extract.

On low speed, beat in the flour mixture in three additions. Using a wooden spoon, stir in the oats, chocolate chips, and lemon zest. The dough will be stiff at this point.

Drop evenly spaced mounds of dough, about 3 tablespoons each, onto the prepared baking sheets and bake until just beginning to set 10 to 12 minutes. Be careful not to overbake.

MESQUITE CORNBREAD

This recipe is a truly Southwestern version of cornbread. You can also add 1 cup of fresh or frozen corn kernels to this recipe, along with ¼ cup of chopped green onions.

Serves 8

Unsalted butter, for greasing

¾ cup cornmeal

¾ cup all-purpose flour

½ cup mesquite flour

2 teaspoons baking powder

½ teaspoon baking soda

½ teaspoon salt

1 cup buttermilk

2 large eggs

3 tablespoons unsalted butter, melted

2 tablespoons honey

¾ cup shredded pepper jack cheese

Preheat the oven to 400°F. Butter an 8-inch square baking pan.

In a medium bowl, whisk together the cornmeal, flours, baking powder, baking soda, and salt. In another medium bowl, whisk together the buttermilk, eggs, butter, and honey until smooth. Stir in the dry ingredients until just combined. There can be some small lumps. Stir in the cheese. Spread the mixture into the prepared pan. Bake until firm and just beginning to brown, 20 to 25 minutes. Cut into squares to serve.

COCONUT-MESQUITE SMOOTHIES

Coconut water has made a huge splash in American markets in recent years. You'll also often see fresh young coconuts with the dark hard outer shell removed. The coconut water inside, along with the tender white meat (it takes a little effort to separate it from the inner shell), makes a delicious drink, and mesquite flour adds a honey-like sweetness.

Serves 2

1 fresh young coconut

1 cup crushed ice

2 to 3 tablespoons palm or light brown sugar

2 tablespoons mesquite flour

1 teaspoon vanilla extract

½ cup chopped pitted dates (optional)

Open the coconut and drain the water into a blender. Carefully scoop the flesh into the blender as well. You should have about 1½ cups water and 1 cup white flesh.

Add the ice, palm sugar, mesquite flour, vanilla extract, and dates, if using. Blend thoroughly until completely smooth and creamy. Pour into tall glasses. No umbrella, please.

TARAHUMARA PINOLE MIX

This recipe is adapted from *The Splendid Grain* (William Morrow) by Rebecca Wood, a wonderful book on how to cook with various unusual grains. The Tarahumara, a Native American people who ran incredible hundred-mile mountain races, ate a mixture similar to this. For a natural energy beverage, dissolve two tablespoons of pinole mix in one cup of water or nut milk of your choice and simmer for ten to fifteen minutes. Drink hot or cold.

Makes about 1½ cups

1 cup blue cornmeal or flour

¼ cup mesquite flour

¼ cup pumpkin or sunflower seeds

2 tablespoons chia seeds

Large pinch of salt

In a heavy skillet over medium heat, stir the cornmeal for a couple of minutes until it becomes aromatic and a shade darker. Be careful not to burn it. Transfer to a bowl. Toast the mesquite flour in the same way for a minute or so and add to the bowl. Toast the pumpkin seeds in the same pan until golden brown, then grind them in a spice grinder and add to the bowl. Stir in the chia seeds and salt until blended. Store in an airtight container. Eat in pinches for energy.

PINE

THE TREES OF THE PINE FAMILY, WITH OVER TWO HUNDRED SPECIES INCLUDING FIR and spruce, have long been used as building materials, but they can also be used for food and are valued for their high content of vitamin C. As wild forager Euell Gibbons tells us, the needles can be steeped to make tea, the young needles can be eaten as a snack or chopped to use as an herb, and the cambium (the layer just under the bark and before the wood) can be boiled, roasted, fried, or dried and ground for flour. The peeled roots are also edible, and the seeds of the piñon pine were harvested by Native Americans and are highly valued by cooks today. Even the pollen can be ingested (if you're not allergic) as an energy booster.

To make pine tea à la Euell Gibbons, just pour two cups of boiling water over one ounce of finely chopped pine needles (Gibbons suggests using white pine needles). Add lemon and sugar if you like. This brew is high in vitamins A and C. Gibbons also makes a pine cough syrup, with the addition of whiskey and honey.

SPATCHCOCKED PINE CHICKEN

A spatchcock was once another name for a young male chicken, but today, the term refers to the technique of removing the backbone of a chicken and flattening the bird before cooking, which allows it to cook more evenly. Adding pine needles to this dish provides a fresh, minty, pine-like flavor. Use younger needles, as they tend to have a milder flavor and are softer than older needles.

Serves 4

1 (3½ pound) whole roasting
or large broiler-fryer chicken

¼ cup olive oil

3 tablespoons freshly squeezed lemon juice

2 tablespoons chopped young
pine needles or shoots

1 teaspoon finely chopped garlic

¼ teaspoon red pepper flakes

Kosher or sea salt

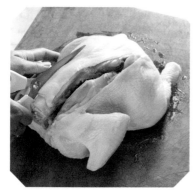

Remove any excess fat from the chicken. Place the chicken breast-side down on a cutting board and, using poultry shears, cut completely along the backbone, starting at the neck. Repeat on the other side of the backbone. Cut off the wing tips and save both the backbone and tips for stock.

Spread the two chicken halves apart like a book and press down on the breast with the heel of your hand to crack the breastbone so the chicken lies flat. In a small bowl, whisk together the oil, lemon juice, pine needles, garlic, and red pepper flakes. Rub this mixture all over the chicken and under the skin, then refrigerate the chicken for at least 2 hours. Season the chicken liberally with salt.

Prepare a charcoal grill or preheat a gas grill for medium indirect heat.

Place the chicken skin-side down over the cooler side of the grill with the legs closest to the heat. Cover the grill and cook until the skin is nicely browned with grill marks, about 25 minutes. Using tongs, turn the chicken over so it is skin-side up and transfer to the hot side of the grill with the breast facing away from the heat. Cover the grill and cook until the chicken is well browned, about 15 minutes. Finally, flip the chicken skin-side down over the hot coals and cook, moving the chicken as necessary to prevent flare-ups, until the skin is well crisped and an instant-read thermometer inserted into the thickest part of a thigh registers 165°F, 5 to 10 minutes. Transfer the chicken to a cutting board and loosely tent with aluminum foil to keep the chicken warm for about 10 minutes before carving and serving.

PINE CARAMEL SAUCE

This is delicious served on ice cream or yogurt or drizzled on a cake like
Brown Butter Polenta Cake (page 47). The addition of fresh young pine needles provides
a minty pine-like flavor, which complements the sweetness of the caramel.

Makes 2 cups

1 cup heavy whipping cream

3 tablespoons chopped fresh pine needles

1¾ cups granulated sugar

¼ cup (½ stick) cold unsalted butter, cut into
small cubes

2 teaspoons freshly squeezed lemon juice

1 teaspoon vanilla extract

⅛ teaspoon salt

2 tablespoons rum, brandy, or bourbon,
or more to taste (optional)

In a small saucepan, combine the cream and pine needles. Cook over low heat until the mixture steams and small bubbles form around the edges of the pan. Set aside to let the pine flavor infuse for at least 15 minutes.

In a deep, heavy saucepan, combine the sugar with ¾ cup water. Cover and bring to a simmer. Uncover and increase the heat to maintain a simmer. Do not stir, but wash down any sugar crystals clinging to the sides of the pan with a pastry brush dipped in water. Watch the pan carefully, swirling it from time to time, until the syrup turns a deep golden brown (325°F on a candy thermometer), about 10 minutes.

Remove from the heat and gradually stir in the cream mixture in a steady stream; the caramel and cream will bubble dramatically, so stir carefully. Gradually stir in the butter until completely combined. Stir in the lemon juice, vanilla extract, salt, and rum, if using. Strain through a fine-mesh strainer to remove the needles.

The caramel may be made up to several days in advance and refrigerated in an airtight container until ready to serve. Warm gently over low heat before serving.

BROWN BUTTER POLENTA CAKE

Using cornmeal in cakes adds an interesting chewy-crunchy texture
and is traditional in northern Italy.

Serves 6 to 8

1 cup (2 sticks) unsalted butter

2⅓ cups confectioners' sugar

¾ cup cake flour

1 cup almond flour

½ cup yellow cornmeal

7 large egg whites

Zest of 1 lemon

Preheat the oven to 350°F. Butter and flour a 13 x 9-inch cake pan or dish.

In a small saucepan, melt the butter over low heat. Continue cooking the butter until it turns golden in color and brown flecks form on the bottom of the pan, about 5 minutes. Scrape the brown butter into a large bowl and set aside.

Sift together the confectioners' sugar and cake flour into a medium bowl. Whisk in the almond flour and cornmeal. In the bowl of an electric mixer fitted with a whisk attachment, whip the egg whites to stiff peaks. Adding about 1½ cups at a time, gently fold the dry ingredients into the egg whites. Mix one-quarter of the batter into the reserved brown butter. Stir in the lemon zest. Fold the brown butter mixture into the remaining batter, pour into the prepared pan, and use a spatula to spread the batter out evenly. Bake until golden brown and a knife inserted into the center of the cake comes out clean, about 30 minutes. Let cool and cut into squares to serve.

MUGOLIO ICE CREAM

Mugolio is an intense dark-brown syrup made from the buds, or miniature pinecones, of Mugo pines in the Dolomite Mountains of Italy. Forager Eleonora Cunaccia picks the buds in early spring and then macerates them in sugar water through the summer until September. The must is then filtered, and the liquid is cooked with more sugar until it is thickened. Like chestnut honey or maple syrup, mugolio can be drizzled over roasted or grilled meats, ripe cheeses, or desserts. It is available online from Zingerman's Mail Order, Dean & DeLuca, and other gourmet sources.

Makes about 1 quart

1½ cups whole milk

1½ cups heavy whipping cream

¾ cup granulated sugar, divided

1½ tablespoons Mugolio pinecone/bud syrup

5 large egg yolks

Position a strainer over a medium bowl set in a larger bowl of ice water. This is your "insurance policy" to help quickly cool down the custard mixture to prevent it from scrambling.

In a medium saucepan, heat the milk, cream, ½ cup of the sugar, and the mugolio over medium heat until the mixture steams and small bubbles form around the edges. In a medium bowl, whisk the egg yolks with the remaining ¼ cup sugar until pale yellow.

Gradually whisk the warm milk mixture into the egg yolks until combined. Return the mixture to the saucepan and cook over medium heat, stirring constantly with a heatproof spatula, until it begins to thicken and steam appears. Be careful not to boil the mixture, or the eggs will scramble. Immediately strain the custard into the bowl set in the ice bath, stirring occasionally to help it cool down. Cover and refrigerate for at least 2 hours to chill.

Freeze in an ice-cream maker according to the manufacturer's instructions. Transfer to an airtight container, press plastic wrap directly onto the surface, cover the container, and freeze for up to 3 days.

Pine-Infused Vinegar

To make a pine-flavored vinegar for use in vinaigrettes or shrubs (page 176), combine equal parts cider vinegar and pine needles along with sugar to taste in a large lidded glass jar. Allow to sit in a dark place for at least four weeks. Strain a couple of times through cheesecloth or a coffee filter, discarding the pine needles. This vinegar will keep indefinitely.

PURSLANE: THE DELICIOUS WEED

T O MOST GARDENERS, PURSLANE (*PORTULACA OLERACEA*) IS A WEED, BUT IT'S EATEN as a vegetable in Asia, the Mediterranean, and Mexico and has become a trendy ingredient among chefs in this country in the past few years.

Even if you don't know purslane by name, I bet you've seen it. It's a low-growing, spreading plant with succulent leaves that looks like a miniature jade plant. It grows just about everywhere and thrives in the warm-to-hot weather of late spring and summer. You can eat the entire plant: leaves, stems, and tiny flowers. It has a tart, lemony flavor with a juicy, sticky texture. Look for it in sunny places with poor or disturbed soil, especially in parks and farmlands. Purslane is a very hardy plant that can even grow in cracks in the sidewalk or roadway. If you are wild gathering, be careful, of course, to avoid picking purslane around areas treated with pesticides or by polluted roadsides. You'll find cultivated versions in farmers' markets during the summer.

Purslane is rich in omega-3 fats and melatonin—more than any other edible plant!—as well as vitamins A and C and other important nutrients. In fact, it may the most obscure superfood that is considered to be a weed.

Purslane Serving Tips

Fresh, raw leaves can be used in salads or made into a vegetable juice. Gently sautéed, steamed, or stewed stems and leaves are great to serve as a side dish with fish and poultry. Purslane can be stir-fried and mixed with other similar greens such as spinach. It is also traditionally used in soups and curries and eaten with rice.

MOROCCAN TOMATO AND PURSLANE SALAD

This red-and-green salad is tossed with a sweet-hot dressing made with harissa, the Moroccan hot sauce. You can buy prepared harissa, but it will taste better if you make your own (page 51). It's a potent condiment, so use with discretion.

Serves 4

3 tablespoons freshly squeezed lemon juice

1 teaspoon harissa, or more to taste (page 51)

1 teaspoon honey, or more to taste

12 ounces cherry tomatoes, halved (quartered if large)

1 cup purslane leaves

¼ cup finely chopped green onions (white and green parts)

2 tablespoons chopped fresh mint

Kosher or sea salt to taste

In a medium bowl, whisk together the lemon juice, harissa, and honey. Add the tomatoes, purslane, green onions, and mint. Gently toss to coat. Season with salt to taste and more harissa, if desired. You can make this a few hours ahead and store covered in the refrigerator.

HARISSA

There are as many variations of the recipe for this Moroccan hot sauce as there are people who make it. At its simplest, harissa is just ground dried chiles mixed with olive oil. This version has some other flavors added to give a little more dimension. You could also add something tart, like lemon juice, vinegar, or sumac, and/or green herbs such as mint or cilantro.

Makes about ½ cup

1 ounce (about 2 cups) dried chiles
    (any kind you like; either single variety
    or a combination)

2 teaspoons coriander seeds

1½ teaspoons cumin seeds

2 tablespoons finely chopped garlic

1 teaspoon kosher or sea salt,
    plus more for seasoning

⅓ cup extra-virgin olive oil,
    plus more as needed

Place the chiles in a bowl, cover with warm water, and soak until softened, about 1 hour. Drain and cut the chiles in half, discarding the stems and seeds. Coarsely chop the chiles and set aside.

In a small, dry skillet, stir the coriander and cumin seeds over medium heat until they turn a shade darker and are fragrant. Grind to a fine powder in a spice grinder.

Add the reserved chiles and the spice mixture to a blender with the garlic and 1 teaspoon salt. With the blender running, gradually add the olive oil to make a purée. Scrape down the sides with a rubber spatula if necessary to make sure the mixture is evenly puréed. Spoon into a clean jar and top with enough olive oil to completely cover. Store covered in the refrigerator for up to 2 weeks or freeze up to 1 month.

CHILLED GREEN PEA SOUP WITH PURSLANE

This beautifully green chilled soup welcomes all kinds of substitutions, such as broccoli for some or all of the peas; watercress or spinach for some or all of the romaine; and basil, dill, or tarragon for some or all of the mint. It's perfect on a hot summer day.

Serves 4

3 tablespoons olive oil, divided

½ cup chopped green onions (white and green parts)

2 teaspoons chopped garlic

3 cups fresh or frozen and thawed green peas (about 12 ounces)

2 cups chicken stock

1½ cups packed finely chopped romaine or other lettuce

3 tablespoons chopped fresh mint

⅔ cup buttermilk (preferably Bulgarian)

Sea salt

Freshly squeezed lemon juice

Hot sauce

1 cup tender purslane leaves and stems

¼ cup crème fraîche

In a stockpot, heat 2 tablespoons of the oil over medium heat and sauté the green onions and garlic until softened but not brown, about 3 minutes. Add the peas and stock and bring to a simmer. Cook until the peas are tender, about 4 minutes. Remove from the heat to cool for a few minutes, then purée with a standard or immersion blender. Add the romaine and mint and purée again until smooth. Add the buttermilk and blend again until combined. Season to taste with salt, lemon juice, and hot sauce. Strain through a medium-mesh strainer and let cool. Cover and refrigerate until chilled, at least 2 hours or up to 24 hours. Taste again for seasoning, since chilling mutes flavor a bit.

To serve, toss the purslane with the remaining 1 tablespoon of olive oil and season with a little salt. Ladle the soup into flat soup plates and top with the purslane and squiggles of crème fraîche.

NOTE: If using fresh peas, you may want to add a little sugar, depending on their maturity. Young peas are generally a little sweeter than older ones, which tend to be starchier.

COUSCOUS RISOTTO WITH PURSLANE

This recipe uses Israeli couscous, which can be found in most markets, especially those that have bulk bins. It is made with the same semolina flour used in regular Moroccan couscous, but instead of being granular, it is round and about the size of a whole peppercorn. The great thing about Israeli couscous is that you can make a risotto in half the time of a rice-based version.

Serves 4 to 6 as a main course

½ cup chopped shallots or green onions (white parts only)

1 tablespoon slivered garlic

2 tablespoons olive oil

2 cups large Israeli couscous

½ cup dry white wine

4 cups chicken or vegetable stock, divided

2 to 2½ cups tender purslane leaves

½ cup coarsely chopped pitted olives, such as Cerignola

½ cup sun-dried tomatoes

½ cup freshly grated Parmesan cheese, plus more for garnish

¼ cup chopped fresh chives

2 tablespoons lemon zest

In a large sauté pan, sauté the shallots and garlic in olive oil over medium heat until lightly colored. Add the couscous and sauté for a minute or two longer until toasty. Add the wine and ½ cup of the stock, and stir occasionally until the liquid is nearly absorbed. Add the remaining stock in ½-cup increments, and continue to cook and stir until each stock addition is nearly absorbed. Continue in this manner until the couscous is tender but still has some texture, about 10 minutes total. Stir the purslane, olives, tomatoes, cheese, chives, and lemon zest into the risotto. Serve immediately in warm bowls topped with more cheese, if desired.

RAMPS

THE RAMP (*ALLIUM TRICOCCUM*), AS IT'S CALLED IN THE CENTRAL AND SOUTHERN Appalachian Mountains, is known as wild leek in the northern part of its range. Ramps are found on the East Coast, from Georgia all the way up to Nova Scotia and New Brunswick, and west to Missouri and Iowa. Festivals honoring ramps are held in many parts of the South and Canada, especially Quebec, and they are popular in farmers' markets in the spring.

Ramps appear early in the spring for only a few weeks, and most of their growth appears before the leaves of their canopy trees are formed. They typically grow in large clumps, which may be several decades old. Because ramps are relatively slow to reproduce, they are susceptible to overharvesting. If you gather them, be sure to leave a good part of the clump behind for next year's harvesting.

Ramps are part of the allium family, which includes onions, garlic, chives, and shallots. Cut into one and you'll understand its family connections. Although they are smaller than cultivated leeks, ramps have a stronger flavor with a garlicky edge. Ramps are very recognizable in the wild, with broad, flat leaves a bit like a donkey's ears.

Ramps may be substituted for green onions or leeks in other recipes. You don't need to clean them as carefully as you do cultivated leeks. Just trim the root ends and rinse off any dirt. Chop and freeze ramps if you come across many during their short season. As with green onions, the green leaves are milder in flavor than the white bulb.

RAMP SOUP

This soup shows off ramp's garlicky flavors and tames some
(but not all!) of its pungency.

Serves 4 to 6

4 strips of thick-cut bacon

1 tablespoon finely chopped fresh
    flat-leaf parsley

2 teaspoons lemon zest

2 pounds whole ramps

2 tablespoons unsalted butter

Sea salt and freshly ground pepper
    (preferably white)

1 small sweet onion, such as Walla Walla
    or Vidalia, chopped

½ cup dry white vermouth or dry white wine

1½ cups peeled and diced russet potato
    (about 1 medium)

7 cups chicken stock

½ cup freshly grated
    Parmigiano-Reggiano cheese

In a large, heavy saucepan, cook the bacon over medium heat until crisp. Using tongs, transfer to paper towels to drain (reserve the pan), then chop finely. In a small bowl, combine the bacon with the parsley and lemon zest; set aside.

Trim the roots from the ramps and rinse them, slipping off the outer skin on the bulb if loose. Cut the green tops from the ramps and coarsely chop enough greens to measure 4 cups (reserve the remainder for another use). Thinly slice all the ramp bulbs, including the pink stems.

In the same saucepan, melt the butter over medium heat and sauté the ramp bulbs and onion until soft but not browned, about 8 minutes. Season with salt and pepper to taste. Add the vermouth and bring to a boil over high heat, stirring occasionally, until nearly evaporated. Add the potato and pour in the stock. Partially cover, and simmer until all the vegetables are very soft, about 20 minutes. Stir in the ramp greens and boil for 1 minute.

Purée the soup with a standard or immersion blender, working in batches if necessary, until very smooth. Return the soup to the pot and bring just to a simmer. Whisk in the cheese until smooth. Taste and adjust the seasoning. Ladle into warmed bowls and top with the reserved bacon mixture.

GRILLED RAMPS WITH ROMESCO

This recipe is based on a dish from a Catalonian festival called *calçotada*, which celebrates the harvest of a kind of green onion known as the *calçot*. They are grilled until smoky and darkly browned and served in big heaps with *salsa romesco*. If you have a grill basket, this is a great time to use it. If not, lay the ramps perpendicular to the grill grates so they don't slip through.

Serves 4

12 ounces whole ramps

Olive oil, for coating

Sea salt and freshly ground black pepper

Romesco Sauce (page 56)

Prepare a charcoal grill for medium-high heat or preheat a gas grill.

Trim the roots from the ramps and rinse them, slipping off the outer skin on the bulb if loose. Toss the ramps with olive oil to coat and season with salt and pepper. Grill, turning often, until the leaves and bulbs are lightly charred, about 4 minutes. Serve with romesco sauce on the side for dipping the grilled ramps. Have napkins at the ready.

ROMESCO SAUCE

Makes about 2 cups

6 plum tomatoes

1 large red bell pepper

1 head garlic, halved,
    papery outer skin removed

1 red onion, halved

5 tablespoons olive oil, divided,
    plus more for coating

6 dried nora or cascabel chiles or 2 ancho chiles

¼ cup raw almonds

1 thick slice of white bread, crust removed,
    cut into small dice

1 tablespoon sherry vinegar

1 teaspoon sweet *pimentón*
    (Spanish smoked paprika)

Sea salt

Prepare a charcoal grill for high heat or preheat a gas grill or broiler.

Lightly coat the tomatoes, bell pepper, garlic, and onion with olive oil. Grill or broil until vegetables have softened and are nicely marked on all sides, about 8 to 10 minutes on a hot grill or 4 to 5 minutes under the broiler. Transfer the vegetables to a cutting board and let cool.

While the vegetables are cooking, put the chiles in a bowl and cover with hot water. Let soak for 15 minutes. Drain and remove the seeds and stems. Set aside.

In a small skillet, heat 1 tablespoon of the olive oil over low heat. Add the almonds and toast until fragrant, about 1 minute. Remove to a bowl and set aside.

Increase the heat to medium and add 2 more tablespoons of the oil to the pan. Add the bread and stir until lightly browned, about 1 minute. Remove to a bowl and set aside.

Add the soaked chiles to the skillet and cook over medium heat for 30 seconds. Remove from the heat.

When the vegetables are cool to the touch, peel, core, and stem them. Working in batches if necessary, put the roasted vegetables in a blender or food processor along with the reserved almonds, bread, and chiles. Add the vinegar, *pimentón*, and the remaining 2 tablespoons of olive oil. Blend until the mixture forms a thick sauce. Season with salt to taste.

RAMP KIMCHI

With their pungent flavor, ramps are a good addition to an intensely flavored kimchi of cabbage and daikon. This spicy condiment complements Asian foods and will keep for up to a month in the refrigerator. Be sure to soak the ramps in cold water before using to loosen any dirt. This will also help in removing the outer skin of the bulbs.

Makes 6 cups

1 pound whole ramps

4 large garlic cloves, thinly sliced

3 tablespoons *gochujang*
   (Korean chile bean paste)

3 tablespoons granulated sugar

2 tablespoons peeled and finely chopped
   fresh ginger

4 teaspoons kosher salt

1 tablespoon Asian fish sauce

1 tablespoon soy sauce

1 napa cabbage, cut into 1-inch cubes
   (about 6 cups)

1½ cups daikon radish, peeled, halved
   lengthwise, and thinly sliced into half-moons

Trim the roots from the ramps and rinse them, slipping off the outer skin on the bulb if loose. Separate the pink ramp stems and the greens from the bulbs. Chop the bulbs, stems, and leaves, and set aside.

In a large bowl, whisk together the garlic, *gochujang*, sugar, ginger, salt, fish sauce, soy sauce, and 1 tablespoon water until smooth. Add the cabbage, daikon, and the chopped ramp bulbs, stems, and leaves. Toss to combine. Massage the vegetables with your fingers to lightly crush them and release the liquid.

Transfer the mixture to a large glass jar, leaving at least 2 inches of headspace. Pack down the vegetables to eliminate air gaps and keep them submerged in the liquid. Weight them down with a smaller glass jar or saucer if necessary to keep the vegetables submerged. Cover the jar with cheesecloth and secure with a rubber band.

Let sit at room temperature, packing down the vegetables once a day to keep them submerged, until the kimchi tastes tangy and releases bubbles when stirred, 3 to 5 days. Move to a smaller jar if needed for longer storage and discard the cheesecloth. Seal with a lid and store in the refrigerator for up to 1 month. This kimchi will grow tangier the longer it sits.

SCRAMBLED EGGS WITH RAMPS AND MORELS

This simple recipe highlights the flavor of both ramps and morels (page 106).
You can also use dried morels that have been softened in warm water for
a few minutes, or any other mushroom that you like.

Serves 4

4 large whole ramps

2 tablespoons unsalted butter

2 ounces (about 1 cup) fresh morels, thinly
sliced lengthwise

2 tablespoons heavy whipping cream

8 large eggs, beaten

Sea salt and freshly ground black pepper

⅓ cup freshly grated Parmigiano-Reggiano
or Asiago cheese

Trim the roots from the ramps and rinse them, slipping off the outer skin on the bulb if loose. Thinly slice the ramp bulbs and pink stems (you should have about ¾ cup). Slice about 1½ cups of the greens. In a large nonstick skillet, melt the butter over medium heat. Add the ramp bulbs and stems to the skillet and sauté for 3 minutes. Add the green tops and the mushrooms and sauté until the ramps are soft, about 6 minutes. Reduce the heat to medium-low.

Whisk the cream into the eggs, season well with salt and pepper, and add the eggs to the skillet. Stir with a wooden spoon until the eggs are very softly set, about 4 minutes. Taste and adjust the seasoning. Divide the eggs among warmed plates. Sprinkle the cheese over top and serve immediately.

SEA BEANS

EVERAL SPECIES OF *SALICORNIA* (ALSO CALLED SAMPHIRE, SALTWORT, PICKLEWEED, glasswort, and sea asparagus), grow along both coasts of North America and around the seacoasts of Europe, where they've long been a favorite of foragers. They grow in that never-never land of brackish marshes that border the sea. The sea bean has an unusual appearance; the plant looks a bit like coral. It's made up of succulent capsules on branches ten to twelve inches long. This vegetable is at its best in early summer. Usually, only the top six inches or so of the plant is harvested because it is the most tender. Avoid sea beans with a hard stringy core inside the stem, which develops later in summer as the plant matures. Sea beans are fragile, so walk carefully and avoid stepping on them when harvesting.

Sea beans have become a favorite wild food for chefs in America because of their beautiful deep green color, and because they have a wonderful snap-like texture similar to green beans. They are crisp and juicy like celery but with a salty and slightly gluey interior. They taste like a cross between spinach and asparagus. Sea beans can be eaten raw (which I think is best) or steamed, stir-fried, or sautéed. (Take care not to overcook them or they'll lose their delightfully crisp texture.) They have a high salt content, so season carefully when pairing them with high-sodium ingredients such as soy sauce. You can reduce some of their saltiness by soaking them for 30 minutes in cold water, changing the water twice.

SPRING SMOKED SALMON SALAD WITH SEA BEANS

The beautiful color of salmon is complemented by the bright green sea beans in this spring dish. This recipe calls for smoking the salmon in a stove-top smoker with the skin on, because the skin adds a lot of flavor. If you don't have a smoker, it's easy to make your own using a wok.

Serves 4

4 (5-ounce) skin-on wild salmon fillets, pin bones removed

1 recipe Honey-Lemon Vinaigrette (page 63)

8 ounces raw or briefly steamed sea beans

2 to 3 cups loosely packed young wild arugula leaves

2 large oranges (preferably navels), peeled and segmented

1 large grapefruit or medium pomelo, peeled and segmented

1 blood orange, peeled and segmented (optional)

Microgreens, for garnish (optional)

Brush the salmon with ¼ cup of the vinaigrette and let sit at room temperature for 30 minutes. If using a stove-top smoker, place the drip tray on top of 1 heaping tablespoon of hardwood chips, such as apple or alder. Place a wire rack covered with aluminum foil on top. There should be room around the sides of the rack for the smoke to circulate. If using a wok, line it with foil and place the wood chips in the center.

Place the salmon skin-side down on top of the rack and slide the top of the smoker almost closed, or partially cover the top of the wok with foil or a lid. Place over medium heat. When the first wisps of smoke appear, fully close the lid of the smoker, or press the foil down snugly around the edges if using a wok. Reduce the heat to low and allow the salmon to smoke for 8 minutes. Check once or twice to see if the chips are still actively smoking. Remove from the heat and leave the smoker covered for 5 minutes longer to finish cooking the salmon to your preferred doneness.

Toss the sea beans and arugula with about ⅓ cup of the vinaigrette, or more to taste, and mound attractively on plates. Arrange the citrus segments around the salad. Place the salmon on top and drizzle with more of the remaining vinaigrette. Top with the microgreens, if using.

NOTE: If you prefer your salmon with a little less smoke, you can smoke it for 4 to 5 minutes, then roast it in a preheated 375°F oven until it is just cooked through, 5 to 6 minutes.

HONEY-LEMON VINAIGRETTE

Makes 1 generous cup

6 tablespoons rice vinegar

¼ cup freshly squeezed lemon juice

2 tablespoons honey, or more to taste

2 tablespoons finely chopped shallot

Large pinch of cayenne pepper

Sea salt

¼ cup extra-virgin olive oil

In a small bowl, whisk together the vinegar, lemon juice, honey, shallot, cayenne, and salt to taste. While whisking, add the olive oil in a slow, steady stream until well combined. Store covered in the refrigerator for up to 5 days.

FRESH SCALLOPS WITH SEA BEANS

This recipe for crudo—marinated raw fish—uses sea scallops, but any sushi-grade fish or shellfish can be substituted. The contrast in color as well as texture makes this dish sing.

Serves 4

½ cup sea beans (a nice handful)

2 tablespoons seasoned rice vinegar

4 large (10 per pound) sushi-grade dry-pack scallops

4 shiso leaves

Extra-virgin olive oil, for drizzling

Freshly squeezed lemon juice, for sprinkling

Sea salt

2 ounces fresh salmon caviar, rinsed very briefly to remove excess salt

Fill a large bowl with ice water. Bring a pot of salted water to a boil. Add the sea beans and cook for 10 seconds. Drain and immediately plunge the beans into the ice-water bath to stop the cooking and set the color. When cool, drain and set aside.

When ready to serve, toss the blanched sea beans with the vinegar. Rinse and pat the scallops dry. Thinly slice each scallop into rounds. Place a shiso leaf on each plate and arrange the scallop slices on top. Drizzle with olive oil and sprinkle with drops of lemon juice. Sprinkle just a little salt over each scallop (remember, the sea beans and caviar are salty). Top with the sea beans and scatter salmon caviar around each plate.

Dry-Pack/Day Boat/Diver Scallops

Scallops that are refrigerated without any additives are labeled as "dry pack." Because these scallops have not been soaked or injected with any additional liquids, they shrink less during cooking. They are highly perishable, and only those that can be quickly transported from boat to shore (within one day) are sold as dry-pack scallops, which is why they are often called day boat or diver scallops.

Scallops that have been injected with a liquid mixture containing the preservative STP (sodium tripolyphosphate) are labeled "wet pack." STP is added to maintain moisture and give the scallops a longer shelf life. Unfortunately, STP makes scallops difficult to sear, gives them a rubbery texture, and obscures their naturally sweet flavor. Don't buy them!

STINGING NETTLES

F YOU'VE EVER WANDERED INTO A NETTLE PATCH, YOU HAVE EXPERIENCED THE PAINFUL sting of their prickly leaves. Yet stinging nettles are both good tasting and good for you. The sting comes from formic acid in the hairy leaves, which is neutralized when cooked. Nettles are greens with amazing culinary and medicinal properties. The nutrients the provide include iron, potassium, manganese, calcium, and vitamins A and C. Some medicinal uses of this plant are the alleviation of arthritis, hay fever, anemia, and kidney problems. Nettles are widely distributed around the world and are found throughout the continental United States, where they proliferate in woodsy areas, grasslands, and fields in spring and early summer.

Choose young plants (less than knee high) when foraging, and be sure to protect yourself by wearing gloves, pants, and long sleeves. Pick just the top four leaves. They can be stored in the refrigerator in a resealable plastic bag for up to four days.

To cook, rinse nettles well, then drain and stem. Blanch them in salted boiling water for one or two minutes, then drain and press to remove excess water. This process will make them sting-free.

NETTLE PESTO

This sauce is delicious with pasta, but also try dolloping it on creamy soups as a garnish or folding it into softened butter as a delicious topping for meats, fish, and vegetables.

Makes 1½ cups

5 cups fresh stinging nettle leaves

3 garlic cloves

½ cup extra-virgin olive oil, plus more as needed

½ cup freshly grated
  Parmigiano-Reggiano cheese

¼ cup pine nuts or blanched almonds,
  lightly toasted

2 teaspoons lemon zest

Salt and freshly ground black pepper

Fill a large bowl with ice water. Bring a large pot of salted water to a boil. Using tongs, add the nettles and garlic and cook for 1 to 2 minutes. Drain and immediately plunge them into the ice-water bath to stop the cooking and set the nettles' color. When cool, drain and wring dry in a clean kitchen towel. Chop both the nettles and garlic coarsely. You should have about 1¼ cups.

In a food processor or blender, combine the nettles, garlic, olive oil, cheese, pine nuts, and lemon zest. Pulse to chop coarsely until a thick, green sauce forms. The mixture can be as smooth or coarse as you prefer. If the sauce is too thick, add a little more olive oil. Season with salt and pepper to taste.

Pour the sauce into a glass jar or other container and top with a thin layer of olive oil to prevent the surface from discoloring. Cover tightly and refrigerate for up to 1 week or freeze for up to 3 months.

STINGING NETTLE
AND GOAT CHEESE QUICHE

You can also combine nettles with lamb's-quarter (page 33)
or any other leafy green, such as spinach, for this quiche.

Serves 6

5 cups fresh stinging nettle leaves

1½ cups heavy whipping cream

2 large eggs

2 large egg yolks

Kosher salt and freshly ground black pepper

½ cup finely crumbled goat cheese,
   such as Bûcheron

⅓ cup grated Parmigiano-Reggiano cheese

3 tablespoons finely chopped green onions
   (white and green parts)

1 tablespoon finely chopped fresh tarragon

⅛ teaspoon ground nutmeg

1 recipe All-Butter Savory Crust (page 71),
   parbaked in a 10-inch tart pan with
   removable bottom

Adjust an oven rack to the middle position and preheat the oven to 375°F.

Fill a large bowl with ice water. Bring a large pot of salted water to a boil. Add the nettles and cook for about 20 seconds, check to make sure they are tender, and then drain. Plunge the nettles into the ice-water bath. When cool, drain and wring the nettles dry in a clean kitchen towel. You should have about ¾ cup. Chop well and set aside.

In a medium bowl, combine the cream, eggs, and egg yolks. Season with salt and pepper and whisk until thoroughly blended. Whisk in the cheeses, green onions, tarragon, nutmeg, and chopped nettles.

Set the parbaked tart shell on a rimmed baking sheet. Pour the custard into the tart shell, being careful that it doesn't overflow. Bake until the filling is nicely puffed and browned, 40 to 50 minutes. Let cool for at least 15 to 20 minutes. Remove the sides of the pan and cut the quiche into wedges to serve.

ALL-BUTTER SAVORY CRUST

This recipe can be doubled for a double crust; divide the dough into two balls
and form into two disks before chilling.

*Makes one 9-inch single piecrust
or one 10-inch tart shell*

1¼ cups all-purpose flour

¼ teaspoon salt

10 tablespoons cold unsalted butter,
cut into ½-inch pieces

3 to 5 tablespoons ice water

In a food processor, briefly pulse together the flour and salt. Add the butter and pulse until the mixture forms pea-size pieces. Add the ice water 1 tablespoon at a time and pulse until the mixture is just moist enough to hold together.

Form the dough into a ball, wrap in plastic wrap, and flatten into a disk. Refrigerate for at least 1 hour before rolling out and baking.

TO PARBAKE THE CRUST: Preheat the oven to 375°F.

On a lightly floured surface, roll out the dough into a 12-inch round. Transfer the crust to a 9-inch pie plate or 10-inch tart pan. Trim the edges to 1 inch, fold the dough under, and crimp the edges. Prick the crust all over with a fork. Place the pie plate in the freezer for 15 to 30 minutes to relax the gluten in the dough. Fit a square of aluminum foil inside the pie plate and fill with dried beans or pie weights. Bake for 15 minutes. Remove the foil and beans, then bake until pale golden, 5 to 7 minutes more. Let cool on a wire rack.

WILD ARUGULA

Wild arugula (*DIPLOTAXIS TENUIFOLIA*) is a relative of commercially grown arugula (*Eruca sativa*). It has narrower leaves with deeper lobes and is more intensely peppery than its cultivated cousin. Arugula is a member of the *Brassicaceae*, or mustard, family and is native to Italy, where it's called *rucola* and has been foraged and cultivated for centuries. Its common name in the United Kingdom is rocket.

In the States, wild arugula may be found in farmers' markets. It is a very capable "weed," and once grown, it will propagate itself wherever there is water and sun. In Northern California, we often find it in meadows and along fence lines and ditches from early spring until the weather gets hot.

Arugula is much more than just a salad green. It can be sautéed in olive oil with garlic for a simple side dish. Blend it with pine nuts, olive oil, and Parmesan or pecorino cheese for a distinctive pesto-like sauce that can be tossed with either pasta or warm potatoes. To really appreciate its zingy flavor, I think it's best eaten raw. Toss it in a salad with salty prosciutto and sweet watermelon, or scatter it on top of pizza (see recipe on page 74) or inside a hot, gooey grilled cheese sandwich smeared with olive tapenade or fig jam. Yum!

GRILLED PIZZA

To successfully grill pizza, you will need a little patience to master the technique. It may take a few practice runs before you get a pizza you want to serve, but persevere! Pizza is fun to make with a crowd; it's really pretty simple and definitely worth the effort. I've done a simple Margherita (named after the Italian queen) with wild arugula here, but add whatever toppings you like. Remember that in Italy the dough is as important as the toppings, so don't overload. You can make the dough and toppings ahead and then just put them out and let everyone create their own pizza masterpieces.

Makes six 10-inch pizzas

All-purpose flour, for dusting

1 recipe pizza dough (page 75),
   divided into six portions

¾ cup extra-virgin olive oil, or more as needed,
   for brushing and drizzling

3 cups canned crushed tomatoes in purée
   with basil (preferably San Marzano),
   from a 28-ounce can

2 cups loosely packed shredded Sonoma
   or Monterey Jack cheese

½ cup freshly grated pecorino cheese,
   or more as desired

6 ounces fresh mozzarella, drained and sliced

½ cup coarsely chopped fresh
   wild arugula leaves

6 large pinches red pepper flakes

Prepare a charcoal grill or preheat a gas grill for indirect medium heat, with one side hotter than the other, setting the grill rack about 4 inches above the coals if using charcoal.

Lightly flour a work surface and rolling pin, and roll each portion of the dough into a free-form circle about 10 inches in diameter, getting the dough about ¼ inch thick (or as thin as you can). Don't worry about the shape, even thickness is the goal here. Place them on a sheet pan separated by parchment or waxed paper so they don't stick to each another.

When the grill is hot, brush one portion of the dough with olive oil and place it oiled-side down over direct heat, onto the hotter part of the grill. Within a minute or so, the dough will puff and bubble, the underside will stiffen, and grill marks will appear.

Using tongs or a spatula, check to see that the crust is not burning. If it is cooking too quickly, move it to the cooler part of the grill (indirect heat). Flip the crust over and place on the cooler part of the grill, then quickly brush the grilled surface lightly with olive oil. Spread a thin layer of the tomatoes on the crust and then quickly top with a bit of each of the cheeses, some arugula, a pinch of the red pepper flakes, and any other toppings you might like to add. Remember that you shouldn't cover the entire surface of the pizza.

Immediately cover the grill and cook until the cheeses are melted, 1 to 2 minutes longer. Transfer the pizza to a cutting board, cut into wedges, and serve immediately. Prepare the remaining pizzas in the same manner.

NOTES: If after a couple of minutes the cheese hasn't melted and bubbled a bit, either the grill was not hot enough or you have used too much cheese and toppings. A longer time on the grill will only dry out the pizza and toughen it. The ideal crust should be both chewy and crisp. This is why a good indirect fire is so important.

PIZZA DOUGH

*Makes about 24 ounces of dough or
enough for six 10-inch pizzas*

1 package (2¼ teaspoons) active dry yeast

2 teaspoons granulated sugar

2 cups warm water, or more as needed

½ cup finely ground cornmeal
  or whole wheat flour

1½ teaspoons table salt
  or 1 tablespoon kosher salt

3 tablespoons olive oil, divided

4 to 4½ cups all-purpose flour

In the bowl of an electric mixer fitted with a dough hook, stir the yeast and sugar into the warm water and set aside. After 5 minutes it should begin to bubble; then stir in the cornmeal, salt, and 1 tablespoon of the olive oil. Add 4 cups of the flour, stirring at low speed until the dough forms a rough ball and pulls away from the sides of the bowl, about 4 minutes. You may need to add a little flour or water at this point if the dough is too sticky or too dry. Let the dough rest in the bowl for 15 minutes. The dough should be fairly soft.

Remove the dough from the bowl and divide into six equal pieces. Gently round each piece into a ball, and brush or rub with a little of the olive oil. Place each ball into a resealable plastic bag, drizzle the remaining olive oil (about 1 teaspoon) over each ball, and seal the bags closed. Let the balls sit for at least 30 minutes before rolling out or refrigerate overnight and roll out the next day, taking them out of the refrigerator at least 1 hour before you plan to make the pizzas. (Sitting overnight actually improves the dough's flavor.) Alternatively, you can freeze the dough for up to 3 months; let the dough thaw and come to room temperature before using.

SALAD OF WILD ARUGULA, BABY ARTICHOKES, AND FENNEL

This salad invites substituting or adding whatever seasonal ingredients you have on hand. Try using thinly sliced Jerusalem artichokes in place of or in addition to the fennel.

Serves 4

2 teaspoons finely chopped shallot or green onion (white part only)

1 teaspoon honey

5 tablespoons freshly squeezed lemon juice, divided

⅓ cup extra-virgin olive oil

Sea salt and freshly ground black pepper

4 baby artichokes

1 small head fennel, trimmed

8 ounces wild arugula

½ cup shaved Parmigiano-Reggiano cheese

Edible flowers, such as borage or calendula, for garnish (optional)

In a medium bowl, combine the shallot, honey, and 3 tablespoons of the lemon juice. Gradually whisk in the olive oil to emulsify. Season the dressing with salt and pepper to taste and set aside.

Fill a medium bowl with water and add the remaining 2 tablespoons lemon juice. Using a sharp knife, peel the artichokes down to the tender white core. Using a mandoline or sharp knife, cut the artichokes into very thin slices. Put them in the lemon water to keep them from turning brown. Cut the fennel into similarly thin slices in the same way.

Add the arugula to the bowl with the dressing and toss to coat. Drain the artichokes and pat dry. Add the artichokes and fennel to the bowl and toss to coat.

Divide the salad among four salad plates. Top with the cheese, garnish with the edible flowers, if using, and serve immediately.

WILD ARUGULA AND RICOTTA GNUDI

Ricotta gnocchi are called *gnudi* ("nudes" in Italian) because they're made of the same mixture that's used to fill a classic cheese ravioli, without the pasta. I'm serving them here with a simple marinara sauce, but a quick sauté in a sage and brown butter sauce would be equally good.

Serves 4 to 6

1 pound whole-milk ricotta
  (do not use part-skim ricotta)

12 ounces young wild arugula

1 large egg, lightly beaten

⅓ cup freshly grated pecorino Romano
  or Toscano cheese

Zest of 1 large lemon, divided

Kosher salt and freshly ground pepper

½ cup all-purpose flour, plus more for shaping

2 tablespoons unsalted butter

1 cup fresh breadcrumbs

1 teaspoon finely chopped fresh rosemary
  or pine needles, or more to taste

1 recipe Simple Marinara Sauce (page 79),
  kept warm

Drain the ricotta in a fine-mesh strainer or cheesecloth bag suspended over a bowl for at least 2 hours at room temperature. Discard the whey.

Meanwhile, fill a large bowl with ice water. Bring a pot of salted water to a boil, add the arugula, and cook 2 minutes. Drain and then immediately plunge the arugula into the ice-water bath to stop the cooking and set the color. When cool, drain, squeeze out as much water as you can, and chop finely. You should have about ½ cup.

Transfer the drained ricotta to a large bowl and beat with a whisk until fluffy. Stir the egg and cheese into the ricotta. Stir in the lemon zest, reserving 1 teaspoon, and season with salt and pepper to taste.

Add the chopped arugula and the ½ cup flour to the ricotta mixture and stir until the flour is completely incorporated and the arugula is evenly distributed throughout.

Line a baking sheet with parchment paper. Lightly flour your hands and scoop out a rounded tablespoon-ful of the ricotta mixture. Gently roll it into a sphere about the size of a large gumball. (**NOTE:** I suggest that you cook a "tester" in boiling salted water at this point to make sure it will hold together and that seasoning is to your liking.) Place on the prepared baking sheet and repeat until you have used all of the mixture. You should have 20 to 24 gnudi. Cover and refrigerate the gnudi until you are ready to cook them, or freeze them on the pan and then store in the freezer in a resealable plastic bag.

In a small skillet, melt the butter over medium heat. Add the breadcrumbs and stir well, then cook until they are browned and crisp. Transfer the breadcrumbs to a bowl and toss with the rosemary and the reserved lemon zest; set aside.

Bring a large pot of salted water to a boil. Add the gnudi and cook until they rise to the surface; let cook for 2 minutes more, then, using a slotted spoon, transfer to a colander and drain well.

To serve, spoon the warm marinara sauce into bowls. Top with the warm gnudi, sprinkle with some of the breadcrumb mixture, and serve immediately.

SIMPLE MARINARA SAUCE

If you like your sauce a little spicy, add a pinch of red pepper flakes along with the tomatoes.

Makes about 3 ½ cups

2 tablespoons olive oil

½ cup finely chopped yellow onion

2 teaspoons finely chopped garlic

1 (28-ounce) can crushed tomatoes with basil

1 cup dry red wine

1 bay leaf

Salt and freshly ground black pepper

In a deep saucepan, heat the oil over medium heat and sauté the onion and garlic until softened and just beginning to brown, about 5 minutes. Add the tomatoes, wine, and bay leaf. Partially cover, and simmer for about 15 minutes. Discard bay leaf. Season with salt and pepper to taste.

WILD ASPARAGUS

HAVE FOND MEMORIES OF FORAGING FOR WILD ASPARAGUS ON MY GRANDPARENTS' ranch in Colorado. The ranch was at the base of Mount Princeton, one of Colorado's "fourteen-ers" (mountains more than fourteen thousand feet high). At about eight thousand feet, winters at the ranch were pretty harsh. When the wild asparagus appeared, usually in early to mid-April, it was a sure sign that the weather was finally going to warm up and summer was on the horizon. My grandmother and I picked and ate much of it raw, right on the spot. If you've never had just-picked wild asparagus, know that it has an amazing sweet, green flavor, not at all like that of culti-vated asparagus. Raw is still one of my favorite ways to eat wild asparagus, but it must be enjoyed right after picking to take advantage of its natural sweetness. On the ranch, we cooked it, too, and we ate it every day until its short season was over. The recipes for wild asparagus that follow were inspired by my grandmother's ways of cooking it.

Wild asparagus (*Asparagus prostratus*) is one of the great treats of spring. It grows where there is a lot of light and moisture, so look for it along the banks of irrigation ditches or small streams. The main part of the asparagus, a network of rhizomes, is below ground, and it will continually send up shoots for several weeks during its growing season. Wild asparagus spears are thinner and daintier than their cultivated cousins, and their flavor is a bit more subtle but sweeter. It sometimes can be hard to spot, but a good way of finding it is to go out in the fall and look for yellowed dead spears leftover from spring; then come back to that spot the next spring and you'll find fresh, green tender shoots to harvest. Note: When harvesting wild asparagus, don't take it all. Leave some of the green stalks behind so they can grow and provide energy for the rhizomes, allowing the plant to produce again in the following year.

Asparagus cultivation is recorded as far back as ancient Egypt. In addition to its value as a food, it has long been considered a medicine, primarily a diuretic to help flush toxins from the liver and kidneys. It also has a reputation as an aphrodisiac (see "Food as an Aphrodisiac" on page 81), proba-bly due more to its erect appearance and growth pattern than anything else. But give it a try and see what happens, anyway.

Food as an Aphrodisiac

For all of recorded history, claims have been made that certain foods increase sexual potency and desire. I've never found a complete listing of these, but there must be hundreds. The Chinese tout soups made with shark fins and actual birds' nests. The Scottish swear by haggis, a mixture of finely chopped sheep innards, oatmeal, and spices stuffed into a sheep's stomach and boiled for four hours (the Scots obviously have a different idea of sensuality!). The Aztecs valued cocoa and chocolate (which were forbidden to their women). The Greeks revered pine nuts, according to Ovid. Pliny mentions hippopotamus snout and hyena eyes, and every culture seems to have considered oysters a potent food. Additionally, caviar, snails, and the eggs, glands, and genitals of all kinds of birds, animals, and fish have been thought to provide special powers. Even prunes were so highly regarded as an aphrodisiac in Elizabethan times that they were freely served in brothels.

In the garden, apples, asparagus, figs, bananas, cucumbers, leeks, peppers, tomatoes, avocados, eggplant, and potatoes have all been believed to possess special sexual potential at one time or another, the obvious connection being that many of them resemble human genitalia! Herbs and edible flowers, including roses, lavender, catnip, passionflower, saffron, savory, and ginseng root have also been celebrated for their special powers.

Anthropologist Peter Farb has observed that the association between food and sex has existed since humans started walking upright. Eating brings couples into close proximity in a situation that does not call for defensive tactics. When you think about it, eating can bind a couple more effectively than sex, simply because people eat more often and predictably than they have sexual relations.

Physiologically, our nervous system deals in a similar way with both hunger and sexual excitement. Sensitive structures called Krause's end-bulbs are found both in the taste buds of the mouth and in the sensitive parts of our sexual organs. This could explain why sexual desire and a delicious aroma of food both cause our mouths to water!

M. F. K. Fisher notes in her wonderful little book *An Alphabet for Gourmets* that gastronomy has always been connected with its sister art of love: Passion and sex is the "come-and-go, the preening and the prancing, the final triumph or defeat, of two people who know enough, subconsciously or not, to woo with food as well as flattery."

GRILLED ASPARAGUS WITH LEMON OLIVE OIL, PECORINO, AND PROSCIUTTO

My favorite way to prepare asparagus (besides eating it raw) is to grill it, which emphasizes the fresh flavor of the vegetable itself. Of course, you can use cultivated asparagus as well. Lemon-infused olive oil is available in Italian markets and specialty food stores. Look for the Agrumato brand from Italy or the "O" brand from California.

Serves 4

1 pound fresh asparagus, trimmed

2 tablespoons extra-virgin olive oil

Flaky sea salt such as Maldon

Freshly ground black pepper

3 tablespoons Italian or California lemon-infused extra-virgin olive oil

2 ounces pecorino or Parmigiano-Reggiano cheese, thinly shaved with a vegetable peeler

8 very thin slices of prosciutto

3 tablespoons drained capers, patted dry and fried in olive oil until crisp

Lemon wedges, for serving

Prepare a charcoal grill for or preheat a gas grill to medium-high heat.

Brush the asparagus with the extra-virgin olive oil and season generously with salt and pepper to taste. Grill the asparagus, turning as needed, until lightly browned on all sides but still green and crisp. Place on a plate and drizzle with the lemon olive oil. Scatter the cheese over the asparagus, arrange the prosciutto attractively on top, and sprinkle with the capers. Serve with the lemon wedges.

ASPARAGUS SOUP

This simple soup is a perfect use for spring asparagus and greens.
It also makes a wonderful base for a nice piece of pan-seared Alaskan rockfish
or sablefish (both of which are managed sustainably).

Serves 4 to 6

2 tablespoons unsalted butter

¼ cup finely chopped shallots

½ teaspoon fennel seeds

Pinch of red pepper flakes

Salt

1 pound fresh asparagus,
    trimmed and chopped, tips reserved

1 small Yukon Gold potato,
    peeled and chopped (about 1 cup)

4 cups chicken stock

2 cups loosely packed spinach leaves
    or tender wild greens

⅓ cup crème fraîche or sour cream

In a deep saucepan, melt the butter over medium heat. Add the shallots, fennel seeds, red pepper flakes, and salt to taste. Cook, stirring occasionally, until the shallots are translucent, about 4 minutes.

Add the chopped asparagus and potato and cook for 1 minute. Stir in the stock and 1 cup water; bring to a boil. Reduce the heat to a simmer and cook until the vegetables are tender, about 10 minutes.

Meanwhile, fill a large bowl with ice water. Bring a small saucepan of salted water to a boil. Add the asparagus tips and cook until just tender, about 2 minutes. Using tongs, transfer the spears to the ice-water bath to stop the cooking and set the color. When cool, drain and set aside.

Remove the soup from the heat, add the spinach, and stir until wilted. Using a standard or immersion blender, carefully purée the soup. Return to the heat and cook until heated through. Adjust seasoning to taste. Ladle the soup into bowls and garnish with the asparagus tips and a swirl of crème fraîche.

WILD GINSENG

GINSENG, FROM THE CHINESE FOR "MAN ROOT," IS SO CALLED BECAUSE IT OFTEN divides into two roots that look like legs, causing it to resemble a human body. The roots of Asian ginseng have been used in Korean and Chinese herbal medicine for centuries, while Native Americans prized both the plant and root for medicinal uses. American ginseng (*Panax quinquefolius*) usually grows to one to two feet in height and is found in hardwood forests from southern Canada as far west as South Dakota and as far south as Georgia. The ginseng plant prefers cool conditions, so it often grows at high altitudes and in shady forests in the southeastern states. It is legal to harvest ginseng in nineteen of the United States.

Ginseng is one of the most studied herbal remedies, and many claims are made for its various stress-relieving, energy-producing, longevity-promoting benefits. It has also been said to enhance sexual performance and to increase the immune function. What more could you want from a wild food?

Wild American ginseng is particularly desirable and valuable because it is larger than Asian ginseng; in fact, it has been exported to Asia for centuries. Ginseng is commercially grown in the States, but wild ginseng is thought to have superior potency. Therein lies a cautionary tale: Because ginseng is so highly prized, it has become a valuable cash crop and its gathering is highly restricted. Because the plants and their valuable roots are so slow growing (it takes five years or more for a plant to mature), eighteen states require that harvested plants be at least five years of age, and Illinois requires that they be ten years old.

Ginseng harvest season is from September 1 to November 30, and diggers must choose only plants with mature red berries. A ginseng plant is not legal to harvest in eighteen of the nineteen states unless it has three prongs; Illinois requires four (prongs are compound leaves, or leaf stems with three to five leaflets). Most states prohibit harvest on state lands. To check the laws and regulations in your state, download a free brochure from the American Herbal Products Association's website (www.ahpa.org).

Make sure to double-check the age of a ginseng plant before you dig it up. This plant has two stems: the upright one, above ground, and an underground stem, or rhizome. When the plant dies back each fall, a scar forms on the upper part of the rhizome, which is also called the "neck" of the ginseng root. To check for age, carefully dig around the bottom of the upright stem to examine the top of the neck. If the plant is five years old, it should have four scars; if six years old, it should have five (though there are exceptions to this rule). Harvest the root carefully, with the rhizome attached; take care not to damage either the root or the rhizome. Also be careful not to disturb the nearby plants. The red berries should be planted, about one-inch deep, near the dug-up plant.

Clean ginseng roots by rinsing them in a container of cool water. Take care not to scrub them or handle them roughly, as their surface is fragile. Dry them, in a single layer and not touching, on wire racks or screens in a warm room.

If you can't find them in the wild, ginseng roots (both wild and cultivated, which are also called cultivated wild) are also sold fresh, dried, and preserved in brandy, as well as in powdered form, as an extract for making tea, and in capsules as a dietary supplement. Cultivated ginseng is much less expensive than the wild roots.

TRADITIONAL KOREAN GINSENG JUJUBE TEA

Tea is a popular way to get the health benefits of ginseng. The following recipe concentrates ginseng's power. Be sure to check with your health care advisor before using this.

Makes three 6-cup pots of tea

3 large fresh or dried ginseng roots

10 jujubes (Chinese red dates),
   rinsed and patted dry

Honey

Pine nuts

Put the ginseng roots and the jujubes in an earthenware pot. Add 6 cups water and bring to a boil slowly, then boil over medium-high heat for 15 minutes. Lower the heat and simmer until the liquid turns brownish red and is reduced by one-third, about 4 cups. Remove from the heat.

To serve, pour the tea into a cup, add honey to taste, and stir well. Sprinkle with a few pine nuts and serve hot.

You should be able to steep this tea twice more, depending on the quality of the ginseng and jujubes. Store the ginseng mixture covered in the refrigerator until ready to steep.

KOREAN GINSENG AND CHICKEN SOUP

This is a recipe from my good friend chef Mei Ibach, who teaches Asian cooking classes all over the world. She notes that this signature Korean soup is revered both for its flavor as well as its medicinal value. It is traditionally cooked in a clay pot, but you can use a metal stockpot.

Serves 4

1 cup cooked sweet (glutinous) rice

5 chestnuts, shelled, skinned, and halved

8 jujubes (Chinese red dates), rinsed and patted dry

4 garlic cloves, silvered

2 fresh or brandy-packed ginseng roots (about 2 inches long), thinly sliced

1 young spring (broiler/fryer) chicken (about 2½ pounds)

6 cups chicken stock

6 to 8 whole white peppercorns

Kosher salt

1 ounce maitake or other wild mushrooms, thickly sliced (about 1 cup)

Korean red pepper powder, for garnish

Fine strips of peeled fresh ginger, for garnish

1 green onion (white and green parts), thinly sliced on the bias, for garnish

Put the rice in a bowl and add the chestnuts, jujubes, garlic, and ginseng roots. Form the sticky rice mixture into a ball and stuff it inside the body cavity of the chicken.

Truss the chicken to hold in the mixture and so the chicken keeps a nice shape. There are all kinds of tutorials online for how to truss a chicken. At its simplest, tuck the wings behind the back and tie the legs together with kitchen twine. Place the stuffed chicken in a clay pot or a medium stockpot and add the chicken stock, peppercorns, and 2 cups water. Bring the liquid to a boil over medium-high heat, then immediately reduce the heat to low, partially cover, and simmer for 1½ hours. Season with salt to taste. Add the mushrooms and cook until just tender, a few minutes longer.

Present the whole chicken at the table, then serve portions of it and the stuffing in individual bowls along with the stock. Garnish each bowl with a pinch of red pepper powder, ginger strips, and green onion.

WILD
MUSHROOMS

Before we delve into the incredible world of wild mushrooms, you must take this caution very seriously:

Make sure you know the wild mushrooms you have are edible. If you don't know for certain, do not eat any!

There are at least ninety-five mycological societies in North America, along with a few regional clubs and a national club. A professional organization called the Mycological Society of America organizes conferences and publishes the journal *Mycologia*. Before you go hunting for wild mushrooms, join one of the clubs that regularly organize hunts. Most mycological societies have a scientific advisor affiliated with the club who instructs the members on regional identification. This is important because the toxicity of mushrooms can vary according to their habitat, age, and method of preparation, and because mushroom identification books can be deceptive.

What are mushrooms? Well, here is the geeky answer: They are part of very large group of organisms that includes yeasts and molds, as well as the more familiar mushrooms. These organisms are classified as a kingdom, called Fungi, which is separate from plants, animals, bacteria, and the like. The discipline devoted to the study of fungi is called mycology. The biggest part of the mushroom, by far, is what we don't see; the part underground, called the mycelium, is a large body of feathery threads that exist beneath our feet. The mushroom, or the aboveground fruiting body, is like the apple on a tree—showy but not the most important part of the organism. This fruiting body appears only when conditions are right, and when that happens, it can almost magically pop up overnight. Many mushrooms are mycorrhizal, which means they help trees obtain nutrients and water from the soil. Mycorrhizae are the reason why forests exist. That's because fungi perform an essential role in the decomposition of organic matter and are critical in nutrient cycling and exchange. We need fungi and mushrooms to survive. Without them, we'd be deeply covered in dead plant material. The trees also help the mushrooms, which lack chlorophyll and are unable to photosynthesize. Mushrooms depend on trees and plants to convert the sun's energy into food.

Other mushrooms, known as saprobes, such as oysters and shiitakes, get their nutrients from dead trees and plants. A third type, such as the lobster mushroom, is parasitic and survives by draining the life out of a plant host.

The world of mushrooms is vast. Of the 1.5 to 5 million species of fungi projected to be out there, perhaps 5 percent have been identified. Of that 5 percent, maybe 10,000 species produce fleshy mushrooms, and about 400 of them are poisonous. As the field is constantly evolving, these numbers are speculative, but in general, of the 400 species that are poisonous, 20 are commonly found, 6 of which are lethal (and of the 2,000 or so species that are probably edible, 100 are widely picked and 15 to 30 are commonly eaten). The challenge, to reiterate, is to know your mushrooms!

Mushrooms have long been used as a direct source of food, as a leavening agent for bread, and in the fermentation of various food products, such as cheese, wine, beer, and soy sauce.

There are regional North American wild mushroom favorites that are dependent on where you live. We can't include them all here, but the cream of the crop include morels, porcini, maitakes, oyster mushrooms of various types, and, of course, truffles. Recipes and notes follow for all of these. I did not include recipes for button mushrooms or cremini (the younger sibling of the portobello), because these come to us primarily from cultivated sources. They were once wild, however.

Foraged wild mushrooms should always be cleaned, despite the conventional wisdom about not washing mushrooms. Wild mushrooms can be pretty dirty, depending on where they were gathered, what animals may have paid them a visit, and so forth. A quick soak in a bowl of fresh water is all you need. The debris will sink to the bottom, leaving you with clean mushrooms. If the mushrooms are exceptionally dirty, you may need to soak them several times. Also make sure to remove any excess moisture from the mushrooms. Giving them a gentle spin in a salad spinner or blotting them with paper towels should do the trick.

Don't store mushrooms (wild or cultivated) in a plastic bag. They need to breathe, so use a brown paper bag and store them in the refrigerator. If you washed them vigorously, a couple of days in the refrigerator in paper will help to dry them out and make sautéing or roasting much more efficient.

It's best not to eat mushrooms raw. The single exception is truffles. Even raw cultivated mushrooms contain a small amount of toxin that can cause stomach distress in some people. The toxins in both cultivated and raw mushrooms are destroyed by cooking.

BLACK TRUMPETS

RELATED TO THE CHANTERELLE, *CRATERELLUS CORNUCOPIOIDES* IS CALLED "THE trumpet of death" because of its color, but it's actually delicious rather than deadly. It's smaller than the orange chanterelle, with funnel-shaped caps and hollow stems. Black trumpets are secretive mushrooms with a habit of growing in dark places under bushes, which makes them hard to find. This mushroom's look-alikes are not toxic, so it's a good quarry for beginning foragers.

Black trumpets, unlike their golden cousins, are easy to clean. Simply cut or tear them in half and quickly wash and pat dry. Add to soups or stews for texture and flavor, or like any other mushroom, just sauté them in butter with some finely chopped shallots or garlic.

Black trumpets dry very well with no loss in flavor. In fact, I find the dried ones a little tastier than the fresh ones. You can also grind the dried mushrooms into a powder. This powder is very versatile. Add it to casseroles or soups for a rich mushroom flavor, sprinkle it over fresh pasta, or stir it into risotto. If you can't find black trumpets, look for morels, either dried or fresh.

CHAWAN MUSHI WITH BLACK TRUMPETS

Chawan mushi is a Japanese comfort food that combines eggs and dashi (the Japanese version of basic chicken stock) to make a light custard, which is then steamed or baked in a hot-water bath. Chicken, shrimp, mushrooms, and green vegetables are typical additions, but you can add whatever you like. *Chawan* means "teacup," the vessel in which the custard is steamed; you can find *chawan mushi* cups, which have lids, in Japanese grocery stores. You can easily substitute heatproof ramekins or small bowls and cover them tightly with aluminum foil.

Serves 4

2 ounces fresh black trumpet mushrooms, cleaned, or ½ ounce dried

1 tablespoon unsalted butter

Sea salt and freshly ground pepper (preferably white)

3 large eggs

2¾ cups Mushroom Dashi (page 96) or chicken stock

½ teaspoon sake (optional)

4 medium shrimp (21 to 25 per pound), peeled and deveined

2 teaspoons Japanese soy sauce (such as Kikkoman)

1 teaspoon peeled and grated fresh ginger

Fresh cilantro or mitsuba (Japanese parsley) leaves, for garnish

If using dried mushrooms, soak them in hot water until softened, about 15 minutes, then drain. Tear fresh or soaked dried mushrooms into thick lengthwise strips. In a medium skillet, melt the butter over medium heat and sauté the mushrooms until just cooked through, about 3 minutes. Season lightly with salt and pepper and set aside.

In a small bowl, beat the eggs thoroughly and stir in the dashi and sake, if using, and season with salt. Cut the shrimp in half lengthwise and toss them in another bowl with the soy sauce. Divide the shrimp and the reserved mushrooms among four 8-ounce custard cups. Gently pour the egg custard mixture equally into the cups and skim off any bubbles. Cover each cup securely with aluminum foil.

Place the cups in a single layer in a steamer basket set over boiling water, partially cover, and steam over medium heat until the custards are just firm, 15 to 20 minutes. Top each with a little of the ginger and garnish with a cilantro leaf.

MUSHROOM DASHI

Traditional dashi is made with kelp (kombu) and dried bonito flakes (smoked and dried skipjack tuna). You'll find recipes online for the stock, which could be used here. A simple alternative is to use a reconstituted dried granular base called *hon dashi*, which you'll find in Japanese and Asian markets. (You'll also find the kombu and dried shiitake there, too, as well as in natural food stores.) For maximum mushroom flavor, however, a good mushroom dashi is best.

Makes about 4 cups

Four (4-inch) pieces kombu seaweed
6 dried shiitake mushrooms, rinsed

Place the kombu in a pot with 6 cups water and very slowly bring to a simmer over medium-low heat, but do not boil, about 10 minutes. Remove the kombu just before the water boils and add the dried mushrooms.

Raise the heat and boil for 1 minute, then turn off the heat and let the pot sit, uncovered, for 30 minutes. Remove the mushrooms, and store the dashi covered in the refrigerator for up to 1 week. This dashi can be used as the base for a simple soup by adding a tablespoon or so of soy sauce and a sprinkling of chopped green onions.

Candy Caps

Also known as maple caps, candy caps are from the genus *Lactarius* and produce a type of latex (or "milk") when cut or bruised. Noting the color of this liquid, or the way it changes color (from orange or red to green or blue when exposed to air or handled), is an important method of identifying this mushroom. When dried indoors, the candy cap smells like maple syrup (hence its name). When you encounter these mushrooms in the woods, the fragrance is faint, so the dried version is the one that cooks generally seek out. Candy caps are also used in desserts, either chopped fresh, or dried and ground into a powder, because of their maple flavor. They also make a delicious counterpoint to savory dishes, especially those using smoked meats.

Unfortunately, candy caps are found only in Northern California in the United States, and they are not easy to find because they blend in so well with the rest of the forest floor. Though fairly expensive, dried candy caps are worth seeking out.

CANDY CAP CUSTARD SAUCE

With an intense maple-sugar taste, this sauce is delicious for fruit and cakes.
It may also be used as an ice-cream base.

Makes about 2½ cups

2 cups half-and-half

¼ cup dried candy cap mushrooms, rinsed

4 large egg yolks, lightly beaten

½ cup granulated sugar, or more to taste

Freshly squeezed lemon juice

In a small saucepan, combine the half-and-half and mushrooms. Bring to a simmer over low heat. Remove from the heat and let sit for at least 20 minutes.

Meanwhile, in a medium bowl, beat the eggs and sugar until light and smooth. Gradually whisk in the cream mixture and return to the saucepan. Cook over medium heat, stirring constantly, until the sauce thickens just enough to coat the back of a spoon, about 4 minutes. Be careful not to boil the sauce or the eggs will scramble. Immediately remove from the heat and strain through a fine-mesh strainer into a cool bowl. Add the lemon juice to taste. Let cool for at least 2 hours, and store covered in the refrigerator for up to 3 days before churning in an ice-cream maker according to the manufacturer's instructions.

CHANTERELLES

CHANTERELLES ARE A FAVORITE OF CHEFS. THE WORD CHANTERELLE COMES FROM the Latin *canthir*, which means "tankard," a vessel for drinking. When mature, chanterelles are shaped so much like goblets that they can resemble shot glasses of rainwater. These mushrooms grow all around the world. The European and Asian ones are small, but in the United States, they grow quite large, especially on the West Coast.

Chanterelles are called *girolle*s in France and "egg mushrooms" in this country because of their beautiful golden egg-yolk color. They are one of the first mushrooms I learned to gather because they can be easily identified. We called them "goldies." Again, however, make sure to properly identify them before eating. There are a couple of chanterelle look-alikes that, although not fatal, can cause some really unpleasant intestinal adventures.

Chanterelles are mycorrhizal and grow in a symbiotic relationship with trees. They will reappear in the same place year after year if carefully harvested, so take care not to disturb the ground in which the mycelium (the vegetative part of the mushroom) grows. Look for them from September to February on the West Coast, especially after a rain, and in the summer on the East Coast.

Cleaning chanterelles can be unpleasant, especially if they've been harvested just after heavy rains. Try to wash them a couple of days ahead of cooking and store them in a paper bag in the refrigerator. A bonus with the chanterelle, however, is that typically there are no problems with worms.

SABLEFISH WITH CHANTERELLES AND PARSLEY

The parsley sauce can be made a day ahead of time, refrigerated, and reheated. The mushrooms can be cooked an hour or two ahead, making this a pretty simple recipe. Any wild mushroom that you like can be substituted for the chanterelles. Likewise, any firm white fish can be substituted for the sablefish (see more about sablefish, also called black cod, on page 284).

Serves 4

Parsley Sauce

1 garlic clove

1½ cups packed fresh flat-leaf parsley leaves
   with tender stems

½ cup packed fresh basil leaves

½ cup extra-virgin olive oil

Sea salt and freshly ground black pepper

Sablefish

Four (5- to 6-ounce) sablefish fillets

Salt and freshly ground black pepper

2 tablespoons unsalted butter

1 tablespoon extra-virgin olive oil

¼ cup dry white vermouth or dry white wine

2 tablespoons freshly squeezed lemon juice

Chanterelles

2 tablespoons unsalted butter

1 tablespoon extra-virgin olive oil

8 ounces chanterelle mushrooms,
   cleaned and quartered

1 tablespoon finely chopped shallot

Salt and freshly ground black pepper

1 teaspoon lemon zest

TO MAKE THE PARSLEY SAUCE: Fill a large bowl with ice water. Bring a medium saucepan of salted water to a boil. Add the garlic and cook for 1 minute. Stir in the parsley and basil and cook for 10 seconds. Drain and immediately plunge the herbs and garlic into the ice-water bath to preserve their color and flavor. Drain again and squeeze as much water out of the herbs as you can. Transfer the herbs and garlic to a blender. Add the olive oil and purée until smooth. Season with salt and pepper to taste. Set aside in the blender container.

(Continues on page 101)

TO COOK THE FISH: Preheat the oven to 425°F.

Season the fish with salt and pepper. In a large ovenproof sauté pan, melt the butter with the oil over medium heat. Add the fish and cook until nicely browned on one side, about 5 minutes. Turn the fish over and transfer the pan to the oven. Roast until the fish is just cooked through and flakes easily when a fork is inserted in the center of a fillet, 4 to 5 minutes. Remove the fish from the pan and keep warm. Add the vermouth and lemon juice to the pan and cook over high heat to reduce the liquid until syrupy, scraping up any browned bits. Transfer the liquid to the blender with the parsley sauce and pulse to combine.

TO COOK THE MUSHROOMS: While the fish is roasting, heat a large skillet over high heat and add the butter and olive oil. Add the mushrooms and let them sear undisturbed for several seconds, then stir and toss in the pan until they release their liquid. Add the shallot and salt and pepper to taste, then continue to cook and gently turn until the liquid has evaporated and the mushrooms are lightly browned but still holding their shape. Stir in the lemon zest and adjust seasonings to taste.

TO SERVE: Spoon a generous portion of the sauce onto four warmed plates. Place the fish on top, then top with the mushrooms and serve immediately.

Great Mushroom Reference Books

My go-to mushroom books are by David Arora and the National Audubon Society. Arora is an American mycologist who has written two popular mushroom field guides, *Mushrooms Demystified* and *All That the Rain Promises and More*. The *National Audubon Society Field Guide to Mushrooms* is comprehensive, including more than seven hundred mushrooms detailed with color photographs and descriptive text. A companion downloadable app for smartphones and tablets is also available. Becky Selengut's book *Shroom* is a good one, too, and it has lots of wonderful recipes for both wild and cultivated mushrooms.

LION'S MANES

THE FURRY TEXTURE OF THE LION'S MANE, FROM THE GENUS *HERICIUM*, IS UNLIKE that of any other mushroom. They feed on dead and dying trees in North America, Asia, and Europe. They are not widespread, and they grow up high on trees, which makes them hard to find. These mushrooms are known by many colorful names, including bearded tooth, pom-pom blanc, sheep's head, and old man's beard.

When you slice open a lion's mane, the interior looks a lot like a tiny slice of cauliflower: lots of branching structure radiating out from the base. This sponge-like texture makes them soak up liquid more than any other mushroom. Be sure to squeeze them dry after washing.

Like many mushrooms, lion's manes are considered something of a superfood and have been shown to possess antioxidant and lipid-regulating properties. Asian medicine has traditionally prescribed them for stomach problems, including cancer. Some studies have suggested that their benefits might include antibacterial and anti-inflammatory effects and might even heal nerve tissue.

Because lion's manes can contain a lot of moisture, you should cook them slowly to drive the moisture out and crisp the edges. I think they are best simply cooked in a mixture of oil and butter and seasoned with salt and pepper. They have a delicate lobster-crab flavor that makes them terrific with eggs.

BAKED EGGS WITH LION'S MANES AND GOAT CHEESE

Instead of sautéing the lion's manes as I'm doing here, you can also leave them whole,
drizzle them liberally with melted butter, and roast them in a hot oven
until lightly browned. Slice thinly before adding to the ramekins.

Serves 4

12 ounces lion's mane mushrooms

2 tablespoons butter, plus more for greasing

1 tablespoon olive oil

Sea salt and freshly ground black pepper

3 tablespoons chopped fresh chives

½ teaspoon chopped fresh thyme

2 ounces fresh goat cheese (chèvre)

8 large eggs

4 tablespoons light cream or half-and-half

Preheat the oven to 350°F. Bring a teakettle of water to a boil.

Squeeze any moisture out of the mushrooms, and cut or tear them into bite-size pieces. In a large skillet over medium heat, melt the 2 tablespoons butter with the oil. When bubbly, add the mushrooms and cook until any moisture has evaporated and the mushrooms are nicely browned and crispy around the edges, 8 to 10 minutes. Season with salt and pepper to taste, stir in the chives and thyme, and cook for another minute until fragrant. Set aside.

Grease four 8-ounce ramekins with butter. Crumble the cheese and divide among the ramekins. Gently crack two eggs into each ramekin, being careful not to break the yolks. Add one-quarter of the mushroom mixture to each, and top each ramekin with 1 tablespoon of the cream.

Place the ramekins in a deep baking pan or dish, place in the oven, and add boiling water to the pan until the water comes halfway up the sides of the ramekins. Bake the ramekins in the hot-water bath until the egg whites are just set and the yolks are still runny in the center, about 10 minutes. Remove the ramekins from the water bath and allow to cool for a couple of minutes before serving.

MAITAKES

MAITAKES ARE ALSO KNOWN AS HEN OF THE WOODS OR SHEEP'S HEAD MUSH-rooms. They are increasingly available cultivated, and I think they taste as good in that form as they do wild. The cultivated version is usually very clean and requires little trimming. In the wild, maitakes provide all kinds of crevices for debris, so take care to thoroughly clean them. The best method is to first pick off any large debris like leaves and twigs from the mushroom and then brush it off with a kitchen brush to remove as much dirt as possible. Cut off any rotten or bruised parts of the mushroom, and wipe off any remaining dirt using damp paper towels. This is my favorite mushroom, both fresh and dried.

MAITAKE TEMPURA
WITH PONZU DIPPING SAUCE

Don't worry if the mushrooms break up a bit after you've cleaned them.
You can fry all the little pieces, which are my favorite nibbles. If you can't find maitakes,
this recipe works well with other mushrooms such as oyster mushrooms.

Serves 4 to 6

Ponzu Sauce

½ cup freshly squeezed lime or lemon juice,
or a combination

⅓ cup soy sauce

2 tablespoons rice vinegar

2 tablespoons mirin

2 tablespoons packed light brown sugar

½ teaspoon Asian fish sauce,
or more to taste

Tempura Batter

2 cups rice flour

2 cups chilled club soda

1 large egg yolk

Maitakes

Canola oil, for frying

1 pound maitake mushrooms,
cut into ¼-inch slices

1 cup cornstarch

Sea salt

TO MAKE THE PONZU SAUCE: In a small bowl, whisk together the lime juice, soy sauce, vinegar, mirin, sugar, and fish sauce. Set aside.

TO PREPARE THE TEMPURA BATTER: In a medium bowl, whisk together the flour, club soda, and egg yolk. Set aside.

TO FRY THE MAITAKES: Line a wire rack with paper towels. Heat 2 inches of oil in a deep, heavy saucepan or Dutch oven over medium-high heat to 375°F.

Dust the mushrooms with the cornstarch, shaking off any excess. Dredge them in the tempura batter and drop into the hot oil, working in batches without crowding. Fry until golden brown on all sides, about 3 minutes. With a slotted spoon or spider, transfer to a prepared rack to drain. Sprinkle lightly with salt and serve warm with the ponzu sauce.

MORELS

UNIQUE AMONG MUSHROOMS, MORELS HAVE A COMPLEX, UMAMI-PACKED FLA-vor and a conical, honeycomb-textured body. Morels can be found and foraged in most regions in the United States except for desert areas. They like moist soil and warm temperatures, and they rely on dying trees as a food source. The normal season for morels is March through July (or when the weather begins to warm up), which is when they can be found fresh in markets. Although usually dark brown-black in color, some morel varieties are yellow and orange. Morels dry beautifully and are widely available in the dried form year-round.

CRAB-STUFFED MOREL MUSHROOMS

Crab-stuffed fresh morels are one of my favorite hors d'oeuvres. You'll find many variations on the theme. They can be made ahead and then baked just before serving. I think Dungeness crab is the best because I'm a West coast boy, but use whatever crab you like. Be sure to thoroughly wash and dry the morels after cutting them in half. They are notorious for harboring insects and debris. Unlike other mushrooms, morels don't soak up a lot of water and as a result keep their texture.

Makes 24

12 fresh, large morel mushrooms
  of uniform size

1 large egg, beaten

5 tablespoons mayonnaise

1 tablespoon finely chopped green onion

2 teaspoons Worcestershire sauce
  (preferably white)

Salt and freshly ground black pepper

Hot sauce

1 pound cooked fresh Dungeness crabmeat,
  picked over to remove any shells

⅔ cup coarse dry breadcrumbs,
  such as panko, divided

3 tablespoons freshly grated Parmesan cheese

1 tablespoon very finely chopped
  fresh Italian parsley

Clarified butter or olive oil, as needed

Preheat the oven to 375°F. Line a baking sheet with parchment paper or a silicone baking mat. Wash the morels well, cut in half, and pat dry with paper towels.

In a bowl, stir together the egg, mayonnaise, green onion, Worcestershire, and salt, pepper, and hot sauce to taste. Add the crabmeat and ½ cup of the breadcrumbs and stir just to combine. Adjust seasonings to taste.

Fill each morel half with a slightly rounded mound of the crab mixture and place in a single layer on the prepared baking sheet. In a small bowl, mix the cheese, parsley, and the remaining breadcrumbs. Sprinkle the breadcrumb mixture lightly over the top of each mushroom and drizzle each with a little of the clarified butter.

Bake the mushrooms until the tops are golden brown and the mushrooms are tender, about 20 minutes. Serve warm.

OYSTERS

YSTER MUSHROOMS CAN BE FOUND THROUGHOUT THE WILD, TYPICALLY IN fall and winter. I'll bet we've all seen them growing on the sides of fallen trees, of which they are prodigious consumers, helping in habitat restoration. For me, oysters are a great mushroom to serve with meat of any kind. Some believe this mushroom has an oyster- or abalone-like flavor, hence its name. Oysters are one of the most easily cultivated mushrooms, making them available year-round. Oysters are convenient for cooking, because they are very clean. These are the mushrooms I use the most. Look for caps that are firm and moist, with intact edges that are not dried out. The stems are a bit chewier than the caps, and often recipes suggest discarding them. I like that texture difference, so try them both ways and make up your own mind.

HANGER STEAK WITH RED WINE AND OYSTER MUSHROOMS

The hanger steak is better known in France (where it is referred to as *onglet*) than in the United States, but it is becoming increasingly popular here. Known in America by various names including the "hanging tenderloin," this steak is the part of the diaphragm that hangs between the last rib and the loin. US butchers traditionally take hangar steak home as a treat for themselves. The meat's grainy texture and intense flavor make it a first-rate steak. Just be sure not to overcook it.

Serves 4

3 tablespoons olive oil, divided

2 tablespoons finely chopped shallot

12 ounces firm, trimmed oyster mushrooms

Kosher salt and freshly ground black pepper

4 tablespoons (½ stick) unsalted butter, divided

1½ pounds hanger steak, trimmed and pounded to ½ inch thickness

3 garlic cloves, lightly crushed

1 cup dry red wine

1 cup beef or chicken stock

1 tablespoon soy sauce

1 tablespoon chopped fresh tarragon

In a large, heavy skillet, heat 2 tablespoons of the oil over medium-high heat. Add the shallot and cook until tender, about 1 minute. Add the mushrooms and cook, stirring, until lightly browned but still holding their shape, about 5 minutes. Season with salt and pepper to taste. Transfer to a bowl and set aside.

Melt 1 tablespoon of the butter with the remaining 1 tablespoon oil in the same skillet over medium-high heat. Season the steak generously with salt and pepper. Add the steak and garlic to the skillet. Cook about 3 minutes per side for medium-rare. Transfer to a cutting board, tent with aluminum foil, and let the steak rest while preparing the sauce.

Remove the garlic from the skillet and discard. Pour off all but 1 tablespoon of fat. Add the wine, stock, and soy sauce, and deglaze the pan, scraping the bottom to incorporate any browned bits. Cook until reduced to ⅔ cup, about 6 minutes. Strain and return the liquid to the skillet and bring back to a boil. Remove from the heat, and whisk in the remaining 3 tablespoons butter. Stir in the tarragon and the reserved mushrooms and season with salt and pepper to taste. Spoon the mushroom mixture onto plates. Slice the steak thinly and fan over the mushrooms.

PORCINI

Porcini are one of the most prized mushrooms in the world. There is no cultivated version. In France, they are called *cèpes*, and in America, both names are used along with boletes, from their Latin name *Boletus edulis*. In the States, we are most familiar with porcini in their dried form, which can add a very distinctive, deeply earthy flavor to sauces, soups, and more. Porcini are found throughout Europe, the United States, and Canada, and in parts of China and Mexico. They are usually found in late summer or early fall, growing near spruce, pine, hemlock, and birch trees. Take care when foraging, as there are some look-alikes that are not edible.

Italians consider this mushroom to be the king of all wild mushrooms (porcini is Italian for "little piglets"). Fresh porcini are usually grilled and served with a peppery olive oil and parsley. Often known as a "poor man's steak," porcini are much more flavorful and satisfying than a grilled portobello, which is simply an overgrown cremini mushroom.

Fresh porcini are also excellent fried, stewed with tomatoes (*porcini in umido*), or used as the base of a decadent pasta sauce or as a bruschetta topping. If you can get to Italy's central regions of Tuscany, Umbria, and Emilia-Romagna in early September through the end of October, you'll be greeted with mounds of plump porcini being sold from roadside stands and in front of almost every restaurant. Unfortunately, worms also love porcini. When buying this mushroom, check the stem for worm damage. If the stem feels very firm, you are in great shape. If the stem is squishy, then there's probably significant insect damage. Smart sellers will usually slice a porcini in half so you can inspect for insect damage.

FARRO RISOTTO WITH PORCINI, PANCETTA, AND PARMESAN

Farro, a favorite grain in Italy, is one of three ancient wheat varieties first cultivated in the Fertile Crescent and still grown in Italy: *farro piccolo* (also known by the German name einkorn), *farro medio* (also known as emmer, the Hebrew word for "mother"), and *farro grande* (also known as spelt). The imported Italian farro available in the States is usually the emmer variety. It's usually labeled *perlato* or *semi perlato* (pearled), meaning it retains some but not all of its bran and nutrients. Most recipes, including this one, are written for this kind of farro, which requires no soaking and cooks in about twenty-five minutes.

Serves 4

1 ounce dried porcini mushrooms

3 tablespoons extra-virgin olive oil, divided

3 ounces diced pancetta

4½ cups low-sodium chicken stock

1 tablespoon unsalted butter

3 tablespoons finely chopped shallots

1 tablespoon finely chopped garlic

1¼ cups semi-pearled farro (*perlato* or *semi perlato*)

½ cup dry white wine

⅓ cup freshly grated Parmesan cheese, plus more for garnish

1 teaspoon lemon zest, plus more for garnish

Kosher or sea salt and freshly ground black pepper

In a bowl, cover the mushrooms with hot water and soak until softened, about 10 minutes. Drain the porcini, reserving the soaking water, and chop very coarsely.

In a large skillet, heat 2 tablespoons of the olive oil over medium heat. Add the pancetta and cook until nicely browned, about 5 minutes. With a slotted spoon, remove the pancetta to a paper towel–lined plate and set aside. Add the porcini and sauté until they just begin to brown around the edges. Set aside.

In a medium saucepan, bring the stock and the reserved soaking water to a simmer and keep warm. In a large saucepan, melt the butter with the remaining 1 tablespoon olive oil over medium heat. Add the shallots and sauté until they just begin to brown, about 3 minutes. Add the garlic and sauté until fragrant, about 1 minute. Stir in the farro so that it's well coated in the fat, and cook for 3 minutes to lightly toast.

Reduce the heat to low and add the wine. Cook, scraping any browned bits from the bottom of the pan with a wooden spoon, until the liquid is completely absorbed. Ladle 1 cup of the warm stock into the pan so that the farro is just covered with liquid. Cook gently (liquid should be just simmering), stirring occasionally, until the stock is almost completely absorbed. Repeat this process until the farro is al dente.

When the farro is tender, stir in the pancetta and mushrooms. Continue to stir until the risotto is creamy and heated through. Remove from the heat and stir in the cheese and lemon zest. Season with salt and pepper to taste. Top with extra cheese and a sprinkle of lemon zest, if desired.

GRILLED FRESH PORCINI MUSHROOMS

I'm grilling these porcini over wood, but you can also use a grill pan on the stove. If cooking on the stove top, I'd suggest using smoked salt in place of the regular salt to give the porcini a bit of the smoky flavor that an outdoor or fireplace grill provides.

Serves 4, depending on what else you are having

2 teaspoons finely chopped
  fresh flat-leaf parsley

1 teaspoon finely chopped fresh thyme

1 teaspoon finely chopped fresh rosemary

1 teaspoon finely chopped garlic

⅓ cup extra-virgin olive oil

1 pound fresh porcini mushrooms

Kosher or sea salt and
  freshly ground black pepper

Prepare a charcoal grill or preheat a gas grill to medium heat.

In a small bowl, combine the olive oil, parsley, thyme, rosemary, and garlic. Set aside.

Clean the mushrooms with a damp cloth. Cut them into ½-inch-thick slices and brush them lightly with the oil mixture. Season well with salt and pepper. Grill the mushrooms until lightly browned, about 3 minutes on each side. Transfer to a serving platter and brush with any remaining oil mixture. Serve immediately.

PORCINI MUSHROOM BREAD PUDDING
WITH SMOKED TOMATO SAUCE

This dish is grand made with fresh porcini, but any other mushroom or a combination can be substituted. Here, the puddings are baked in individual portions, but you can use a large baking or casserole dish instead; add fifteen to twenty minutes to the baking time if done this way. The smoked tomato sauce is delicious, but if you don't have time to make it, a simple tomato sauce will work perfectly well.

Serves 12, as a first course

1½ pounds fresh porcini mushrooms, cleaned and trimmed

Olive oil, for brushing

Salt and freshly ground black pepper

2 tablespoons chopped fresh chives

3 ounces poached garlic cloves (about 12) (page 117)

2½ cups light cream or half-and-half

5 large eggs

2 teaspoons fresh thyme or 1 teaspoon dried

½ teaspoon finely crushed juniper berry (optional)

1 teaspoon salt, or more to taste

¼ teaspoon freshly ground black pepper, or more to taste

1 tablespoon unsalted butter

1 small (8 ounce) loaf challah, brioche, or other egg bread, cut into ½-inch cubes

1½ cups freshly grated Parmesan, Asiago, or dry-aged Jack cheese

1 recipe Smoked Tomato Sauce (page 117)

Deep-fried basil leaves (see note), for garnish (optional)

Preheat the broiler.

Lightly brush the mushrooms with olive oil and season with salt and pepper to taste. Place the mushrooms on a sheet pan and roast them under the broiler until just cooked through. Chop coarsely, combine with chives, and set aside.

Preheat the oven to 350°F.

In a blender, add the garlic and just enough of the cream to cover, and purée until smooth. Pour the mixture into a bowl and add the eggs, thyme, juniper berry (if using), salt, pepper, and the remaining cream. Whisk until smooth.

Lightly butter twelve 5-ounce ramekins (or use a standard muffin pan), and place three or four bread cubes in each to cover the bottom. Divide the reserved mushrooms evenly among each ramekin and sprinkle evenly with ¾ cup of the cheese. Pour the custard mixture over the top. Add as many more bread cubes as can comfortably fit (you'll want to gently press down on them so they absorb the custard), and top with the remaining ¾ cup cheese.

Place the ramekins (or muffin pan) in a larger roasting pan and pour hot water in roasting pan to reach three-quarters up the sides of the ramekins. Cover with aluminum foil and bake until custard is just set, 25 to 30 minutes. Remove from the oven and allow to rest for 3 minutes before unmolding.

To serve, carefully remove the custards from the pan and unmold in the center of warm plates. Ladle the tomato sauce around the custards and garnish with fried basil, if using.

NOTE: For a beautiful and tasty garnish, deep-fry basil leaves. Make sure the leaves are completely dry. In a heavy, deep saucepan, heat about ½ inch of vegetable oil to 325°F. The tall sides help protect you against hot splatters. Carefully drop a few leaves at a time into the hot oil and cook until they become crisp and look crystalline, about 20 seconds. Remove with a slotted spoon or spider and drain on paper towels. Can be made an hour or two ahead.

SMOKED TOMATO SAUCE

Makes about 1½ cups

4 large tomatoes (2 pounds total), cored

4 large garlic cloves

1½ teaspoons balsamic vinegar, or more to taste

Salt and freshly ground black pepper

Place the tomatoes and garlic in a pan with sides to catch the juices, and smoke in a stovetop smoker on very low heat until they begin to collapse, 30 to 40 minutes.

Transfer the tomatoes and garlic to a food processor. Pulse until the mixture is puréed. Strain through a fine-mesh strainer, pushing down on the solids, and season to taste with the balsamic vinegar and salt and pepper to taste. Keep warm. The sauce can be made up to 3 days ahead and stored covered in the refrigerator; reheat before serving. The sauce can also be frozen for up to 3 months.

NOTE: If you do not have a smoker, you can prepare this sauce on the stove top by placing wood chips or dust in the bottom of an aluminum foil–lined wok. Put the tomatoes in a cake pan that fits inside the wok about 1 inch above the chips (or use a grate). Cover tightly and smoke over very low heat. Be sure you have a good exhaust system if doing this in the kitchen. The same method can be applied in a kettle grill.

Poaching Garlic

Poaching softens and sweetens the flavor of garlic cloves. To poach garlic, separate the cloves but do not peel. Place the cloves in a small saucepan and cover with at least a half inch of cold water. Bring to a boil over high heat, then drain. Repeat the process again. Rinse to cool the cloves, then peel.

TRUFFLES

TRUFFLES ARE MUSHROOMS, BUT UNLIKE REGULAR MUSHROOMS, THEY GROW UNDER the ground. This makes them difficult to find, and as a result, they can be breathtakingly expensive.

Also unlike regular mushrooms, whose spores are carried by air currents, truffles must be eaten by animals to have their spores distributed. Truffles resemble small potatoes, and their name comes from the Latin for "tuber." There are hundreds of truffle varieties, but only a few are prized as food. At the top of the list, in terms of cost, is the Italian white truffle from Piedmont or Alba, followed by the French black truffle from Périgord, and Oregon white and black truffles. Since the early 1800s, truffles have been "cultivated" by inoculating the roots of host trees with spores, and they are now grown in many parts of the world including America, Australia, New Zealand, and China. There have been some problems of adulteration with Chinese truffles, so I'd avoid them.

Want to grow your own truffles? In the United States, the American Truffle Company (www. americantruffle.com) assists those who would like to do so, especially in Northern California.

Traditionally, truffles have been harvested in Europe using female pigs, as Italian and French truffles produce a scent that is similar to that of a sex hormone of the male pig. More recently, dogs have become preferred to pigs because they don't eat truffles and they're easier to train and transport by car.

As with all mushrooms, refrigerate truffles in a paper bag (never plastic). They can also be stored frozen for several months in a glass jar or immersed in olive oil (which flavors the oil) and refrigerated for up to two weeks. Some people store them in rice (which flavors the rice), but this also may leach moisture from the truffles. Storing them in a paper bag with eggs will flavor the eggs for omelets and scrambled eggs. But if you are lucky enough to have one or more fresh truffles, the best idea is to cook them immediately.

Salt and butter flavored with truffles are available in some specialty foods stores and online, as is truffle oil, but be aware that most truffle oil is artificially flavored with a chemical.

FRENCH SCRAMBLED EGGS
WITH SHAVED TRUFFLES

The French technique for scrambling eggs in a double boiler or over very low heat makes
for lovely, soft, custardy curds, unlike the usual tough, sulphury eggs we get when we cook them over high
heat. I learned this technique in my early training in France, and it's still my favorite way to cook eggs.
To gild the lily, use truffle butter in place of regular. And if you're one of those people who somehow has
frequent access to fresh truffles, a truffle shaver is a good tool to have on hand.

Serves 4

2 tablespoon unsalted butter

6 large eggs

⅓ cup half-and-half

Sea salt and freshly ground pepper
  (preferably white)

1 tablespoon chopped fresh chives

1 small impeccably fresh truffle,
  or as much as you can afford

In the top of a double boiler set over very gently simmering water, melt butter, swirling it around the pan.
In a bowl, crack the eggs, whisk together with the half-and-half, and season lightly with salt and pepper.
Add to the pan and begin stirring with a heatproof spatula. Continue to stir until the eggs slowly begin to
form creamy curds. The entire process should take at least 8 minutes. If the curds are forming faster, lower
the heat or remove pan from the heat for about 1 minute while continuing to stir.

When the eggs are creamy, with very small curds and still moist, spoon them into four warmed cups or
bowls and top evenly with the chives. Shave as many slices of truffle as you like over the top of each, and
serve immediately.

A Conversation with Mushroom Forager Dean Robbins

THE TOPIC:

Wild Mushrooms

CHEF: What comes to mind when you hear the words wild mushrooms?

ROBBINS: Flavor. Because wild mushrooms cannot be cultivated on a commercial scale, their flavor is far superior. The textures and shapes of wild mushrooms also lend themselves better to gourmet meals as well as hardy everyday fare. The seasonal nature of wild mushrooms allows us to enjoy them when they are available and crave them when they are not. For the most part, wild mushrooms are healthier and grown with fewer toxins than cultivated mushrooms. The varieties are virtually endless.

CHEF: Can you tell the difference between a wild and cultivated mushroom?

ROBBINS: Because popular gourmet wild mushrooms cannot be raised on a commercial scale, there's not much danger of getting a cultivated mushroom mixed up with a wild mushroom. Varieties like morels, chanterelles, hedgehogs, and porcini are only harvested in the wild. If you find mushrooms like lion's manes, oysters, and tree ears that have been cultivated, they are usually labeled as such.

CHEF: How easy is it to obtain wild mushrooms?

ROBBINS: When I first started harvesting, only people "in the know" were able to enjoy wild gourmet mushrooms. If you didn't know how to find them, or know someone who did, you didn't get to enjoy them. Times have changed, and today, wild mushrooms are becoming much easier to obtain. Dried wild mushrooms are available in stores and online throughout the year. Fresh wild mushrooms are available at specialty grocery stores and farmers' markets when in season. When the chanterelles are flushing heavy on the West Coast, for example, you can buy them almost anywhere, including Costco.

CHEF: Anything in particular we should look for when buying wild mushrooms?

ROBBINS: You should know where the mushrooms are coming from, because some states or countries are more polluted than others. You should also know who is harvesting the mushrooms. Try and deal with a trusted vendor or forager. Fresh mushrooms should smell pleasant and earthy. They should be firm and relatively clean. Watch out for any mold or decay.

CHEF: Talk a little bit about mushroom spoilage.

ROBBINS: Most wild mushrooms are much more fragile than cultivated varieties. They aren't always picked in ideal conditions, and they are difficult to keep fresh in the woods. Spoiled wild mushrooms will look and smell bad. I have seen oyster mushrooms in the store that have been sitting there so long that the mycelium is starting to consume the mushroom. This stage of decay will definitely make you sick.

CHEF: What are some of your favorite wild mushrooms?

ROBBINS: Definitely the morel mushroom. It's also the most popular and well-known wild mushroom, which is sold worldwide both fresh and dried. The chanterelle is another one of my favorites, especially fresh. After that I would say the porcini. This variety can be eaten raw, grilled, fried, or used like button mushrooms, but with an earthy, nutty flavor that is far superior to buttons or portobellos. Dried, they make rich gravies, sauces, and are a wonderful base for soups. I eat dried porcini all winter long.

CHEF: You mentioned both fresh and dried. Is there a difference in the flavor profile?

ROBBINS: There is a big difference in the taste of dried and fresh wild mushrooms. But they both have their place. Fresh morels, for example, are delicious almost any way you cook them. The texture is interesting, and the flavor is earthy and bold. Dried morels are a little chewy when rehydrated, but they make a delicious clear broth that cannot be made with fresh morels. Fresh chanterelles are exotic prepared the right way, but dried chanterelles are chewy and best used for soups or dips. The flavor is intensified with most dried mushrooms. Always keep in mind that dried mushrooms are not cooked and need to be prepared, just like fresh mushrooms, before consuming.

CHEF: Any wild mushrooms you enjoy that we might not be familiar with?

ROBBINS: The lion's mane mushroom is interesting and tasty. They can take on a light seafood flavor if prepared properly. Tree ears are also interesting because they have a unique texture that isn't ruined by cooking. They are wonderful in Asian soups or stir-fries.

CHEF: Any words of advice for those considering foraging wild mushrooms themselves?

ROBBINS: Do your homework and be careful. Foraging for wild mushrooms can be dangerous for the novice. The best way to learn is to find an experienced mentor to show you the way. You can join a local mushroom club and go on forays. Get some good identification guides, and realize that learning wild mushrooms is a slow process and cannot be rushed. Do not eat anything that you are not absolutely sure of the identification. And only eat a small amount, even if you found a bunch. Wild foraging can be accomplished by almost anyone, but should not be taken lightly. I have watched some edible mushrooms come and go [in the wild] for three years before I was confident enough to actually eat them.

WOOD SORREL

MOST OF US HAVE ENCOUNTERED WOOD SORREL EVEN IF WE DIDN'T KNOW WHAT it was. It's a common lawn weed also known as sour grass. Dr. James Duke's *Handbook of Edible Weeds* notes that Native Americans chewed wood sorrel to alleviate thirst on long trips and used it medicinally to alleviate mouth sores and a sore throat and to help with cramps, fever, and nausea. The leaves of the wood sorrel are high in vitamin C. The starchy roots can be boiled and taste a bit like a potato.

Wood sorrel grows almost everywhere in North America. The plant belongs to the genus *Oxalis*, and there are hundreds of different species. The species we typically encounter looks very similar to clover. Wood sorrel grows about a foot tall, with small, heart-shaped leaves in groups of three, like clover. The tiny flowers on the wood sorrel are typically white or yellow, though they can be pink or violet, depending on the species. There are no poisonous look-alikes. To harvest, simply pull the wood sorrel up by its roots. This plant can be harvested from mid-spring through fall. Yellow wood sorrel blooms April through September.

Oxalis is Latin for "sour," and the plant's sour taste is due to it oxalic acid content, a characteristic it shares with other vegetables such as spinach and broccoli.

In addition to making a great seasoning and salad ingredient, the leaves and flowers of wood sorrel can be used to make a tisane, or herbal tea, by adding boiling water and letting them steep.

WOOD SORREL SOUP

Variations of this simple recipe appear in Polish and Russian cookbooks. Known as *schav* in Russia and *zupa szczawiowa* in Poland, this soup can also be made with domestic sorrel. Some recipes call for putting a heaping spoonful of mashed potatoes in the bottom of the bowl and then ladling the soup over top. Sounds good to me!

Serves 6

2 tablespoons unsalted butter

2 cups finely chopped yellow onions

1 pound sorrel leaves, stemmed and finely chopped

6 cups chicken or vegetable stock

1 tablespoon granulated sugar, or more to taste

Kosher salt and freshly ground pepper (preferably white)

Freshly squeezed lemon juice

3 large egg yolks, beaten

Sour cream, for garnish

Sorrel flowers for garnish

In a deep, medium saucepan, melt the butter over medium heat and sauté the onions until soft but not brown, about 6 minutes. Add the sorrel and cook until softened, about 4 minutes.

Add the stock and bring to a boil. Immediately lower the heat and simmer for a few minutes. Season with sugar, lemon juice, and salt and pepper to taste. Remove from the heat.

Beat about ⅓ cup of the hot soup into the egg yolks, then stir the yolk mixture into the soup. Reheat, if desired, but don't let the soup boil or the eggs will scramble. Serve hot or cold, dolloped with sour cream and garnished with flowers.

NUTS, GRAINS, AND SEEDS

AMARANTH

MARANTH HAS BEEN CULTIVATED FOR THOUSANDS OF YEARS, AND THUS YOU might ask why it's being included in a "wild" book. Despite its cultivation, amaranth continues to grow wild, and because of its ability to produce a prodigious amount of tiny seeds, this vigorous plant continually reseeds itself, returning to the wild throughout the world. I believe amaranth and probably dandelions will remain long after humans are gone!

According to author and forager Samuel Thayer, at least forty different species of amaranth (from the genus *Amaranthus*) are found in the wild. Also referred to as wild beet, redroot pigweed, and redroot amaranth, this tall, broad-leafed annual is found all across North America.

Wild amaranth, which can grow many feet tall, is often seen as an annoying weed by gardeners and farmers, but people around the globe eat its leaves as a vegetable and its tiny seeds as a cereal or flour (though amaranth is not a true cereal). Cultivated versions are grown for their flamboyant flowers, which are made up of clusters of spiky blossoms in bright colors of red, purple, and gold. The flowers retain their color and shape when dried.

Amaranth grain has been cultivated for millennia in Latin America and Mexico, where it was a major food source for the Aztecs and was used in religious ceremonies to make sacred cakes in the shape of a god's face. The cakes were broken and eaten as a way of worshipping the god. Because of its ritual symbolism, amaranth was outlawed by the Spanish conquistadors in an effort to convert the natives to Christianity. Amaranth crops were destroyed and anyone possessing the grains was harshly punished. As a result, corn took the place of amaranth as a food crop.

Yet amaranth is still cultivated in Mexico, for it is a quickly growing crop and its grains are remarkably high in protein—about 14 percent, more than any other grain. Unlike corn, which must be eaten with beans to provide complete protein, amaranth grain is a complete protein on its own. It is believed to be highly effective in lowering cholesterol.

Amaranth tolerates hot weather, so the leaves can be harvested in summer, unlike most lettuces, which bolt in the heat. Choose tender leaves for salads and cook older ones for greens. Amaranth seeds are ready to harvest after the first frost; you will notice birds beginning to feed on the grains. To harvest, just bend the blossom heads over a container and shake to release the seeds.

WHITE BEANS
WITH AMARANTH LEAVES

Amaranth leaves often have a beautiful magenta stripe in the center, which turns everything they are cooked with a rosy pink. I often use amaranth as a base for roasted sausages and meats.

Serves 4 to 6

2 cups dried small white beans,
  soaked overnight and drained

2 large bay leaves

Sea salt

12 ounces young fresh amaranth leaves, stems
  discarded

2 tablespoons olive oil

1 cup finely chopped yellow onion

1 tablespoon finely chopped garlic

2 teaspoons dried oregano (preferably Mexican)

½ teaspoon whole fennel seeds

¼ teaspoon ground allspice

Red pepper flakes

Freshly squeezed lime juice

Cilantro sprigs, for garnish

Place beans in a large, deep saucepan and cover with about 2 inches of water. Add the bay leaves, bring to a boil, then reduce the heat to a simmer. Partially cover, and cook until the beans begin to soften, 15 to 20 minutes. Add salt to taste, and continue to cook the beans until they are tender, about 15 minutes more, depending on their age.

While the beans are simmering, fill a large bowl with ice water. Bring a pot of generously salted water to a boil. Wash the amaranth leaves and cook them in the boiling water, 1 to 2 minutes. Immediately plunge them into the ice-water bath to stop the cooking and to preserve their color. Drain, squeeze out excess water, and chop coarsely.

Add the chopped amaranth to the bean mixture and simmer gently to heat through. Drain the beans and keep warm.

Meanwhile, in a small sauté pan, heat the oil over medium heat. Add the onion and garlic, and cook, stirring, until just beginning to brown. Stir in the oregano, fennel seeds, and allspice, then add to the drained beans. Season with salt, red pepper flakes, and lime juice to taste.

Serve immediately, garnished with the cilantro.

POPPED AMARANTH
FOR BREAKFAST

When popped like popcorn, amaranth seeds take on an interesting flavor
and produce an enticing aroma. Serve popped amaranth as cold cereal, with milk,
or sprinkle it over salads or other dishes to add a crunchy texture.

Serves 2

1 cup amaranth seeds, divided

2 cups milk

⅔ cup fresh fruit, such as blueberries
or sliced strawberries, or more as desired

Agave or maple syrup

Heat a large, deep saucepan over medium-high heat. Add 2 tablespoons of the amaranth seeds and cover. Slide the pan back and forth over the heat constantly until most of the grains have popped and those that haven't popped are lightly toasted, about 1 minute. Be careful not to burn. Transfer to a bowl, and continue in the same manner with the remaining amaranth. You should have about 2 cups.

To serve, divide the popped amaranth between two bowls. Pour on the milk. Add the fruit and sweeten with agave to taste.

DULCE DE ALEGRÍA

(Amaranth Bars)

Alegrías (from the Spanish word for "happiness") are often wrapped in colored cellophane and are a treat for *Día de los Muertos*. A similar sweet called *ladoo* is made in India. This recipe calls for amaranth that has been popped (see page 129). You can also buy popped amaranth in natural food stores and some supermarkets, where it is called amaranth cereal.

Makes about 20

Olive oil or unsalted butter, for greasing

8 ounces amaranth cereal (popped amaranth)

⅓ cup toasted pumpkin seeds

¼ teaspoon ground cinnamon

4 ounces *piloncillo* (Mexican raw sugar) or dark brown sugar

Freshly squeezed lime juice, as needed

Grease a 9-inch square cake pan and line with parchment paper. In a bowl, combine the amaranth, pumpkin seeds, and cinnamon and set aside.

In a deep, heavy pot, combine the *piloncillo* and 1 cup water and cook, stirring frequently, until the syrup has reached the hard ball stage, 245ºF on a candy thermometer. Add a few drops of the lime juice, remove from the heat, and add the reserved amaranth mixture, stirring with a wooden spoon or paddle to combine.

Immediately spread the mixture in the prepared cake pan. Using a heatproof spatula, press the mixture to a uniform thickness of about ½ inch. Cool for a couple of minutes, until just set. Cut it into finger-size strips or squares. Wrap the pieces individually in cellophane or waxed paper and store in a tin for up to 1 month.

HICKORY NUTS

THERE ARE SEVENTEEN VARIETIES OF HICKORY TREES (*CARYA LACINIOSA*) IN THE world, and thirteen of them are native to the United States, mostly in the eastern part of the country. Hickory wood was important in the early years of our country for construction and especially for gunstocks and tools because the wood is so hard and durable.

Hickory nuts are closely related to pecans and walnuts and are truly America's wild nut. They are easy to forage by simply scooping them up after they've fallen from the trees in autumn after a frost.

This nut has never been a commercially viable product due to its small size (like a small walnut) and the hardness of its shells. On top of this, the meat is difficult to extract. Many kinds of tools and techniques have been suggested for shelling hickory nuts. Here's one from an old edition of *Mother Earth News*: If you hit a hickory nut on the "bulls-eye," a point about one-third of the way down from its stem, the husk should fracture in thirds.

Though hickory trees don't grow where I live in California, I have gone foraging with friends in Tennessee, where the trees abound. For shelling, I've found the Kenkel Hardshell Nutcracker to be a handy tool to get at the meats.

Like walnuts, hickory nuts are hidden inside a fleshy husk or bur ranging in size from a golf ball to a tennis ball. The husk isn't too much of a problem to remove, especially if you've allowed the nuts to dry a bit. Be prepared for stained hands, however.

Once you've peeled off the outer husk, discard any nuts that look moldy, are discolored, or have a hole, which means some kind of insect has drilled into them. With the nuts that remain, try the old trick of throwing them into a large pot of water. The nuts that float are suspect, as they are lighter and may have been eaten by the nut weevil (a grub that exits by a perfectly round hole) or have become dried out and shriveled. Set the floaters aside to crack immediately, because many of them are still good. The nuts that don't float can be dried and stored unshelled in the refrigerator or frozen for a longer shelf life.

Hickory nuts have an excellent rich flavor with a buttery quality thanks to their high fat content. Like walnuts, raw hickory nuts usually have a slightly bitter taste that nips at you at the end; subtly in some, stronger in others. The flavor improves when the nuts are dried, toasted, or roasted. (Preheat the oven to 225°F and roast for 10 minutes.) Hickory nuts can be used in a variety of baked goods and in any recipe as a substitute for walnuts or pecans.

HICKORY NUT TORTE

This torte from Jeff Cox is unimaginably good if the nuts are fresh and their volatile oil
is at full flavor. The nuts are best prepared in a hand-cranked nut shredder that turns the meat
into thin, slender, fluffy threads. A blender, food processor, or Magic Bullet will work,
but these machines simply reduce the meat to a coarse meal.

Serves 8

Unsalted butter, for greasing

All-purpose flour, for dusting

12 large egg yolks, at room temperature

1 cup granulated sugar

2 cups shredded or finely ground hickory nuts

8 large egg whites, at room temperature

½ teaspoon cream of tartar

Slightly sweetened whipped cream, for serving

Mugolio (page 48), for serving

Adjust the oven rack to the middle position and preheat the oven to 350°F. Butter and flour the bottom and interior sides of a 10-inch springform cake pan. Alternatively, you can butter the bottom and line it with parchment paper. Simply set the bottom on a length of the paper and cut around its circumference with a very sharp knife or razor blade.

In the bowl of an electric mixer, beat the egg yolks on medium-high speed for 1 minute. Gradually add the sugar in a thin stream while continuing to beat until all the sugar is incorporated and the mixture turns a light yellow, about 2 minutes. Remove the beaters and place in the sink. Add the hickory nuts and stir in well.

Clean the beaters thoroughly. In a very clean bowl, whip the egg whites and cream of tartar on medium-high speed until stiff peaks form. Fold one-third of the beaten whites into the yolk mixture until well incorporated, and then fold in the rest of the beaten whites.

Pour the batter into the prepared pan and bake until a toothpick inserted into the center of the cake comes out clean, about 40 minutes. Cool the cake in the pan set on a wire rack.

After the cake cools, run a knife around the inside of the pan to loosen the cake, and then remove the sides. Serve slices of the cake with whipped cream (and a drizzle of mugolio, page 48).

PINE NUTS

PINE NUTS, THE EDIBLE SEEDS OF PINES, ARE HARVESTED FROM SEVERAL DIFFERENT species of these trees, especially in Asia and Europe. Prized by cooks for their buttery richness and delicate taste, pine nuts are harvested from the stone pine in Europe and were brought to this country by Italians, who use them in many dishes, most famously Genoese pesto sauce and *pignoli* cookies. A revered old Italian American dessert *Torta della Nonna* (literally "Granny's Cake") is still very popular today. (See page 139.)

But pine nuts have also been gathered for centuries from three different species of the piñon tree by Native Americans, including the Shoshone and the Hopi, as a nutritious food source.

Pine nut coffee, known as *piñón* (Spanish for pine nut), is a specialty found in the southwest United States, especially New Mexico, and is typically a dark roast coffee having a deep, nutty flavor. In addition, pine nuts are widely used in Middle Eastern dishes, such as *kibbeh* and *sambusak*, and desserts, including baklava.

Pine nuts are expensive in part because they can take up three years to mature. They are also very difficult to harvest. They reach maturity about ten days before the green cone begins to open. The cones are dried in a burlap bag in the sun for twenty days to speed up the process of drying and opening. The cones are then smashed (as a way to quickly release the seeds), and the seeds are separated by hand from the cone fragments. All of this takes a lot of time and patience.

Furthermore, the pine cone is only the pine nuts' first shell. They have a second shell, which also has to be removed before eating. The shell can be thick and challenging to remove.

DUKKA

Dukka has its roots in Egypt but has become an international favorite. I first encountered this mixture of nuts and seeds in South Africa, where it is a very popular snack; good bread is dipped into extra-virgin olive oil and then into the dukka. This is also delicious sprinkled over salads, roasted or grilled vegetables, or fruits. The following quantities of ingredients can be adjusted to your own taste.

Makes about 1 cup

1 cup pine nuts or hazelnuts

½ cup sesame seeds

⅓ cup coriander seeds

2 teaspoons ground cumin

1 teaspoon salt, or more to taste

1 teaspoon granulated sugar, or more to taste

Freshly ground black pepper

In a small, dry saucepan, toast the pine nuts over medium heat, until golden, 3 to 4 minutes. Shake the pan occasionally so that the nuts don't burn. Let cool, chop finely and transfer to a bowl. (If using hazelnuts, be sure to remove the skins before chopping.) Using the same pan, repeat the process to toast the sesame seeds and then the coriander seeds until fragrant (or toast in a preheated 375°F oven for 3 to 5 minutes). Add the sesame seeds to the bowl with the pine nuts. With a spice grinder (or a clean coffee grinder), grind the coriander in short bursts until reasonably fine, and add to the bowl. Grind the cumin, salt, and sugar and black pepper to taste together until very fine. Adjust seasonings to taste. Refrigerate in an airtight container for up to 3 weeks.

PIÑON BREAD

I collected this recipe in New Mexico many years ago; its author is unknown.
This is a simple yeast bread recipe that showcases the rich flavor of the piñon.

Makes 1 loaf

1½ cups pine nuts

1 package (2¼ teaspoons) active dry yeast

2 teaspoons agave or granulated sugar

2 cups warm water

4½ cups all-purpose flour

1 cup whole wheat flour

1 teaspoon salt

Olive oil, as needed

Cornmeal, as needed

2 teaspoons ground red chile powder
(preferably New Mexican)

In a small, dry skillet, toast the pine nuts over medium heat, until golden, 3 to 4 minutes. Shake the pan occasionally so that the nuts don't burn. Let the pine nuts cool, then chop finely by hand or in a food processor to make a fine meal. Be careful not to overprocess, or the pine nuts will become nut butter. Set aside.

In the bowl of an electric mixer fitted with a paddle attachment, stir the yeast and agave into the warm water and set the mixture aside for 10 minutes, or until the surface is covered with bubbles. Stir in the ground nuts, flours, and salt. Attach a dough hook, and stir on medium speed until the dough comes away from the sides of the bowl and is smooth and not sticky, about 4 minutes. Add a bit more all-purpose flour, if needed.

Alternatively, you can do all of this by hand. After mixing with a wooden spoon, turn the dough out onto a lightly floured surface and knead it until it is smooth and silky, about 8 minutes, incorporating extra flour as needed.

Lightly brush the inside of a large bowl with oil. Add the dough, cover with a damp towel or a piece of plastic wrap, and let rise for about 45 minutes. When the dough has doubled in size, turn it out onto a lightly floured surface on the counter and knead it briefly. Shape the dough into a round ball and set it aside to rise again on a peel or counter dusted with cornmeal or flour. While it is rising, preheat the oven to 375°F. If you're using a baking stone, heat the stone at the same time.

When the dough has risen again, after about 30 minutes, cut four or five deep slashes across the top. Mix the chile powder with a few spoonfuls of water, and paint it over the surface of the bread. Slide the risen bread onto the baking stone or a baking sheet and bake until the bread is firm on top and lightly browned on the unglazed parts, about 40 minutes. Set the bread on a wire rack to cool.

NOTE: You can also bake the piñon bread in a 10-inch cast-iron skillet.

PINE NUT COOKIES

These are a simple, classic cookie found in Italy, particularly Sicily. They are easy to make even if you aren't a baker. They were also the first cookie my grandmother taught me to make. Almond paste is generally available in large supermarkets. Don't use marzipan, which contains a lot more sugar than almond paste does.

Makes about 24 cookies

8 ounces almond paste

¾ cup granulated sugar

2 large egg whites, lightly beaten

2 cups pine nuts

In a food processor, combine the almond paste and sugar and pulse until the mixture is relatively smooth with the texture of coarse sand. Set aside.

With a fork, beat the egg whites until frothy. Add the egg whites to the almond paste mixture, stirring well with a fork so that it comes together and holds its shape. If there are any lumps, use the fork to smooth them out. Cover and refrigerate the mixture up to 2 hours ahead.

Preheat the oven to 350°F. Line a baking sheet with parchment paper or a silicone baking mat.

Spread the pine nuts in a pie plate and drop 3 rounded teaspoons of the chilled almond dough on top. Use your fingers to coat each piece with as many of the pine nuts as you can and then form into balls. Place the balls at least 2 inches apart on the prepared baking sheet, working in batches, if necessary. Bake until cookies have spread a little and are golden brown, 18 to 20 minutes.

Remove from the oven and let the cookies cool for a few minutes to firm up, then transfer to a wire rack to cool completely. The cookies are best when eaten the day they are made, or you can store them in an airtight container for up to 3 days.

TORTA DELLA NONNA

(Grandmother's Cake)

This is a recipe inspired by author Frances Mayes's version in *The Tuscan Sun Cookbook*.
Like most Italian recipes, there are as many variations of the cake as there are bakers who make it.

Makes one 10-inch torta

⅓ cup pine nuts

2½ cups milk

⅔ cup granulated sugar

4 large egg yolks, beaten

Zest and freshly squeezed juice of
 1 lemon, divided

⅓ cup all-purpose flour, plus more for dusting

1½ teaspoons cornstarch

1 teaspoon vanilla extract

1 recipe *Pasta Frolla* (Italian short pastry),
 page 140

1 teaspoon yellow cornmeal, divided

2 tablespoons confectioners' sugar

In a small, dry skillet, toast the pine nuts over medium heat, until golden, 3 to 4 minutes. Shake the pan occasionally so that the nuts don't burn. Let the pine nuts cool and set aside.

In a medium saucepan, whisk together the milk, granulated sugar, egg yolks, and lemon zest over medium heat. Cook, stirring, until slightly thickened, about 5 minutes. Reduce the heat to medium-low and slowly sift in the flour and cornstarch, whisking continuously. When the mixture becomes a very thick and creamy custard, stir in the lemon juice and vanilla extract. Remove from the heat and allow to cool while you roll out the pastry.

Preheat the oven to 350°F.

On a floured surface, roll out one ball of dough and fit into a 10-inch tart pan. Sprinkle ½ teaspoon of the cornmeal over the dough for a little crunch. Pour in the filling, then roll out the other ball of dough to cover. Crimp the dough around the overlapping edges.

Press the toasted pine nuts into the dough and sprinkle on the remaining ½ teaspoon cornmeal. Bake until the crust is golden, about 30 minutes. Let the torta rest for 5 minutes before sifting the confectioners' sugar over the top. Serve slightly warm or at room temperature.

PASTA FROLLA

(Italian Short Pastry)

Frolla means "friable" or "crumbly." It's a short crust, and if you are rolling pin–challenged, you can press the crust into the pan with your fingers. Any leftover dough can be baked as cookies with a couple of pine nuts or a dab of jam on top.

Makes one 10-inch double piecrust

¾ cup (1½ sticks) cold unsalted butter, cut into small cubes

⅔ cup granulated sugar

Pinch of salt

2 large eggs

Zest of 1 lemon

2¼ cups all-purpose flour, sifted, plus more for dusting

In a food processor, combine the butter, sugar, and salt, and pulse once or twice. Add the eggs and lemon zest, and then gradually add the sifted flour, pulsing just to blend, until the dough forms.

Transfer to a lightly floured surface. Roll the dough into a ball, dust it with flour, and divide into two balls, one slightly larger than the other. The dough will be sticky. Refrigerate the dough wrapped in plastic for at least 1 hour or up to overnight before rolling out.

TO FORM THE PIECRUSTS: Dust the rolling pin and a cool work surface with flour. Roll out one ball of dough into a circle to fit your pie plate. Flip the pastry over the rolling pin and fit it into the pie plate. Or, simply press the pastry into the pan with your fingers. Repeat with the remaining dough.

WILD RICE

WILD RICE (*ZIZANIA PALUSTRIS*) IS NOT RICE AT ALL BUT THE GRAIN OF A MARSH grass. In this country, it grows wild in the northern part of the Great Lakes region and is gathered by Native Americans and other licensed gatherers. But it also grows in Asia, especially in China. It's an ancient grain that has been harvested for thousands of years. Another kind of "wild" rice is cultivated in Minnesota and California and is known as "paddy rice." Developed by the University of Minnesota in the 1960s, this hybrid rice is less expensive and more widely available than truly wild rice, which is often known as "organic" wild rice, even though it's not certified organic because it's foraged in the wild! True wild rice is highly expensive because it requires exact conditions for growth: a specific water level and rate of flow, plus a certain kind of soil and temperature range.

Like quinoa, millet, amaranth, and buckwheat, true wild rice is much closer to its original state than most grains. Some people think it has more nutrients than its hybridized version, and many believe it to be far more flavorful. Both kinds of rice are available online, and I suggest you try some of both and decide which you like better.

Harvesting true wild rice has remained unchanged for centuries. In Minnesota, laws are in place to make sure traditional Native American harvesting methods are used. Licenses are required for anyone looking to forage wild rice. It's still a romantic picture: Two foragers sit in a canoe, one of them poling it through the rice beds, while the second person bends the rice stalks over the canoe with a cedar stick, and, with a second stick, knocks the rice grains off the stalks. The rice is then bagged and taken to a rice mill to be dried.

Wild rice is rich in nutrients, low in fat, and contains no gluten. It takes longer to cook than regular rice; thirty-five to fifty minutes, with a rice-to-liquid ratio of one to three. It helps to soak it overnight, which renders the rice more digestible. The long straight grains of true wild rice, dark brown to black in color, have a deep, earthy and nutty fragrance and flavor that are incomparable in cooking. It is a precious food that's worth the high cost.

ROAST PHEASANT STUFFED WITH WILD RICE

Like other upland birds (page 239), pheasant can be dry if it's not roasted with care. This stuffing keeps it moist and lends a rich, deep flavor that complements the slightly gamy taste of the pheasant.

Serves 2 to 4

1½ cups wild rice

2 tablespoons unsalted butter

1½ cups finely chopped yellow onions

½ cup finely chopped celery

2 teaspoons finely chopped garlic

Salt and freshly ground black pepper

1 ounce dried porcini mushrooms, soaked in warm water for 30 minutes, drained, and chopped

¾ cup sliced cremini mushrooms, or whatever mushrooms you prefer

⅓ cup chicken stock

¼ cup dry white wine

½ cup golden raisins

¼ cup chopped fresh flat-leaf parsley

1 tablespoon chopped fresh thyme or 1 teaspoon dried thyme

1 whole pheasant (about 2½ pounds)

In a medium saucepan, bring 4½ cups water to a boil over high heat. Add the rice and return to boil. Cover, reduce the heat to a simmer, and cook until the rice is tender, 40 to 50 minutes. Drain the rice, and set aside.

Meanwhile, in a large, heavy skillet, melt the butter over medium heat. Add the onions, celery, and garlic. Season lightly with salt and pepper to taste, and cook, stirring, until the onions just begin to brown, 4 to 5 minutes. Add the mushrooms and cook until all the liquid released from the mushrooms has evaporated, about 5 minutes. Add the stock and wine and stir, scraping the bottom of the pan to incorporate any browned bits. Cook until most of the liquid is evaporated. Set aside.

Preheat the oven to 425°F.

Transfer the cooked rice to a bowl and stir in the reserved cooked vegetables along with the raisins, parsley, and thyme. Season with salt and pepper to taste.

Season the pheasant inside and out with salt and pepper. Stuff the cavity loosely with the rice mixture, then arrange on a rack set in a roasting pan. Place in the oven and roast for 10 minutes, then reduce the oven temperature to 350°F and roast until the juices in the thigh run clear when pierced with a knife and an instant-read thermometer inserted into the thickest part of the thigh reaches 160°F, about 40 minutes. Let the pheasant rest for 5 minutes before carving.

WILD RICE PANCAKES

I love to use these pancakes in place of blini for caviar or smoked salmon.
They are used in the quail with mustard butter recipe on page 247.

Makes 12 to 16 cakes

⅔ cup finely chopped red onion

2 tablespoons melted unsalted butter

2 large eggs, separated

1¼ cups cooked wild rice (page 142)

⅓ cup chicken stock

¼ cup finely chopped walnuts

3 tablespoons all-purpose flour

1 teaspoon fresh thyme or oregano leaves,
  or a combination

1 teaspoon sea salt

¼ teaspoon freshly ground white pepper

Vegetable oil or clarified butter, for sautéing

In a medium saucepan, sauté the onion in 1 tablespoon of the melted butter over medium heat until soft but not brown, 3 to 4 minutes. Let cool. In a medium bowl, beat the egg yolks until light. Stir in the cooked onions, wild rice, stock, walnuts, flour, thyme, and the remaining 1 tablespoon melted butter. Season with the salt and pepper.

In a separate bowl, beat the egg whites with a whisk until stiff but not dry. Gently fold into the yolk mixture.

In a hot skillet or on a griddle, sauté heaping tablespoon-size dollops of the mixture in oil. Cook until lightly golden, then turn and cook on the other side, about 3 minutes total. Do not overcook; the cakes should still be moist in the center. Serve warm.

WILD RICE AND MUSHROOM SOUP

The wild rice in this dish is cooked with a little baking soda,
which helps to decrease the cooking time.

Serves 6 to 8

¼ ounce dried porcini or shiitake mushrooms

1 teaspoon fresh thyme

1 teaspoon salt, plus more to taste

¼ teaspoon baking soda

1 large bay leaf

2 teaspoons finely chopped garlic, divided

1 cup wild rice

¼ cup (½ stick) unsalted butter

1 tablespoon olive oil

1 pound cremini mushrooms, trimmed
and sliced ¼ inch thick

2 cups chopped yellow onions

1 teaspoon tomato paste

Freshly ground black pepper

⅔ cup dry sherry, such as amontillado

7 cups low-sodium chicken stock

1 tablespoon soy sauce

½ cup heavy whipping cream

¼ cup finely chopped fresh chives

2 teaspoons lemon zest

2 tablespoons cornstarch dissolved
in ⅓ cup water

Grind the dried mushrooms in spice grinder until finely ground. You should have about 3 tablespoons.

In a medium saucepan, combine the thyme, salt, baking soda, bay leaf, and ½ teaspoon of the garlic with 4 cups water and bring to a boil over high heat. Add the wild rice and return to a boil. Cover, reduce heat to a simmer, and cook until the rice is tender, 35 to 40 minutes. Drain the rice, discard the bay leaf, and set aside.

In a deep, heavy stockpot, melt the butter with the olive oil over high heat. Add the cremini mushrooms, onions, tomato paste, and salt and pepper to taste. Cook, stirring occasionally, until the vegetables are browned; add the remaining ½ teaspoon garlic and cook for another minute, about 15 minutes total. Add the sherry and stir, scraping the bottom of the pan to incorporate any browned bits, and cook until reduced and almost evaporated, about 3 minutes. Add the stock, soy sauce, and the reserved ground mushrooms and bring to boil. Reduce the heat to low, cover, and simmer for 15 minutes. Stir in the cream, chives, lemon zest, and the reserved cooked rice. Stir the cornstarch mixture into the soup 1 teaspoon at a time in 1- to 2-minute intervals until you reach the consistency of a thin paste. You may not end up using all of the cornstarch mixture. Adjust seasonings to taste.

FRIED WILD RICE

The secrets to good fried rice are starting with cold leftover rice, cooking in
a preheated large wok or skillet, and using the right amount of the liquid ingredients
(overdoing it will make the rice too wet). Almost any vegetable, meat, or fish
can be added to fried rice; it's a perfect way to use leftovers.

Serves 4

4 cups leftover cooked and
   refrigerated wild rice

1 to 2 tablespoons vegetable oil, such as canola,
   plus more as needed

1 cup chopped carrots

½ cup chopped red or white onion

2 teaspoons finely chopped garlic

3 large eggs

1 cup chopped cooked shrimp, tofu,
   or other protein of your choice

½ cup fresh or frozen and thawed peas

2 tablespoons oyster sauce

2 tablespoons soy sauce or Asian fish sauce

Salt and ground pepper (preferably white)

Break up any clumps of rice and separate the grains; set aside. Preheat a 14-inch wok or 12-inch skillet over high heat for about 1 minute. Swirl in the oil and heat until it shimmers but is not smoking.

Reduce the heat to medium, add the carrots and onion, and cook, stirring, until the vegetables just start to become tender, about 3 minutes. Add the garlic and stir until fragrant, about 1 minute more.

Move all of the ingredients to one side of the wok. Break the eggs into the wok, and stir to scramble until they are almost cooked through but still a little wet, about 2 minutes. Add the protein, stirring and tossing to combine. Repeat with the peas and then with the wild rice, stirring and tossing between each addition. Use a spatula to break up any clumps. Add the oyster sauce, soy sauce, and salt and pepper to taste. Stir everything swiftly around the wok until the rice is well coated, with little bits of white here and there, and heated through, about 3 minutes. Add more oil if the rice begins to stick to the wok; reduce the heat if it starts to scorch. Adjust the seasonings to taste and serve immediately.

WILD RICE AND
TURKEY MINI MUFFINS

This is a recipe from my good friend Jennifer Bushman, who is an excellent cook.
Any leftover cooked bird meat could be used here. I prepare them as mini muffins
because a regular size muffin might be too much, as these are pretty rich.

Makes 24 mini muffins

½ cup (1 stick) unsalted butter,
   plus more for greasing

¼ cup finely chopped white onion

2 garlic cloves, finely chopped

1 cup of your favorite wild mushroom, chopped

2 cups all-purpose flour

1 tablespoon baking powder

2 teaspoons sea salt

¾ teaspoon freshly ground black pepper

2 large eggs, at room temperature

1 cup whole milk

1 cup cooked wild rice (page 142)

⅔ cup finely diced cooked turkey or other
   poultry or game bird (white or dark meat)

½ teaspoon chopped fresh thyme

In medium sauté pan, melt the ½ cup butter over medium-high heat. Sauté the onion and garlic until soft, 3 to 4 minutes. Add the mushrooms and cook until tender, about 5 minutes more. Remove from the heat and set aside to cool.

Meanwhile, heat the oven to 350°F. Grease 24 mini muffin cups with butter.

Sift the flour, baking powder, salt, and pepper into a large bowl. In a medium bowl, whisk together the eggs and milk. Stir in the wild rice, turkey, thyme, and the reserved cooked vegetables. Pour the mixture over the sifted dry ingredients and stir until just blended; the batter will be thick.

Spoon or scoop the batter into the prepared mini muffin cups. Bake until the muffins are no longer moist in the center or a toothpick comes out with only slight crumbs on it, about 25 minutes. Let cool on a wire rack for 15 minutes before removing muffins from cups.

FRUITS AND SWEETENERS

WILD GRAPES AND LEAVES

THERE ARE DOZENS OF WILD GRAPE SPECIES GROWING IN ALMOST ALL PARTS OF North America. They are one of the most abundant fruits on the North American continent, where they grow in sunny areas in hardwood forests and disturbed sites like roadsides and urban lots. Wild grapes are so similar to cultivated grapes in appearance and growing habit that they're easy to find. These perennial vines can grow to more than eighty feet by using their forking tendrils to climb up trees or ravines. The fruit of wild grape varies in size, but it is recognizable because of its bunching characteristics. Both the young tendrils and the young leaves of wild grape are also edible. To harvest grape leaves, target the medium-size leaves growing from wild vines, as they are much more tender and flavorful than the cultivated variety. Pick the leaves at their base. Don't worry about picking part of the stem; you can trim that later. When you get home, gently wash the leaves in cold water and pat them dry with paper towels. Store the leaves in an open plastic bag in the refrigerator. They should last for several days. If you freeze the leaves, make sure you first wrap them tightly in plastic wrap before sealing them in a freezer bag to avoid freezer burn. These should last about six months to one year.

Incidentally, two plants are wild grape look-alikes: the Virginia creeper (also called woodbine, of the genus *Parthenocissus*), and Canada moonseed (*Menispermum canadense*). Both are considered inedible, and moonseed is toxic. Be sure to learn how to identify wild grapes so you don't mistake them for one of these plants.

Collecting wild grapes is pretty simple. In autumn, when the fruit is ripe, simply pick the whole clusters. The stems keep the grapes from being mashed in the bucket or whatever you're using to gather them. When you get home, pick the fruit off the stems and immediately process it. You'll often see a white dusty substance on a grape. This is yeast, which will begin to ferment the juice immediately after the skin is broken. Grapes are made to become wine! If you want to store them in the refrigerator for a couple of days, leave the grapes attached to the stem.

The different species of wild grape have different flavor characteristics, so find one you like and you'll be able to return to it each season. Most wild grapes are turned into juice, and then into jelly or wine. You'll find many recipes online and in books for wild grape pie (*Stalking the Wild Asparagus* has an excellent one).

Let's start with making juice. Samuel Thayer, in his excellent book *The Forager's Harvest*, talks about an important step in making juice: Be sure to gently crush the grapes after stemming. You can do this by hand, or I like to use the Roma food strainer and sauce maker, which you can buy online. If you crush the seeds, the resulting juice will be very bitter.

Strain the resulting juice through cheesecloth or a fine-mesh strainer to remove any bits of skin or seed, and gently wring out the beautiful dark juice, which will be as tart as lemon juice. If you drink this juice as is, it will make your mouth and throat sore within just a few minutes. This is caused by tartrates in the juice. Thank goodness you can easily get rid of tartrates. Simply put the juice in the refrigerator for a day or two, and the tartrates will settle on the bottom like sludge. Pour off the good juice, like decanting an old, fine wine, and discard the tartrates, which will appear as sediment. Thayer warns: "Never make anything from fresh-pressed small wild grapes without subjecting the juice to this purification process."

WILD GRAPE JELLY

Once you've had wild grape jelly, you'll never eat the commercial version again.
(I recommend using Tattler reusable canning lids, which are BPA-free and much more
environmentally friendly; www.reusablecanninglids.com.)

Makes 6 half-pint jars
(adapted from the box of Sure-Gel pectin)

1 box Sure-Gel low-sugar pectin

3¼ cups granulated sugar, divided

5 cups prepared wild grape juice
(see discussion on page 152)

Prepare a boiling-water canner and sterilize six half-pint glass canning jars and lids.

In a small bowl, whisk together the pectin and ¼ cup of the sugar. Add to a large nonreactive pot with the wild grape juice and whisk to blend. Bring to a boil over high heat. Stir in the remaining 3 cups sugar and return to a boil. Cook for 1 minute, stirring constantly to keep the foaming mixture from boiling over.

Ladle the hot jelly into the sterilized jars, leaving a ¼-inch headspace. Wipe the rims and seal, then process in the boiling-water canner for 10 minutes.

STUFFED GRAPE LEAVES WITH CUCUMBER-YOGURT SAUCE

Stuffed grape leaves are from the cuisine of Greece, where they are known as dolmades. Generally they are vegetarian, but versions are also made with ground meat such as lamb. Here I'm using fresh grape leaves harvested in the spring, when they are still tender.

Makes 30 stuffed grape leaves

30 young spring wild grape leaves, stemmed

½ cup extra-virgin olive oil, divided

2 medium yellow onions, finely chopped

1¼ cup water, vegetable or chicken stock

¾ cup short- or medium-grain rice, such as arborio

1 large tomato, peeled, cored, and finely chopped

1½ teaspoons tomato paste mixed with 2 tablespoons water

2 tablespoons chopped fresh dill or mint

1 tablespoon chopped fresh Italian parsley

1 teaspoon granulated sugar

⅛ teaspoon ground allspice

Pinch of cayenne

Salt

2 tablespoons dried currants

2 tablespoons pine nuts

2 tablespoons freshly squeezed lemon juice, or more to taste

1 recipe Cucumber-Yogurt Sauce (page 156)

Bring a large pot of salted water to a rolling boil. Add the grape leaves, working in batches, if necessary, and cook until they are softened and pliable, 1 to 2 minutes. Take a little bite to be sure. Drain and set aside.

In a medium pot, heat ¼ cup of the oil over medium heat. Add the onions and cook until soft but not brown, about 8 minutes. Stir in the water, rice, tomato, diluted tomato paste, dill, parsley, sugar, allspice, cayenne, the remaining ¼ cup oil, and salt to taste. Cover, reduce heat to low, and simmer until the rice is al dente or barely cooked through, about 15 minutes. Remove the pot from heat, stir in the currants and pine nuts, cover, and set aside for 10 minutes. Add the lemon juice, adjust the seasonings to taste, and set aside to cool.

Line the bottom of a medium, heavy pot with a tight-fitting lid with 10 of the boiled grape leaves and set aside. Lay one grape leaf, smooth-side down, on a clean surface. Put 1 heaping tablespoon of the rice filling onto the center of the leaf. Fold sides over the filling on either side by about 1 inch to keep the filling from falling out as you roll. Starting with end closest to you, roll up the leaf, encasing the filling. Repeat in the same manner to make 30 stuffed leaves in all.

(Continues on page 156)

Arrange 2 or 3 layers of stuffed leaves side by side, seam-side down, in the prepared pot, arranging each layer perpendicular to the previous layer. Cover the stuffed leaves with the remaining 10 grape leaves. Add 1 cup water to the pot and weigh the stuffed leaves down with a small plate. Cover and bring to a boil over high heat, then reduce the heat to low and simmer for 1 hour. Remove the pot from heat and set aside to cool. Serve the stuffed grape leaves at room temperature or chilled with the sauce.

CUCUMBER-YOGURT SAUCE

Makes 2 cups

1½ cups plain yogurt (preferably Greek)

2 small cucumbers, peeled, grated, and squeezed in a towel to remove excess moisture

2 garlic cloves, finely chopped

Salt and black pepper

1 tablespoon extra-virgin olive oil

In a medium bowl, stir together the yogurt, cucumbers, and garlic. Season with salt and pepper to taste and top with olive oil. Store covered in the refrigerator until ready to serve.

WILD GRAPE SOURDOUGH STARTER

Wild grapes are a rich source for yeast, as noted on page 151. Pick some wild grapes away from a roadside so they won't harbor any residue from traffic exhaust, and bring them home to create this excellent starter.

2 cups all-purpose flour

1 cup wild grapes

2 cups lukewarm water (preferably distilled)

1 teaspoon granulated sugar

Put the flour in a glass or ceramic bowl and bury the grapes in the flour, being careful to keep them intact. Remember, it's the wild yeast that lives on the grape skins that you want to transfer to the flour.

Cover the bowl with plastic wrap to keep other yeasts out (the air in your kitchen may be full of yeasts, especially if you bake yeasted breads often), and let these characters stay together overnight. The following morning, carefully remove the grapes and stir in the water. If you have access to a spring, terrific; otherwise use distilled water. Stir in the sugar for the yeast to feed on.

Stir your brew together thoroughly, then cover the bowl with a cloth and place in draft-free place for 3 or 4 days, stirring it once every day. It will begin to ferment in the first day or so if the yeast is working. It should develop a yeasty, boozy smell. Store it in a covered jar in the refrigerator. If it molds or looks or smells funny, start over.

NOTE: The starter is what causes the bread to rise and is used in place of yeast. There are many kinds of tutorials online about using starters.

GOOSEBERRIES

GOOSEBERRIES BELONG TO THE GENUS *RIBES* AND ARE CLOSELY RELATED TO CURrants (not the dried small raisins that share the same name). There are approximately two hundred species of both of these kinds of berries in the world, and all are native to the Northern Hemisphere. It is estimated that there are at least eighty species in North America, according to wild-food expert Hank Shaw. Not all of these are wonderful to eat, and some, generally gooseberries, have sharp spines both on the branches as well as on the fruit, necessitating the wearing of gloves when picking and processing. Currants generally have a smooth skin. Gooseberries are thought to be green, while currants are red or black, although this differs among some species.

Gooseberries and currants are much loved by birds, and the flowers of both are favorites of hummingbirds. Domesticated versions are relatively easy to grow in home gardens and not nearly as difficult to please as blueberries. My grandmother had a couple of big bushes of both gooseberries and currants, and we were well rewarded in the fall with lots of fruit from both. In the wild, most gooseberry and currant bushes (officially classified as shrubs) grow from two to five feet high. Some types, particularly the ones found at high elevations (up to ten thousand feet), creep close to the ground and along rocks. The golden currant, which is distributed quite widely throughout the West and much of the East, hangs from trees of up to ten feet tall.

The fruits of both the gooseberry and currant are edible, although there are reportedly more species of currant with an unpleasant, mealy texture or tannic flavor than there are of gooseberries, which are almost universally tart and a little sweet. The "tails" on the bottom of the fruits are remnants of the plant's flowers and are another hallmark of the *Ribes* clan. The little tails are perfectly edible, but you may prefer to remove them.

GOOSEBERRY SYRUP

While harvesting gooseberries in the field, you may encounter some berries that have spines, particularly those of the Sierra gooseberry. The easiest method to deal with the spines is to turn the berries into a syrup, which is delicious on pancakes.

Makes about 1 quart

8 cups fresh gooseberries

Granulated sugar, as needed

Freshly squeezed lemon juice, as needed

Wash the gooseberries well. In a large pot, combine the berries with 4 cups of water, bring to a boil, and cook for 3 minutes. Remove from the heat, and, using a potato masher, crush the berries to a pulp. Do not use a blender of any kind. If you do, you will make the nasty spikes smaller and harder to remove later.

Cover, and let the berries steep until the mixture cools to room temperature. Pour everything through a fine-mesh strainer and into a container, cover, and refrigerate overnight. The sediment at the bottom will be tan, and the juice will be varying degrees of red or purple if you are using ripe gooseberries.

Strain again through a fine-mesh strainer or cheesecloth to create a clear juice, leaving the sediment behind. I personally prefer using a nylon nut milk bag, which can be easily washed. (Mine is the More than a Nut Milk Bag by Rawsome Creations.) Measure the liquid and then add an equal amount of sugar. Transfer to a saucepan and cook over medium heat until the sugar is dissolved. Remove from the heat, and add lemon juice to taste. This will keep almost indefinitely stored covered in the refrigerator.

GOOSEBERRY GRANITA

This is a technique that can be used for any fruit syrup or purée. In Italy, granitas are a staple in cafés, especially during warm-weather months. The word granita comes from the Italian *grano*, meaning kernel or grain. This frozen delight is not made in an ice-cream maker but instead by periodically scraping the mixture as it freezes, which gives it the characteristically grainy texture that is so refreshing on a hot day.

Makes about 1 quart

1 quart gooseberry syrup (page 159)

2 cups fresh or frozen smooth-skinned gooseberries, puréed

In a bowl, stir together the syrup and berries and adjust sweet and tart flavors to your taste by adding more of either ingredient. Transfer the mixture to a nonreactive bowl or pan (preferably of metal) and place in the freezer.

Stir the mixture every 30 minutes; it will develop into a slush. When it is semisolid, scrape it with a tablespoon every 30 minutes until firm but grainy.

To serve, scoop the granita into chilled glasses and serve immediately.

OLD-FASHIONED GOOSEBERRY PIE

This is one of the best pies you'll ever eat! For this recipe, make sure you are using smooth-skinned gooseberries. You can also substitute currants. Be sure to remove the "tail," or flower remnant, if it's still there.

Makes one 9-inch pie

Crust

2½ cups all-purpose flour

3 tablespoons granulated sugar

½ teaspoon salt

1 cup (2 sticks) very cold unsalted butter, cut into ⅛-inch-thick cubes

¼ cup very cold milk, plus more if needed

1 large egg beaten with 1 tablespoon milk, for glazing crust

Filling

6 fresh cups whole smooth-skinned gooseberries

1½ cups granulated sugar

⅓ cup instant tapioca

2 tablespoons peeled and grated fresh ginger

Zest and freshly squeezed juice of 1 lemon

3 tablespoons unsalted butter

TO MAKE THE CRUST: In a food processor, combine the flour, sugar, and salt. Add the butter and pulse 10 to 12 times, until the mixture resembles coarse crumbs.

Add the milk and pulse 4 or 5 times, until a crumbly mixture forms. Press the mixture together to form a ball, adding more milk, if necessary, so that it holds together when pressed into a ball. Form into two equal-size disks, wrap in plastic wrap, and chill for at least 30 minutes (and up to 2 days) before rolling out. This allows the gluten in the flour to relax, ensuring a tender crust.

TO PREPARE THE FILLING: In a large saucepan, combine the gooseberries, sugar, tapioca, ginger, lemon juice, and lemon zest while the dough is chilling. Cover, and cook over medium heat until the berries begin to soften and burst, about 5 minutes. Uncover, and keep barely simmering over medium-low heat for 10 minutes longer. Remove from the heat and allow to cool while rolling out the pastry.

TO BAKE THE PIE: Preheat the oven to 375°F.

(Continues on page 166)

Remove the chilled dough from the refrigerator and roll out one disk on a lightly floured surface until large enough to cover the bottom and sides of pie plate, with a ¾-inch overhang. Crimp the edges decoratively. Gently line with a sheet of aluminum foil and set dry beans or pie weights on top of the bottom crust. Bake until golden, about 10 minutes. Do not let the edges of crust burn. Cover with foil or pie guards, if necessary.

While the bottom of crust is baking, roll out the remaining pastry disk to fit the top of the pie, and cut into ¾-inch-wide strips. Refrigerate until ready to use.

Once the bottom crust has baked and filling has cooled, pour the gooseberry filling into the bottom crust. Slice the butter on top of the filling, and arrange the chilled pastry strips attractively on top in a lattice pattern, which is relatively easy to do by "weaving" parallel pastry strips placed across the pie above and underneath a series of perpendicular pastry strips placed in the other direction. Brush the top with the beaten egg mixture. Use foil strips or pie guards over the crust. Place on a rimmed baking sheet to catch any juices, and bake until juices are bubbling, 35 to 50 minutes. Allow the pie to cool completely before serving.

HUCKLEBERRIES

HUCKLEBERRIES GROW IN THE ROCKY MOUNTAINS AND THE PACIFIC NORTHWEST. They resemble blueberries and have a similar, though more intense, taste. However, they are usually smaller and contain more seeds, which gives them a crunchy texture.

Huckleberries have never been commercially farmed and can only be found growing wild or sometimes in small home gardens. Their season is usually June through August. Look for them in an area that has experienced a forest fire in the recent past. Huckleberries freeze wonderfully, and you can often find them online from foragers. If you decide to pick huckleberries, remember that they are the favorite food for a wide range of animals, including black and grizzly bears. Don't forget your bear-repellent spray!

HUCKLEBERRY MUFFINS

This is a simple muffin recipe that can use any of your favorite berries. Again, because
the growing season for huckleberries is so short, frozen can be substituted. If using fresh berries,
a little trick that bakers use to keep the berries from all falling to the bottom of the muffin
is to very lightly dust the berries with flour before gently folding into the batter.

Makes 12 muffins

Unsalted butter, for greasing

2 cups sifted all-purpose flour,
  plus more for dusting

1½ cups fresh huckleberries

⅔ cup packed light brown sugar

1 tablespoon baking powder

1 teaspoon baking soda

½ teaspoon salt

2 large eggs

1 cup buttermilk

6 tablespoons melted unsalted butter

2 teaspoons lemon zest

1 teaspoon vanilla extract

Preheat the oven to 400°F. Grease a standard 12-muffin pan and dust with flour or line with paper cups.

In a large bowl, combine the 2 cups flour, huckleberries, sugar, baking powder, baking soda, and salt. Mix thoroughly and set aside.

In another bowl, whisk together the eggs, buttermilk, melted butter, lemon zest, and vanilla extract. Add to the dry ingredients, and mix together with a few light strokes until moistened. Do not overmix; the batter should not be smooth.

Divide the batter among the prepared muffin cups. Bake until a toothpick inserted into the muffins comes out clean, about 20 minutes. The muffins should be golden and just pulling away from the sides of the cups. Let cool for a few minutes before removing to a wire rack to cool completely.

HUCKLEBERRY TART

Blueberries can be substituted if huckleberries are not available. Look for those labeled as "wild." This recipe calls for blending fresh berries with the cooked berries, but you can certainly substitute uncooked IQF (individually quick frozen) berries if fresh are not available.

Serves 8

Crust

1¼ cups all-purpose flour

½ cup (1 stick) cold unsalted butter, cut into small cubes

¼ cup granulated sugar

¼ teaspoon salt

1 large egg yolk

Filling

½ cup granulated sugar

1 tablespoon freshly squeezed lemon juice

¼ teaspoon ground cinnamon

Pinch of salt

8 cups fresh huckleberries, divided

2½ teaspoons unflavored gelatin (from one ¼-ounce envelope)

2 teaspoons vanilla extract

Lightly whipped cream or crème fraîche, for serving

TO MAKE THE CRUST: In a food processor, combine the flour, butter, sugar, and salt. Pulse until the mixture resembles coarse meal. Add the egg yolk and pulse until dough just begins to come together but is still crumbly. Press the dough evenly into the bottom and up sides of a 10-inch fluted tart pan with a removable bottom. Prick the bottom of crust with a fork and refrigerate for at least 30 minutes.

Adjust the oven rack to the middle position and preheat the oven to 400°F.

Bake the crust until golden, 15 to 18 minutes. Remove and cool on a wire rack.

TO PREPARE THE FILLING: In a heavy, deep saucepan combine the sugar, lemon juice, cinnamon, salt, and 4 cups of the huckleberries. Bring to a simmer and cook, stirring occasionally, for 10 minutes.

Meanwhile, in a small bowl, sprinkle the gelatin over 3 tablespoons water and let soften.

Remove the saucepan from the heat and stir in the softened gelatin and the vanilla extract. Transfer to a metal bowl set in a bowl of ice and water and stir occasionally until thickened to the consistency of raw egg white but not set, about 10 minutes. Fold in the remaining 4 cups berries. Pour the mixture into the cooled crust and spread evenly. Refrigerate the tart, loosely covered, until set, 3 to 4 hours.

Allow the tart to stand at room temperature for an hour before removing from pan. Cut into wedges and serve topped with the whipped cream or crème fraîche.

PAWPAWS: AMERICA'S BEST-KEPT WILD-FRUIT SECRET

THE PAWPAW MAY HAVE BEEN NAMED IN 1541 BY A MEMBER OF HERNANDO DE SOTO'S expedition through the southeastern United States because of its resemblance to papaya. Papaya is a Spanish word, and in English-speaking countries, such as Australia and New Zealand, the tropical papaya is also known as pawpaw, often resulting in confusion between the two species.

George Washington planted pawpaws at his home at Mount Vernon, and Thomas Jefferson cultivated them at Monticello. The Lewis and Clark expedition is said to have subsisted almost entirely on pawpaws for several days during their westward exploration in 1806.

Native Americans have a long history of eating (and growing) pawpaws. And even though white settlers had to clear pawpaw trees to create farmable land, they savored the fruit, which was often the only fresh fruit available in the Western migration. There are towns named Pawpaw in Michigan, West Virginia, Kentucky, and Oklahoma (mid-Atlantic and midwest states make up the pawpaw hot zone). It's the only food source for the zebra swallowtail butterfly, and one of the few fruits that don't require any pesticides. It is also the closest to a tropical fruit that grows in America.

Pawpaw's scientific name has been changed often. It is now known as *Asimina triloba*. The *Asimina* genus includes eight different species, and *Asmina triloba* is the most widespread. The pawpaw grows wild in twenty-six of the eastern United States, ranging from New York to northern Florida and west to eastern Texas, Nebraska, and Kansas. The pawpaw is North America's largest edible-fruit tree.

Though it's a little homely to look at, the pawpaw, when ripe, has flavor that is entirely unique. The fruit's pale-yellow flesh is something like a mash-up of bananas, mangoes, pineapple, and citrus. Its flavor has also been described as subtly yeasty and floral. Eating a ripe pawpaw is a gooey, sensuous experience.

The propagation and cultivation of pawpaws has been studied for decades but is hampered by a short harvesting season (in the fall), small yields, and fruit that bruises easily and lasts only two or three days at room temperature. When ripe, pawpaws generally fall off the tree, so you must gather them quickly before the squirrels get to them. They can be kept in the refrigerator for about one week if fully ripe, or three weeks if a little underripe. Tree-ripened pawpaws are best.

The custardy flesh inside a ripe pawpaw is entirely too soft to be diced. Once you separate the fruit from the seeds and skin, it becomes a purée, akin to the pulp of a ripe Hachiya persimmon. To get at the pulp, halve the pawpaws, scoop out the flesh, and press through a strainer with the back of a large spoon into a large bowl. The pulp freezes well for up to six months. Pawpaws oxidize quickly, so when storing pawpaw pulp in the refrigerator, stir in a little lemon juice and remove the air by pressing plastic wrap directly on the surface. The fresh pulp is best used within one day, and it is delicious spooned over yogurt or ice cream.

PAWPAW BREAD PUDDING

Bread puddings are easy to make and a great way to use up leftover bread or croissants. You can flavor them any way you like. The key to a good bread pudding, in my mind, is to let the bread soak in the custard mixture for at least thirty minutes before baking. At the restaurant, we let them soak overnight in the refrigerator before baking them in the morning. This ensures a moist, custardy pudding.

Serves 8 to 10

4 tablespoons unsalted butter,
    for buttering bread and baking dish

12 (½-inch-thick) slices of Challah
    or other artisan bread with crusts removed,
    or 6 large croissants

3 cups light cream or half-and-half

1 tablespoon lemon zest

2 teaspoons vanilla extract

½ teaspoon salt

½ teaspoon ground cinnamon

4 large eggs

⅔ cup packed brown sugar, divided,
    plus 2 tablespoons for topping

2 cups fresh pawpaw purée (page 172)

2 teaspoons freshly squeezed lemon juice

Caramel sauce or lightly whipped cream,
    for serving (optional)

Preheat the oven to 375°F.

Lightly butter the bread slices on both sides, place on a large baking sheet, and bake, turning once, until lightly toasted on both sides. (If using croissants, you can omit this step.) In a small saucepan, whisk together the cream, lemon zest, vanilla extract, salt, and cinnamon over medium heat until just about to simmer, and remove from the heat. In a separate bowl, whisk together the eggs and ⅓ cup of the brown sugar until smooth. Slowly pour in the warm cream mixture, whisking constantly. This tempers the egg yolks and makes for a more custardy pudding.

Cut the toasted bread into 1-inch squares and put in a large bowl. Pour the cream mixture over top and stir gently. Allow the bread to soak for at least 30 minutes and up to overnight in the refrigerator.

Butter a shallow 2-quart baking dish and bring a teakettle of water to a boil. In a separate bowl, mix the pawpaw purée and lemon juice with ⅓ cup of the brown sugar and stir into the bread mixture. Pour into the prepared baking dish, making sure that the ingredients are evenly distributed. Sprinkle the remaining 2 tablespoons brown sugar over the top of the pudding.

Set the baking dish in a larger pan and transfer to the oven. Add enough boiling water to reach halfway up the sides of the baking dish. Bake until the custard is mostly set, 50 to 55 minutes. It will still be a little jiggly in the center but will set up as the pudding cools. Serve warm or at room temperature with caramel sauce or lightly whipped cream, if desired.

PAWPAW SORBET

Sorbets are best eaten the day they are made. You don't want to keep this particular sorbet around for more than a couple of days. The temperature cycling of typical home freezers will make it too icy after that.

Makes 1 generous quart

¾ cup granulated sugar

4 cups fresh pawpaw purée (page 172)

2 teaspoons freshly squeezed lime juice, or more to taste

½ teaspoon salt, or more to taste

In a large bowl, whisk the sugar into the pawpaw purée until well dissolved. Gradually whisk in the lime juice and salt, adding more to taste.

Refrigerate the purée until very cold, 2 to 3 hours. Churn in an ice-cream maker according to the manufacturer's instructions, then transfer to an airtight container and freeze for at least 4 hours before serving.

PAWPAW QUICK BREAD

This is my go-to simple recipe for quick bread using pawpaw purée. It's very moist and freezes well, for up to a month. Be sure to wrap in plastic and then aluminum foil to prevent freezer burn.

Makes two 9-inch loaves

Unsalted butter, for greasing pan

3½ cups sifted all-purpose flour, plus more for dusting

2½ cups granulated sugar

2 teaspoon baking soda

1½ teaspoons salt

1 teaspoon ground nutmeg

2 cups fresh pawpaw purée (page 172)

2 cups shelled walnuts or pecans, toasted and chopped

2 cups golden raisins

1 cup melted unsalted butter, cooled to room temperature

⅔ cup Cognac, bourbon, or whisky

4 large eggs, at room temperature, lightly beaten

Preheat the oven to 350°F. Butter two 9 x 5-inch loaf pans. Line the bottoms with parchment paper or dust with flour and tap out any excess.

In a large mixing bowl, sift the flour, sugar, baking soda, salt, and nutmeg. Make a well in the center, then stir in the pawpaw purée, walnuts, raisins, melted butter, Cognac, and eggs. Pour the batter into the prepared pans and level the tops.

Bake until a toothpick inserted into the center of the bread comes out clean, about 1 hour. Cool for several minutes, then turn loaves out on a wire rack to cool completely.

RHUBARB

RHUBARB (*RHEUM RHABARBARUM*) IS A SPECIES OF PLANT IN THE FAMILY *POLYGONACEAE*. Though we tend to think of rhubarb as a fruit because it's typically used in sweet preparations such as pies, tarts, and sauces, rhubarb technically is a vegetable. The thick celery-like leaf stalks, or petioles, are the part of the plant that we use for culinary purposes. These stalks can reach two feet in length. Wild-grown rhubarb, sometimes called pieplant, has bright red stalks and deep green leaves, or green stalks that don't turn red at all, while the cultivated version has pink or light red stalks.

Wild rhubarb is one of the first plants of spring, and like spring greens, it is considered a blood thinner in folk wisdom. The short growing season of rhubarb lasts only a few weeks, but the harvest freezes well. The plant grows in open woods, on riverbanks, and in disturbed areas like roadsides. Burdock, which is toxic, is commonly mistaken for rhubarb. The underside of burdock leaves is hairy, while the leaves of rhubarb are smooth. The large triangular leaves of the rhubarb plant are toxic, so cut them off and discard them.

Although rhubarb is extremely sour and needs a lot of sugar to make it palatable, its sweet-tart taste and beautiful color are highly valued in desserts.

Shrubs have been with us for centuries and are basically a mixture of fruits with vinegar and often sugar. They came about before we had refrigeration as a preservation method for fruits and herbs. Vinegar has long been thought of as part of a healthy diet. Growing up with my grandparents, a tablespoonful of apple cider vinegar was part of my daily routine. It was thought to help digestion and a number of other things depending on the folklore of the day. There is some evidence that this is true, and with the recent interest in fermentation of all kinds, shrubs have made a comeback and are part of the new DIY wave of fancy cocktails and other libations. Natural vinegar (not distilled) is considered a prebiotic. That is, it acts as a source for nutrition for those prebiotic bacteria in the gut. Take a walk down any supermarket aisle today, and you'll find the shelves loaded with products that promote gut health.

Shrubs are easy to make and a way of using up over-the-hill or too-abundant fruits, vegetables, and herbs. Once made, the basic syrup can be refrigerated for several months and used to make refreshing beverages of all kinds, including those with alcohol. The great virtue is that there are no hard-and-fast recipes. Fruit (or vegetables or herbs), vinegar, and sugar are combined to your personal taste.

BASIC RECIPE

4 cups rhubarb, cut into 1-inch lengths

2 cups granulated sugar

2 cups white balsamic or rice vinegar (you can also use white wine vinegar)

Aromatics (for herbs: several sprigs or a modest handful of leaves; for spices: 1 to 2 tablespoons, depending on strength/flavor)

Combine the rhubarb and sugar in a large, widemouthed glass jar. Use a muddler or wooden spoon to apply gentle yet firm pressure, enough to break up the rhubarb. Cover the jar with a lid or plastic wrap and let it sit in a cool, dark place for 24 hours.

After 24 hours, add the vinegar and aromatics, stir until the sugar has dissolved, cover, and return to a cool, dark spot (or the refrigerator) for 1 week or slightly longer, until the flavor is fully developed.

After 1 week, or when the flavor is to your liking, press and strain the contents of the jar through cheesecloth or a fine-mesh strainer, pushing down lightly to release all of the liquid from the rhubarb. Store in a clean container in the refrigerator for another week, or until the flavor of the vinegar mellows and fades into the background.

The shrub will keep in the refrigerator for up to 6 months. Serve it with sparkling or still water or over ice, or create your own cocktail by mixing the shrub with a spirit such as gin, rum, or vodka and a dash of bitters, if you like.

RHUBARB COMPOTE

This makes a delicious dessert sauce for cakes, ice cream, and custards, and it can also accompany grilled poultry and pork, sausages, and ham.

Makes about 3 cups

½ vanilla bean, split lengthwise and seeds scraped

¾ cup granulated sugar

2 pounds rhubarb, cut into ¾-inch pieces

⅓ cup Grand Marnier

Large pinch of kosher salt

Cacao nibs, for sprinkling

Preheat the oven to 325°F. In a 13 x 9-inch baking dish, rub the vanilla bean and seeds into the sugar. Add the rhubarb, Grand Marnier, and salt, and toss to coat. Let the rhubarb macerate for 15 minutes.

Tightly cover the baking dish with aluminum foil, and bake until the rhubarb is soft but not falling apart, about 25 minutes. Let cool and discard the vanilla bean.

Drain the rhubarb in a fine-mesh strainer set over a medium saucepan and set the rhubarb aside. Bring the juices to a boil, then simmer over medium-high heat until syrupy, about 5 minutes. Add the rhubarb to the syrup and let cool completely. Cool and store covered in the refrigerator for up to 5 days.

RHUBARB GALETTE

Galettes (French) and *crostadas* (Italian) are rustic free-form tarts that encourage those of us who have a baking phobia to dive in and make one. They are very forgiving, and if the juices happen to leak out during baking, it just lends to their rustic, peasant nature. Any combination of fruits can be used, especially those that are getting a little too soft. This dessert is best eaten the day it is made.

Serves 8 to 10

2 cups plus 3 tablespoons all-purpose flour, divided, plus more for dusting

1 cup granulated sugar, divided

½ teaspoon salt

1 cup (2 sticks) very cold, unsalted butter, cut into teaspoon-size cubes, divided

⅓ cup plus 1 teaspoon ice water, divided

3 tablespoons almond meal

2½ pounds fresh rhubarb, cut into 1-inch lengths

2 tablespoons apricot preserves

2 tablespoons Grand Marnier

Vanilla bean ice-cream, for serving

Preheat the oven to 375°F.

In a food processor, combine 2 cups of the flour, 1 tablespoon of the sugar, and the salt. Scatter three-quarters (1½ sticks) of the cubed butter evenly around the blade and pulse a few times, allowing large clumps of the butter to remain. Drizzle ⅓ cup of the ice water over the mixture and pulse to create a dough that looks like coarse oatmeal. There should still be visible chunks of butter. Remove a bit of the dough and pinch to see if it holds together. If not, add a tablespoon or two of cold water and pulse once or twice. Remove the dough from the processor, gently press into a flat cake, and wrap in plastic wrap. Refrigerate for at least 1 hour or up to 2 days.

In a medium bowl, whisk together the almond meal, ⅓ cup of the sugar, and the remaining 3 tablespoons flour. Add the rhubarb and gently toss to combine.

On a lightly floured work surface, roll out the chilled dough into a 15-inch circle, about ⅛ inch thick. Carefully transfer the dough to a nonstick or parchment paper–lined baking sheet and spread the rhubarb evenly in the middle, leaving a 4-inch border on all sides of the dough. Gently fold the sides of the dough up around the edges of the rhubarb, piecing the dough together to avoid leaving any holes in the edges. Sprinkle the remaining sugar and ¼ cup cubed butter over the rhubarb. Bake until the bottom and edges of the crust are golden brown, 1 hour and 20 minutes, rotating the galette halfway through.

In a small bowl, whisk the preserves with the Grand Marnier and the remaining 1 teaspoon ice water. Use a pastry brush to generously brush the liquid all over the edges of the galette. Return the galette to the oven and bake until a glossy finish forms on the crust, about 10 minutes longer.

Let the galette cool on the baking sheet for 5 minutes, then transfer to a wire rack and let cool completely, about 20 minutes. Serve with ice cream, if desired.

THE TOPIC:

Wild Fruit

Jeff Cox comes from a family of graphic artists, but, in true revolutionary spirit, he went rogue and decided to become a food writer. The James Beard Foundation nominated his book *The Organic Cook's Bible* for a Best Reference award, earning Jeff a ticket to the awards banquet. Jeff's connection to wild fruit began when he was nine years old and his family moved to the Pocono Mountains of eastern Pennsylvania. During the growing season, Jeff discovered all sorts of wild fruits—including some he never knew existed.

CHEF: With all the selective breeding these days to make fruit bigger, prettier, easier to eat, and easier to transport, is there any real [wild] fruit out there? Is nature still capable of producing fruit without human intervention?

JEFF: Wild fruit needs wild places, or, if not quite pristine wild, at least abandoned land. There's plenty of wild fruit if you know where to look and what to look for. Nature's fruiting plants aren't going anywhere. All they need is a space that's left alone.

CHEF: For the health minded, is eating wild fruit more nutritious?

JEFF: It can be. For one thing, if your wild fruit is not growing in or near land or water that's been polluted, it won't carry a load of agricultural chemicals. Some cultivated varieties have been selected or hybridized for extra nutrition, but also carry chemical toxins, unless they're grown organically. Wild fruits tend to be thriftier—that is, more compact because they are not given soluble fertilizers—so ounce for ounce, would have more nutritional bang for your buck than conventional food. Many studies show that some organically grown fruits have more nutrition than conventional fruit, but this isn't categorical. A lot depends on the variety and farming practices.

CHEF: Can a consumer at the market tell the difference between truly wild and modern cultivated fruit?

JEFF: Cultivated varieties tend to be large—big grapes, big strawberries, and so on. Thompson seedless grapes, for instance, grown naturally without the hormone sprays used by big growers, are about the size of your little fingernail or smaller. Wild blueberries are smaller than their plump conventional counterparts. Wild apples are about the size of a pullet egg. If you're not sure, ask the purveyor what variety he or she is selling. If they tell you a name, it's a cultivated variety.

CHEF: In addition to size, what about flavor? I find some cultivated fruits like strawberries and blackberries are tasteless compared to wild varieties.

JEFF: Because wild fruits are more compact and thrifty, and because when grown in the tough conditions of the wild, the plants tend to pack more flavor compounds into the fruit. Most of these compounds are phenolics with sharp flavor profiles. Besides that, when selections are made and fruits hybridized, great weight is not given to flavor.

CHEF: What are some of your favorite wild fruits?

JEFF: When I was a boy growing up in the Poconos, I'd eat wild fruit all day long during the growing season. Here is some of what I'd find cruising around the fields and forests: black raspberries, aka blackcaps; wineberries—still my favorite wild fruit; blackberries, dewberries, wild red raspberries, huckleberries, blueberries, wild grapes—I could smell them fifty yards away; wild strawberries—*Fragaria virginiana*—these are unimaginably delicious—our five acres in the Poconos was filled with them, and every June our place smelled like strawberries; teaberries, aka American wintergreen; elderberries, wild apples, black cherries, mayapples, and, rarely, bunchberries. And I'm probably forgetting some fruits.

CHEF: Can you find/buy wild fruit year-round?

JEFF: Unfortunately, no. Wild fruits are only available when they're in season. And their seasons tend to be short—just a couple of weeks for most of them. They're rarely sold, because they typically don't ship well, although they are sometimes found at roadside stands or farmers' markets. If you have a freezer and live where the wild fruits grow, get out there and get picking. I used to freeze blackcaps, wineberries, and blackberries by the gallons and eat them all winter.

CHEF: What do you think about the future of wild fruit? Do you envision eating them ten, twenty, fifty years from now? Or will the fruits in our stores and markets strictly be cultivated fruit?

JEFF: As long as we don't "pave paradise and put up a parking lot," wild fruit will grow, hungry children will find it and enjoy it, and those children will become adults who will search for those wild fruits for the rest of their lives. The fruits in our stores and markets are almost invariably cultivated, hybridized, or GMO right now. I'd like to see that change, but don't believe it will. Wild fruits are exceedingly delicious, but evanescent and perishable.

HONEY

HONEY HAS PROBABLY BEEN WITH US FOR AS LONG AS HUMANS HAVE WALKED upright. No doubt, wild honey was gathered in the beginning, as written history traces the sticky substance back to 2100 BC. Beekeeping is illustrated in ten-thousand-year-old cave paintings in Spain and was recorded in a sun temple erected in 2400 BC in Egypt, where honey was a royal symbol and used as an ingredient in embalming.

It's not surprising that honey was considered a magical food by primitive peoples. It has been used in rituals throughout history, often to make sculptures in the form of a god, which were then consumed in order to ingest the holy aspect of that god.

Although there are many bees that are native to North America, the honeybee is not indigenous to this continent; it was brought here by European settlers and established in the wild by escaping swarms. Honey was the main sweetener in Europe and then in North America up until the discovery of sugarcane and beets, which provided much more abundant and cheaper sweeteners. Though we don't ordinarily gather honey any longer in the wild, there are some intrepid souls out there who still scout it out. Of course, bears are wonderful foragers of honey.

The honey-making process starts with bees collecting nectar from flower blossoms. They carry it back to their nest, where the worker bees add enzymes and transfer the mixture to honeycombs. The water in the nectar is then evaporated by the action of the bees fluttering their wings (this is the humming you hear inside a hive), which converts the nectar into honey. This substance is a food source for the bees during cold months when flowers are not blooming, but a healthy colony will produce up to three times as much honey as it needs, allowing some to be harvested.

Honey contains about 70 percent fructose and glucose. Honey with a high fructose content will be clear, while the kind with more glucose may crystallize or thicken, but both are a pure food source. To melt crystallized honey, just stand the jar in warm water and it will clear in about an hour. Bees usually have a flight radius of one or two miles, within which they gather nectar from many kinds of flowers (which yields polyfloral honey) or from just one kind (which yields monofloral honey), depending on what is available to them in their gathering territory. The flavor of honey is determined by the type of flower or flowers the nectar comes from, as well as their terroir; the nectar of the same kind of flower will vary depending on where the flower grows. The depth of flavor of a honey can generally be judged by its color, which ranges from very pale in mild honeys to almost black in intensely flavored ones.

Honey has always been valued as a healing substance as well as a food source. Raw honey (see "What Is Raw Honey" below) is both antimicrobial and an antioxidant; historically, it was most commonly applied as a wound dressing. It still makes one of the most effective cough medicines when mixed with lemon juice.

What Is Raw Honey?

Raw honey is simply honey that hasn't been heated over 95°F, the temperature inside a beehive when the bees are at work. This allows the natural enzymes in the honey, which are beneficial nutrients, to remain active.

Look for raw, unfiltered honey in natural food stores. It's a far more nutritious product than mass-market processed honey. Of course, if raw honey is used in cooking or is otherwise heated over 95°F in your kitchen, the enzymes are destroyed. Use unheated raw honey as a topping for desserts and cheeses, but take care not to feed it to a child under the age of twelve months, as it can contain bacteria from dust accidentally added during the honey-gathering process.

PORK KEBABS WITH HONEY AND POMEGRANATE MOLASSES

You can use any meat for this dish, including chicken, semiboned quail,
or even a firm-fleshed fish like swordfish.

Serves 4

1 cup fragrant honey, such as lavender
or orange blossom

⅔ cup extra-virgin olive oil,
plus more for brushing

⅓ cup pomegranate molasses

2 tablespoons freshly ground black pepper,
plus more as needed

2½ pounds lean, well-trimmed pork loin,
cut into 2-inch cubes

2 tablespoons freshly squeezed lemon juice
or rice vinegar

2 large artichokes

Sea salt

In a medium bowl, combine the honey, ⅔ cup olive oil, ⅔ cup water, molasses, and black pepper and mix well. Add the pork, turning to coat. Cover and refrigerate overnight.

When ready to cook, bring the pork to room temperature. Meanwhile, prepare the artichokes. Fill a medium bowl with water and add the lemon juice. Remove the outside leaves of the artichokes down to the pale-yellow leaves. Cut off the tops just above the hearts. Trim off any remaining leaves and scoop out the fuzzy chokes with a spoon. Cut the hearts into quarters, and immediately put them into the bowl of acidulated water to keep them from browning.

Prepare a charcoal grill or preheat a gas grill for medium-high heat.

Thread the pork onto skewers alternating with the artichoke hearts. Pat dry with paper towels, brush lightly with olive oil, and season generously with salt and pepper.

Grill until cooked through but not dry, about 5 minutes per side depending on the grill used.

GRILLED FIGS WITH HONEY AND BLUE CHEESE

Use any blue cheese you like, as long as it's creamy in texture. A couple of my favorites are Point Reyes Farmstead Original Blue and Rogue Creamery Smokey Blue.

Serves 6 as a starter

12 rosemary sprigs (6 inches long)

3 tablespoons raw honey

3 tablespoons unsalted butter

1 tablespoon good-quality brandy or Cognac

1 teaspoon freshly squeezed lemon juice

12 fresh firm-ripe figs

6 ounces creamy blue cheese

Strip the leaves from the bottom 5 inches of the rosemary sprigs to form skewers. Soak in a shallow dish of water for at least 15 minutes. Chop a few of the rosemary needles (you'll need a scant 1 teaspoon). Set aside.

In a small saucepan, combine the honey, butter, brandy, lemon juice, and the reserved chopped rosemary. Cook over medium heat until the butter is melted, about 1 minute. Stir to combine, and set aside.

Prepare a charcoal grill or preheat a gas grill for medium-low heat.

Cut the figs in half through the stem end and thread 2 halves on each rosemary skewer. Brush the cut side of the figs generously with the honey mixture. Grill the skewers, cut-side up, until warmed through. Place the skewers cut-side up on plates, top with a nice piece of blue cheese, and drizzle with any remaining honey mixture.

NOTE: You can also heat the figs under a hot broiler at least 8 inches from the heat source.

HONEY ZABAGLIONE WITH STRAWBERRIES

Zabaglione (Italian) or sabayon (French) is a simple but delicious dessert that can be made at the very last minute and served warm. It's like a soufflé without the dish. I serve this with fresh fruit just spooned on the side, or, for a more dramatic presentation, I arrange the fresh fruit in a shallow bowl, spoon the zabaglione on top, and quickly brown it with a propane torch.

Serves 6

1 pint fresh strawberries, hulled and sliced

2 large eggs

4 large egg yolks

⅔ cup fragrant honey, such as lavender or orange blossom

¼ cup freshly squeezed lemon juice

¼ cup sweet Riesling, Muscat, Sauternes, or other sweet dessert wine (optional)

Mint sprigs, for garnish (optional)

Small crisp cookies, for garnish (optional)

Arrange the strawberries attractively in six shallow bowls or soup plates.

In the bottom of a double boiler, bring water to a simmer. In the top of the double boiler, combine the eggs, egg yolks, honey, lemon juice, and wine, if using, and whisk until the mixture is light and thick. Place over the simmering water and whisk vigorously until the mixture has tripled in volume and is thick and light in color. Total cooking and whisking time will be about 4 minutes. Be careful not to scramble the eggs. Remove from heat, spoon around the strawberries, and serve immediately garnished with mint and a cookie, if using.

BEE'S KNEES

This cocktail dates back to the Prohibition era in the 1930s. The phrase "bee's knees" was slang at the time for "the best." During this period, the addition of ingredients such as citrus and honey covered the less-than-ideal smell and taste of bathtub gin. Pick your favorite monofloral honey to make this drink.

Serves 1

Ice cubes, for shaker

2 ounces good-quality gin

¾ ounce freshly squeezed lemon or lime juice

¾ ounce honey simple syrup (one-to-one ratio of honey to water)

Lemon twist, for garnish

In an ice-filled cocktail shaker, combine the gin, lime juice, and syrup. Shake and strain into a chilled cocktail glass. Garnish with the lemon twist.

Colony Collapse Disorder

You've no doubt heard that bees, including the honeybee, are in trouble. Honeybees are critical to our food supply, but they are dying in huge numbers in this country every year. A tendency to single out one cause for the collapse of bee colonies has confused this issue, which is due to a combination of factors that include: pathogens and pests, pesticides, genetic weakness, and exhaustion and malnutrition caused by the commercial exploitation of bees (which are often trucked from one monoculture to another on large farms and fed with high-fructose corn syrup).

Although some companies and organizations are still arguing that pesticides are not a cause of colony collapse, in the spring of 2015, the EPA placed a moratorium on new uses of neonicotinoid pesticides (which are already banned in Europe). We can help bees survive by not supporting companies that use this poison in their products, by not buying garden pesticides, and by eating organic foods. Gardeners can help by planting such bee-friendly plants as foxgloves and bee balm.

HONEY MUSTARD ROAST CHICKEN

Roast chicken is one of life's great pleasures and it's easy to do. The coating here could also be used for roast pork, and I've also used it successfully with salmon.

Serves 4

1 whole roasting chicken (about 4 pounds)

Salt and freshly ground black pepper

1 lemon

⅓ cup honey

2 tablespoons Dijon mustard

1 tablespoon finely chopped fresh rosemary

1 small yellow onion, quartered

3 garlic cloves, halved

Preheat the oven to 375°F. Season chicken generously inside and out with salt and pepper. Place the chicken on a rack set in a large roasting pan and set aside.

Zest and juice the lemon into a small bowl, reserving the lemon halves after juicing. Add the honey, mustard, and rosemary and stir to combine. Set aside.

Place the juiced lemon halves, onion quarters, and garlic in the cavity of the bird. Using a brush or with your fingers, coat the outside of the bird with the honey mixture.

Place the roasting pan in the oven and baste the chicken every 15 minutes with any remaining glaze. Roast until an instant-read thermometer inserted into the thigh reaches 170°F and juices run clear, about 1 hour. Let stand at least 10 minutes before carving. Carve and serve hot or at room temperature.

MAPLE SYRUP

MAPLE SYRUP IS A SWEETENER MADE FROM THE SAP OF MAPLE TREES. THE SAP from the species *Acer saccharum*, the sugar maple, is used for most maple syrup. Sap can also be harvested from the black, silver, or red maple, but it is not as sweet as that of the sugar maple. Gathering the sap or "maple sugaring," as it's called, has been an activity of native peoples in the Northeast since before the Pilgrims landed. Native Americans taught the colonists how to collect the sweet sap, which they called "Indian molasses." For most early settlers in that region, maple syrup was the only available sweetener, and it was often cooked down into maple sugar because it was easier to store. Folks would hack pieces of maple sugar from tubs or blocks either to use whole or to heat back into liquid form.

Sugar maple trees grow almost exclusively in northeast Canada and the United States. Some trees can be found as far south as Georgia, but the large tracts needed for sugaring are found primarily in the northern forests. Most maple syrup comes from the Canadian provinces of New Brunswick, Ontario, and Quebec. The last is the largest producer, with as much as 75 percent of all maple syrup produced worldwide coming from this one province. In the States, the key producers are Vermont (the largest US producer), New Hampshire, New York, Pennsylvania, Michigan, Wisconsin, and Maine.

The flavor of maple syrup is affected by terroir, weather conditions, the timing of the sap collection, and how the sap is processed. Although maple syrup is less refined than white sugar and thus contains some nutrients, it is not considered more healthful than white sugar for diabetics. Maple syrup is primarily sucrose, although some syrups, usually the darker ones, contain fructose and glucose. The time of year when the sap is gathered makes a big difference in its sweetness level. Generally, the best time is late winter into early spring. When the tree reaches the right temperature (between 40 and 45°F), the starches turn to sugar and the sweet sap begins to flow. Ideally, the temperature should drop below freezing at night, and it is this variation in temperature that keeps the sap flowing. It takes forty gallons or so of sap (depending on the sugar content, or Brix) to make one gallon of syrup, because the sap is mostly water.

Until 2014, the grading of maple syrup was very much a local or regional affair; the syrup was divided by color into three grades: A, B, and C. Today, all maple syrup produced in the United States and Canada is categorized with a unified grading system that relies on taste as well as appearance. All maple syrups for consumption are now called Grade A. The four different categories are golden (delicate taste), amber (rich taste), dark (robust taste), and very dark (strong taste).

Unopened maple syrup will keep at room temperature for at least one year and often much longer, depending on how the syrup was reduced and packaged. Opened maple syrup should be kept refrigerated and used within six months, though I've kept it in my refrigerator for a couple of years with no discernible loss of flavor or quality.

PEPPERED MAPLE WALNUTS

These are delicious as a little snack with cocktails, a topping for salads,
or an accompaniment to a cheese plate.

Makes approximately 3 cups

1 cup maple syrup

¼ cup (½ stick) unsalted butter

2 to 3 teaspoons freshly ground black pepper,
   or in combination with pure chile powder,
   such as ancho

1 teaspoon salt

12 ounces (3 cups) shelled walnuts

Preheat the oven to 300°F.

In a small saucepan, stir together the maple syrup butter, black pepper, and salt and bring to a simmer over medium heat. Simmer until thickened, about 3 minutes. Place the walnuts in a large bowl and pour the butter mixture over top, tossing them to evenly coat.

Line a baking sheet with parchment paper, aluminum foil, or a silicone baking mat, and spread the coated walnuts in a single layer. Bake for 40 minutes, stirring and turning the walnuts every 10 minutes or so. After 40 minutes, the walnuts will appear fairly dry. Slide the walnuts off the tray and onto a wire rack to cool. Resist the temptation to eat the nuts at this point because they will be very hot! Store the walnuts in an airtight container for up to 2 weeks.

MAPLE-GLAZED SALMON

I like to cook salmon and most fish with the skin on. Skin adds flavor and keeps the fish moist, and it can be removed before serving by simply sliding a fish spatula (you definitely should have this tool if you don't already) between the skin and flesh, leaving the skin behind in the pan. You can also place the fillet skin-side up, slide a knife under the skin, and simply pull the skin off. It's worth noting, however, that many people value crisp-cooked salmon skin, and some recipes highlight it.

Serves 4

⅓ cup maple syrup

1 teaspoon freshly ground cardamom

1 teaspoon smoked paprika

Large pinch of cayenne pepper

Freshly ground black pepper

Sea salt

4 (5-ounce) skin-on wild salmon fillets, pin bones removed

Preheat the oven to 450°F.

In a small bowl, combine the maple syrup, cardamom, paprika, cayenne, and black pepper to taste. Whisk until the mixture is smooth. Season with salt to taste.

Arrange the salmon on a cutting board. Brush the syrup mixture evenly over the salmon. Place a large cast-iron skillet in the oven and allow to heat for about 5 minutes while the salmon rests.

Place the salmon skin-side down in the preheated skillet (use caution with hot pan) and cook for 5 minutes. Turn and brush more glaze on the salmon, and cook until the fish just begins to flake but is still juicy pink inside, about 5 minutes more depending on thickness. Remove from pan and serve.

CHIPOTLE-MAPLE BARBECUE SAUCE

This is adapted from a recipe in *Fresh Every Day* by the talented Sara Foster (Clarkson Potter 2005).
I changed the ingredients a bit and added a big glug of rum, which I think adds interesting depth
to the sauce and enhances the maple flavor. Use whenever you want
a good sauce: Ribs and chicken would be a good start.

Makes about 1 quart

1 (28-ounce) can crushed tomatoes

1 cup cider vinegar

¾ cup maple syrup

⅓ cup packed brown sugar

2 tablespoons chopped chipotle peppers
in adobo, or more to taste

2 tablespoons Worcestershire sauce

½ cup apple cider

⅓ cup freshly squeezed lemon juice

½ cup dark rum

2 tablespoons finely chopped garlic

2 tablespoons dry mustard

Salt and freshly ground black pepper

In a deep, heavy saucepan, add the tomatoes, vinegar, maple syrup, brown sugar, chipotle peppers, Worcestershire, apple cider, lemon juice, rum, garlic, dry mustard, and salt and black pepper to taste. Stir well and bring the sauce to a boil over medium-high heat.

Reduce the heat and simmer until the sauce is thick and reduced by about one-third, or as you like it, about 25 minutes.

Store the sauce covered in the refrigerator for up to 3 weeks.

FRISÉE SALAD WITH POACHED EGGS AND MAPLE-ROASTED BACON

A variation on the classic French bistro salad *frisée aux lardons*. The star here is the maple bacon, which I also like serving with French toast. The bacon can be cooked ahead, as can as the eggs. If you cook the eggs ahead, simply place them in ice water to stop the cooking, and when you are ready to eat, reheat in simmering water for a few seconds.

Serves 4

8 strips of thick-cut bacon

½ cup maple syrup

2 tablespoons white wine vinegar

4 large eggs

1 tablespoon finely chopped shallot

1 tablespoon freshly squeezed lemon juice,
   or more to taste

2 teaspoons grainy Dijon mustard

1 teaspoon granulated sugar, or more to taste

3 tablespoons extra-virgin olive oil

Kosher salt and freshly ground black pepper

6 cups loosely packed torn frisée greens
   (medium-size pieces)

Preheat the oven to 425°F. Line a sheet pan with parchment paper or a silicone baking mat. Separate the bacon and blot dry with paper towels. Coat both sides of the bacon liberally with maple syrup. Lay the bacon in a single layer on the prepared pan.

Cook bacon, turning once, until browned and lacquered, about 12 minutes. Transfer to a lightly oiled plate to cool. Break slices into quarters and set aside.

Bring a 4-quart saucepan of water to a boil. Add the vinegar, and reduce the heat to medium-low. Crack each egg into its own ramekin and set aside.

In a medium bowl, whisk together the shallot, lemon juice, mustard, and sugar to taste. While whisking, add the olive oil in a slow, steady stream until well combined. Season with salt and pepper to taste. In a large bowl, toss the frisée with the vinaigrette. Divide the frisée and reserved bacon among four plates.

In the saucepan, gently slide the eggs one by one into the water and cook until just firm, about 2 minutes. Use a slotted spoon to drain the eggs and place one on top of each of the salads. Season with salt and pepper to taste. Serve immediately.

MAPLE FLAN

Simple to make, flans are a desert staple in Mexico and Spain. The maple syrup adds interesting flavor different from the typical sugar-based recipe. I'm doing it here in individual ramekins, but you could also use a 6-cup metal or ceramic mold.

Serves 6

½ cup granulated sugar

1 cup maple syrup

5 large eggs

2 large egg yolks

1 quart whole milk

1 teaspoon vanilla extract

Fresh seasonal fruit, attractively cut, for serving

In a small, deep saucepan combine the sugar with ½ cup water, bring to a boil, and cook, stirring occasionally, until the mixture turns a deep golden color. Carefully divide the hot syrup among six 6-ounce ovenproof ramekins, and turn to coat the bottoms of each.

Adjust the oven rack to the middle position. Preheat the oven to 350°F.

In a large bowl, whisk together the maple syrup, eggs, and egg yolks. Heat the milk in a saucepan and bring just below a simmer. Slowly whisk the hot milk and vanilla into the egg mixture and pour through a fine-mesh strainer into the prepared ramekins.

Put the ramekins in a deep roasting pan and place in the middle of the oven. Add enough hot tap water to the pan to reach three-quarters of the way up the sides of the ramekins.

Bake until the centers of the flans are gently set but still a little wiggly, about 40 minutes. (If using one large mold, increase the cooking time by 10 to 15 minutes.) Transfer the flans to wire rack and cool. Refrigerate until cold, about 2 hours. Cover and refrigerate overnight. Can be made a day ahead.

To serve, run a small, sharp knife around the flan to loosen. Turn over onto a plate. Shake gently to release the flan. Carefully lift off the ramekin, allowing the caramel syrup to run over the flan. Repeat with remaining flans and serve with the fresh fruit.

Chapter 4

MEAT AND BIRDS

BISON

THE ANIMAL WE USUALLY CALL A BUFFALO IS ACTUALLY A BISON. ALTHOUGH BOTH animals look alike and belong to the *Bovidae* family, they are different in genus and species. When this country was first settled by Europeans, bison were found on much of the continent, from what is now southern Canada to northern Mexico. The animal we think of as a buffalo is a plains bison; there are also wood bison, whose range is in Canada and Alaska.

But why call them buffalo at all? Presumably it's because of their resemblance to the Asian water buffalo or the African buffalo, which really are buffalo; both have been domesticated on their respective continents for more than five thousand years. Unfortunately, a name change was not the only thing that happened to the bison when Europeans arrived here. These creatures were hunted sustainably by the Native Americans, who stampeded them over cliffs (in the absence of guns) and then used every part of the animal, not just the meat. The hides, bones, sinews, etc., were used to make clothing, food, and ritual objects. The Europeans brought guns to this country and then built railroads; the combination resulted in the slaughter of bison for sport, although not everyone would define shooting animals from the window of a passing train as sport.

Bison were replaced on the central plains by cows, which are much easier to raise, although they are more destructive to rangeland than are bison. For one thing, bison refuse to be herded; they are also capable, despite their huge size, of jumping high fences, and they can carry a disease called brucellosis, which can be transmitted to cows. (Ironically, this disease was originally transmitted from cows to bison.) A movement to restock the American plains with bison is ongoing, although it has been strenuously opposed by many Western ranchers.

Bison meat is deliciously sweet, with the flavor of the grass the animal grazes. It's also very lean in comparison with beef, as it doesn't the same marbling of fat (it also has more protein and less cholesterol than beef). For this reason, tender cuts of bison shouldn't be cooked at as high a temperature or as long as beef. It's a good idea to rub cuts of bison with oil before cooking. When roasting bison, reduce the oven temperature by about 50°F; when broiling, use a lower heat and keep the bison at least six inches from the heat source. Indirect heat is the best choice for grilling. Use an instant-read thermometer to check for doneness; medium-rare is 125° to 130°F.

BISON AND BLACK BEAN CHILI

A good chili recipe should be in everyone's repertoire.
This is a fun one that uses both coffee and chocolate.

Serves 6

3 tablespoons olive oil

1 pound coarsely ground bison

3 cups diced yellow onions

2 tablespoons chopped garlic

2 large fresh poblano chiles, stemmed,
  seeded, and chopped

½ cup bulgur wheat

2 tablespoons pure chile powder, such as ancho

2 tablespoons unsweetened cocoa powder

1 tablespoon dried oregano
  (preferably Mexican)

1 tablespoon ground cumin

2 teaspoons chopped chipotle in adobo,
  or more to taste

1 teaspoon instant espresso powder
  or instant coffee

Salt

2 (15-ounce) cans black beans,
  drained and rinsed

1 (14-ounce) can diced tomatoes

5 cups beef stock

In a Dutch oven, heat the oil over medium-high heat. Add the bison, onion, and garlic. Cook, stirring and breaking up the meat with a wooden spoon, until the meat is no longer pink, about 5 minutes.

Add the poblanos, reduce the heat to medium, and cook, stirring frequently, until the vegetables are beginning to color, 5 to 7 minutes. Add the bulgur, chile powder, cocoa powder, oregano, cumin, chipotle, espresso powder, and salt to taste and cook, stirring, until aromatic, about 2 minutes.

Add the beans and tomatoes, then stir in the stock and bring to a boil. Reduce the heat to simmer, partially cover, and cook, stirring occasionally, until the liquid is reduced and thickened and the bulgur is tender, about 50 minutes. If you're not serving immediately, cover and refrigerate the chili for up to 3 days, or freeze for up to 3 months.

CORNED BISON BRISKET

Corning is an old English term that refers to curing meat with pellets of salt, called corns. If you've ever looked at the ingredient list on a package of commercially corned beef, you'll see that way too many chemicals and preservatives have been used in the corning process. Homemade corned beef is easy to make and much more delicious, and bison takes to this technique well, as it serves to tenderize the meat.

This recipe can easily be doubled or tripled. The only uncommon ingredient is pink salt, which is available in spice shops and online. This is not Himalayan pink salt but a curing salt that contains sodium nitrite and sodium chloride. It is sometimes called Prague powder No. 1. Pink salt accounts for the deep red color of corned beef and offers a distinctive flavor.

Serves 8

1½ cups kosher salt

½ cup granulated sugar

4 teaspoons pink curing salt (sodium nitrite)

3 garlic cloves, finely chopped

5 tablespoons pickling spice

2 (2-pound) bison briskets

8 ounces carrots

8 ounces yellow onions

8 ounces celery

8 ounces fennel

8 ounces potatoes

8 ounces cabbage (vegetables can be varied according to preference)

½ cup prepared horseradish sauce, for serving

½ cup grainy mustard, for serving

In pot large enough to hold the briskets, combine the kosher salt, sugar, sodium nitrite, garlic, and 3 tablespoons of the pickling spice with 8 cups water. Bring to a simmer, stirring until the salt and sugar are dissolved. Remove from the heat, add another 8 cups water, and let cool to room temperature, then refrigerate until chilled.

Place the briskets in the brine, weighted with a plate to keep them submerged, and cover. Refrigerate for 4 to 5 days. Remove the brisket from the brine and rinse thoroughly.

To cook the bison, place in a pot just large enough to hold both briskets. Cover with water and add the remaining 2 tablespoons pickling spice. Bring just to a boil over high heat, then reduce heat to low and cover. Simmer gently until the brisket is fork-tender, about 3 hours, adding water if needed to keep the brisket covered.

Cut the carrots, onions, celery, fennel, potatoes, cabbage, or any vegetables you'd like to add into similar-size pieces. During the last 20 minutes of cooking, add the vegetables to the pot and cook until tender.

Keep warm until ready to serve. The brisket can be refrigerated for several days in the cooking liquid. Remove any congealed fat, and reheat in the liquid. Alternatively, you can drain the brisket, chill it, and slice it for a slider or sandwich. Any leftovers are excellent for breakfast hash, too!

BRAISED BISON SHANKS

Here's a rich, earthy version of the Italian classic osso buco.

Serves 6

6 meaty sliced bison shanks
   (about ¾ pound each)

All-purpose flour, for dusting

Salt and freshly ground black pepper

⅓ cup olive oil

6 cups sliced yellow onions, divided

2½ cups bias-cut carrots, divided

1 cup thinly sliced fresh fennel, divided

2 tablespoons slivered garlic

1 teaspoon fennel seeds

2 bay leaves

6 cups beef stock

2½ cups hearty red wine, such as cabernet

2 teaspoons cornstarch whisked in
   2 tablespoons red wine

Gremolata, for garnish (page 206)

Preheat the oven to 325°F. Using kitchen twine, tie the shanks individually to retain their shape. Lightly dust the shanks with flour and season well with salt and pepper.

In a heavy bottomed casserole dish or Dutch oven, heat the oil over medium-high heat and brown the shanks on all sides, about 4 minutes. Remove the shanks to a plate and add 1½ cups of the onions, 1¼ cups of the carrots, and ½ cup of the fennel. Cook until the vegetables just begin to brown. Add the garlic, fennel seeds, and bay leaves, then stir in the stock and wine and bring to a boil. Return the shanks to the dish, cover, and place in the oven. Braise for until meat is very tender when pierced, 2 to 2½ hours.

Transfer the shanks to a platter. Strain the cooking liquid into a large glass bowl pressing on the vegetables to extract all the juices. Discard the pressed vegetables and bay leaves. Skim the fat from the surface, reserving 2 tablespoons, and discard the rest. Place the fat in a heavy skillet, add the remaining onions, carrots, and fennel, and cook over medium heat until crisp-tender and lightly browned.

Meanwhile, bring the strained cooking liquid to a boil over high heat and cook until reduced by half. Stir in the cornstarch mixture and cook 2 minutes to thicken. Seasoning with salt and pepper to taste. Add the cooked vegetables and shanks, and heat through. Arrange the shanks and vegetables attractively on warm plates. Garnish with a generous sprinkling of gremolata on top.

GREMOLATA

This is a traditional garnish for classic Italian veal shanks. The bright flavor of the lemon and parsley help cut through and balance the rich flavor of the meat.

Makes 6 servings

¼ cup finely chopped fresh flat-leaf parsley

2 large garlic cloves, very finely chopped

1 tablespoon lemon zest

In a small bowl, combine the parsley, garlic, and lemon zest, up to one hour before using.

Braising

Braising is a great way to cook tough cuts of meat, so it's perfect for bison, which is much lower in fat than beef. In this method, meat is usually first browned in fat, then baked or cooked on top of the stove in a covered pot with some kind of liquid, such as stock, along with flavorful vegetables like carrots, onions, and celery. The meat is cooked at a low temperature for a relatively long time, until the collagen in the meat dissolves into gelatin and releases the muscle fibers, which makes the meat tender. Tougher cuts of bison, such as the shanks and brisket, will need even longer braising times compared with beef, but the results will be richly flavorful and succulent.

WILD BOAR

WILD BOAR IN THE UNITED STATES HAVE AN INTERESTING LIFE STORY. THEY ARE THE result of the coming together of two related species. The first is the domestic pig, introduced in the 1500s to what is now the southeastern United States by Spanish explorer Hernando de Soto. These pigs proved so successful as domesticated animals that as America expanded, people took pigs right along with them. Later, these domesticated swine were either given free range or they escaped into the wild and spread across the country as feral pigs.

Then there is the Eurasian or Russian wild boar (*Sus scrofa*), brought to the United States in the early 1900s to provide a new, huntable game. The two pig species were sympatric, meaning closely related and often occupying the same geographical areas. Nature's laws kicked in, and the two pigs crossbred. This continuous crossbreeding and hybridization has made it difficult to pin down clean genetic profiles for wild boar in the many locations they reside. In addition, domestic pigs have often been released and wild ones relocated to provide new sources for hunters. Wild boar have been reported in at least forty-five states, including Hawaii.

In the past few decades, Eurasian wild boar have been reintroduced into the States at least twice for the purposes of breeding. No proof exists that they have been deliberately released into the wild for hunting purposes, but the likelihood of this is high. This means that "wild pigs" can be feral domestic hogs, a genetic mixture of domestic hogs and wild boar, or purely wild boar.

Wild boar can be very destructive to the environment, especially in vineyards and cultivated fields, which they can destroy in no time while rooting for food. Vineyard owners in Sonoma County, California, where I live, are in constant battles with wild boar, and they encourage hunters to control them.

Wild boar meat is a delicious and flavorful alternative to domestic pork, which it of course resembles. The meat is incredibly lean. This means that tender cuts such as the loin need to be watched carefully during cooking so they don't dry out and become tough. The rest of the animal takes well to slow-cooking methods such as braising (page 206). Unlike other game animals like venison, wild boar meat needs to be fully cooked before eating, as it can carry the Trichinella larvae that cause trichinosis. Cooking the meat to an internal temperature of 160° to 170°F is important. Wild boar meat is a great way to experiment with exotic meats. A slow-roasted whole bone-in leg is impressive.

SLOW-ROASTED LEG OF BOAR

Serving an entire boar leg is a dramatic presentation for a special occasion. You can do the same with a whole leg of lamb. Boar leg is readily available through mail-order or found in specialty stores if you haven't wild-harvested your own. You'll need to begin this recipe one day ahead in order to marinate the boar. Wild boar legs are traditionally marinated for a day or two to tame their gaminess, as the meat can have a strong flavor, while the farmed version is much milder and closer to conventional pork in taste. With farmed boar legs, the marinating step is optional, though it does add flavor.

Serves 6 to 8

4 tablespoons olive oil, divided

1 medium yellow onion, roughly chopped

2 stalks celery, roughly chopped

1 medium carrot, roughly chopped

3 large garlic cloves, roughly chopped

4 cups hearty red wine, such as cabernet

½ cup balsamic vinegar

2 teaspoons sea salt

6 whole peppercorns, crushed

2 bay leaves

6 whole juniper berries, crushed

1 (5- to 6-pound) bone-in boar leg

⅓ cup Dijon mustard

In a large skillet, heat 2 tablespoons of the olive oil over medium-high heat. Add the onion, celery, carrot, and garlic and sauté until lightly browned. Add the wine, vinegar, salt, peppercorns, bay leaves, and juniper berries and bring to a boil. Simmer for 10 minutes, then cool completely before using.

Once the marinade is cool, put the boar leg in a rimmed pan large enough to hold the leg. Pour the marinade over the leg. Cover with plastic wrap and refrigerate overnight, turning the leg several times to evenly marinade.

One hour before roasting, remove the boar leg from the refrigerator and bring to room temperature. Transfer the leg to a rack set in a roasting pan. Strain the marinade, discarding the solids, and set aside.

Preheat the oven to 450°F.

In a small bowl, mix the mustard and remaining 2 tablespoons olive oil, and smear the mixture all over the boar leg. Pour the reserved marinade into the pan under the boar leg. Place in the oven and roast for 20 minutes. Reduce the oven temperature to 275°F. Continue cooking the leg until an instant-read thermometer inserted into the thickest part registers 150°F. For a 5- to 6-pound leg, expect a cooking time of 4 to 5 hours (a 10-pound leg can take 8 hours or longer). A good rule of thumb is about 1 hour per pound.

Transfer the boar leg to a cutting board. Tent loosely with aluminum foil and let rest for 30 minutes before carving. Make a sauce out of the pan drippings, if desired.

BOAR BRAISED IN RED WINE WITH FRESH BLACK PEPPER PASTA

This is a hearty peasant-style dish for fall and winter. Some roasted or sautéed wild or cultivated exotic mushrooms would make a nice accompaniment.

Serves 4 to 6

1 ounce (1 cup) dried porcini mushrooms

1½ pounds wild boar meat, cut into 1½-inch cubes

Salt and freshly ground black pepper

¼ cup olive oil

1 cup sliced yellow onion

½ cup diced carrots

½ cup thinly sliced celery

3 tablespoons slivered garlic

4 cups chicken stock

2 cups hearty red wine, such as cabernet

2 cups seeded, diced tomatoes or canned diced tomatoes

2 teaspoons finely chopped fresh sage or 1 teaspoon dried sage

½ teaspoon fennel seeds

Basil or mint sprigs, for garnish

1 recipe (1 pound) fresh Black Pepper Egg Pasta (page 211)

Freshly grated pecorino or Parmesan cheese, for garnish

In a bowl, cover the mushrooms with warm water and soak for 10 minutes.

Meanwhile, season the boar meat liberally with salt and pepper. In a large, heavy saucepan, heat the oil over medium-high heat and quickly brown the meat on all sides, about 10 minutes. Remove to a plate and set aside. Sauté the onion, carrots, celery, and garlic, and sauté until very lightly browned, about 5 minutes. Drain the mushrooms, reserving the soaking water, and chop. Stir in the mushrooms and sauté for another couple of minutes until they just begin to color.

Return the boar meat to the pan, and add the mushroom soaking water (pouring carefully to leave any sediment behind), stock, wine, tomatoes, sage, and fennel seeds. Bring to a simmer. Cover and simmer until the meat is tender, about 45 minutes. Remove the boar meat and set aside. Strain the cooking liquid, discarding the vegetables, and return the liquid to the pot. Bring to a boil over high heat and cook until reduced and thickened slightly, 8 to 10 minutes. This helps concentrate the flavors. Season with salt and pepper to taste. Add the reserved meat and heat through. Stir in the basil just before serving.

Meanwhile, bring a large pot of salted water (so it tastes like the sea) to a boil, and add the pasta. Cook until the pasta is just tender (**NOTE:** cooking time depends on thickness of pasta being used), drain, and toss with the boar sauce. Garnish with grated cheese, and serve.

NOTE: You can also add a little dissolved cornstarch or arrowroot to the reduced braising liquid if you prefer it thicker.

BLACK PEPPER EGG PASTA

This simple, handmade pasta can be prepared ahead and dried. Try substituting fresh herbs such as finely chopped rosemary or chives for the black pepper.

Serves 4 (makes 1 pound)

2 cups all-purpose flour, or more if needed

1½ teaspoons coarsely ground black pepper

3 large eggs, beaten

½ teaspoon kosher or sea salt

In a food processor, pulse the 2 cups flour and black pepper to aerate. Add the eggs and process until the dough forms a rough ball, about 30 seconds. If the dough is not coming together, add water 1 teaspoon at a time. If the dough sticks to the sides of the work bowl, add additional flour 1 tablespoon at a time, and process until the mixture forms a rough ball.

Turn out the dough, and any small bits, onto a dry work surface, and knead until the dough is smooth, about 2 minutes. Cover with plastic wrap, and set aside for at least 30 minutes for the gluten in the dough to relax.

Roll out the dough with a pasta roller, and cut into fettuccine or a similar noodle shape with a pasta machine following the manufacturer's directions. If not cooking immediately, pasta can be dried using a pasta drying rack or even draped over plastic coat hangers and allowed to air dry.

WILD BOAR TERIYAKI MEATBALLS

You can use any ground game meat, such as venison, in this recipe.
Serve these meatballs as an hors d'oeuvre or with steamed rice as a main course.

Makes about 24 meatballs

1½ pounds finely ground wild boar

⅔ cup panko breadcrumbs, or more if needed

1 large egg

3 tablespoons finely chopped green onions
   (white and green parts)

2 tablespoons peeled and finely chopped
   fresh ginger

2 tablespoons soy sauce

1 teaspoon salt

¼ teaspoon red pepper flakes, or more to taste

Vegetable oil, for frying

1 recipe teriyaki sauce (see below)

Toasted sesame seeds, for garnish

In a bowl, mix together the boar meat, ⅔ cup panko, egg, onions, ginger, soy sauce, salt, and red pepper flakes until just combined. Don't overmix. Form the meatballs with rounded tablespoon-size portion of the mixture and place on a parchment paper–lined baking sheet. Refrigerate for a few minutes to firm up the meatballs. If they seem too soft, work in a few more breadcrumbs.

TO COOK THE MEATBALLS: In a large pot, heat 3 inches of vegetable oil over medium-high heat until it reaches 360°F. Deep-fry the meatballs until cooked through, about 5 minutes. (Alternatively, poach them in simmering water until they float. You can also bake the meatballs in a preheated 400°F oven for about 20 minutes.)

Warm the teriyaki sauce in a large skillet. Add the meatballs and turn them to coat with the sauce. Cook for a minute or two to glaze the meatballs. Serve hot topped with toasted sesame seeds.

TERIYAKI SAUCE

I typically use the entire amount when making the meatballs, but use as much as you like.

Makes 1 generous cup

⅓ cup soy sauce

⅓ cup mirin

⅓ cup sake

2 tablespoons granulated sugar

1 teaspoons peeled and grated fresh ginger
   (optional)

2 teaspoons cornstarch dissolved in
   2 tablespoons cold water

In a small saucepan, combine the soy sauce, mirin, sake, sugar, and ginger, if using, and bring to a simmer over low heat to dissolve the sugar. Whisk in the cornstarch mixture a little at a time until you reach the desired consistency. Keep warm.

WILD BOAR BREAKFAST SAUSAGE PATTIES

If the boar meat you are using doesn't contain enough fat to reach 70 percent lean, ask your butcher for some ground fatback or unsmoked bacon to incorporate into the meat mixture.

Serves 6

1 dried bay leaf

1 teaspoon red pepper flakes

1 tablespoon finely chopped fresh sage

1 teaspoon dry mustard

¼ teaspoon ground nutmeg

1 pound ground wild boar (70% lean)

2½ teaspoons kosher salt, or more to taste

2 teaspoons freshly ground black pepper

1 tablespoon olive oil

Using a spice grinder, grind the bay leaf and red pepper flakes to a fine powder. Add the sage, dry mustard, and nutmeg to the grinder, and pulse twice to combine.

In a large bowl, combine the spice mixture with the ground boar, salt, and pepper, and mix gently with your hands until the spices are evenly distributed throughout the meat.

Form the mixture into six patties, each about 3 inches wide and ½ inch thick. Make a small depression in the center of each patty with your thumb and forefinger. (This helps to keep the patties flat as they cook.) Refrigerate for at least 1 hour or overnight so the flavors can meld. The raw patties may be kept covered in the refrigerator for up to 4 days, or frozen up to 3 months if wrapped well in plastic wrap.

To cook the patties, in a 12-inch skillet, heat the oil over medium-high heat. Add the patties and cook, turning once, until well browned, 8 to 10 minutes. Transfer the patties to a paper towel–lined plate and keep warm.

Javelina

If you've ever driven in Arizona and seen a road sign saying "Watch for Javelina," you may have wondered what you were supposed to look for. The javelina (*Tayassu tajacu*) is similar in appearance to a wild pig but is smaller; javelinas weigh 45 to 80 pounds, while wild pigs start around 80 pounds and can grow as large as 350 pounds. Javelinas are peccaries, a distant cousin to the wild boar. They are also called New World pigs and are native to the Americas. Javelinas have a distinct appearance because of their cropped beard. Unlike wild pigs, they have no tails, and they travel in herds of about ten members. They root for food like pigs do, but their favorite foods are prickly pears and agaves. Their range extends from the American Southwest to northern Argentina. Like wild pigs, they are a favorite quarry of hunters. However, javelinas pose some butchering and cooking challenges. They have a scent gland on their rump that, if breached, can taint the meat; it's the reason they are sometimes called skunk pigs or musk pigs. Even if you butcher them cleanly, the meat has a strong gamy flavor. For this reason, brining and marinating are highly recommended. I've only eaten javelina a couple of times, and by far the best preparation was slow cooking the meat with many spices and seasonings and then barbecuing it for pulled sandwiches.

VENISON

THOUGH WILD TURKEY IS SAID TO HAVE BEEN SERVED FOR THE FIRST THANKSGIVING, certainly venison appeared on the Pilgrims' table, too. There is evidence, in fact, that it may have been the main course. Humans have eaten deer since prehistory; archeological evidence indicates that deer were hunted in China and Borneo half a million years ago. And in the early days of this country, deer was the most readily available red meat.

The word venison refers to the edible flesh of a game animal, particularly deer. Deer belong to the family *Cervidae*. Most deer are herbivores and generally eat grasses, weeds, leaves, twigs, lichens, and herbs. Many species lack the upper front row of incisors and have only a hard palate. They are ruminants, meaning they are cud-chewing mammals like cows: They can eat a variety of foods quickly and digest them later. To aid in this process, they have four-chambered stomachs, with each chamber serving a different digestive purpose.

Deer can be found in all climatic and geographical zones of the world, ranging from freezing tundra and the plains, mountains, and grasslands to equatorial forests. There are at least 100 different deer species in the world. In North America, these include white-tailed deer, mule deer, black-tailed deer, elk, caribou, and moose. Though they differ in size (the moose being the largest deer in the world), their culinary uses are similar. All have keen senses of smell, hearing, and vision (in that order). All prefer to browse when they can, consuming soft vegetation in summer while relying primarily on brush in winter. All give birth to their young from late spring through early summer.

Deer have never been fully domesticated, though humans have tried and have exerted some control over them from ancient times. This has usually amounted to keeping herds in fenced areas or forests so there would be an adequate meat supply when needed.

Wild venison, unfortunately, is one of the most abused meats in America. Many who have tried venison complain that it's both tough and gamy. The age of the deer, how it was killed, how it was handled after the kill, and whether it was properly "hung" and aged will all affect the venison's taste and level of tenderness. Naturally, younger deer will be more tender than older ones, and those that are killed quickly and cleanly and are immediately field-dressed will provide superior meat. Unfortunately, some hunters are just after trophies. My grandfather, who introduced me to deer hunting, always said, "Don't go after those big, testosterone-soaked bucks shot during the rut. They're terrible to eat! Go for a young buck or better yet, a doe."

Aging is a great way to tenderize venison. Right after any animal is killed, the muscles enter rigor mortis and become stiff. Then, natural enzymes in the flesh begin to naturally tenderize, or decompose, the meat. A controlled aging process will yield tender meat. High-quality beef, for example, may be aged for two to four weeks before reaching the market. But the aging process must be done carefully, following specific rules for cleanliness, air temperature and humidity, and circulation of air. See the interview with Chris Hughes of Broken Arrow Ranch in Texas on page 222 for more information on aging meat.

From a nutritional standpoint, deer surpasses beef mightily. Three ounces of lean beef contains 247 calories and 15 grams of total fat, while the same amount of venison has 134 calories and only 3 grams of total fat. More important, venison contains about one-sixth the amount of saturated fat found in beef. Venison also has more protein: 26 grams to beef's 23 grams. According to Livestrong.com, the only category in which venison loses is cholesterol: 95 milligrams to 76 milligrams in beef. And according to Harvard School of Public Health, we now know that cholesterol in food has little to do with cholesterol in our body. Venison has more vitamins and minerals per serving than beef. It also has more iron, vitamin B6, niacin, and riboflavin. Another attractive feature of venison is that deer aren't shot full of hormones or antibiotics to stimulate growth and protect from disease. In these times of "natural," "free-range," and Paleo concerns, more venison on the table just might be the ticket!

When cooking venison, here are a couple of pointers to keep in mind. Because venison is much lower in fat without the internal marbling found in beef, it will dry out much more quickly, so keep an eye on it. Cook tender cuts like the loin quickly at high heat just until medium-rare. This is best done by grilling, broiling, or sautéing. For less tender cuts, such as shoulder or leg meat, braising or stewing is the way to go.

VENISON TARTARE

In my mind, this is better than beef tartare. A couple of things to remember: Choose one whole piece of meat to minimize bacteria. Bacteria don't exist on the interior of meat, so you only need to deal with the exterior. Further, do not make tartare if the animal has been shot in the gut, since this could contaminate the meat from inside the abdominal cavity. Only animals that have been cleanly killed with a shot in front of the diaphragm should be considered. Sirloin can also be used in this recipe if there is no indication that the tenderloin has been contaminated.

Serves 4

1 pound venison backstrap (tenderloin) or sirloin

Kosher salt, as needed

2 tablespoons finely chopped
  fresh Italian parsley

1 tablespoon drained and chopped capers

1 tablespoon finely chopped shallot

2 teaspoons lemon zest

2 teaspoons Dijon mustard

1 tablespoon extra-virgin olive oil,
  or more to taste

1 teaspoon Worcestershire sauce

Sea salt and freshly ground black pepper

4 small egg yolks or quail eggs

Toast points, for serving

With clean hands, rinse the meat thoroughly under running water, then give it a uniform coating of kosher salt; you can't use too much. Next, refrigerate the meat for 1 hour. Rinse the meat well to remove the salt. Then place the venison in the freezer for about a half hour while you gather the remaining ingredients.

Remove the venison from the freezer and slice thinly. Stack the slices and cut into thin strips, then cut across the strips to make very small cubes. Slicing by hand gives a much more uniform and pleasing texture than using a food processor or meat grinder.

In a bowl, combine the meat, parsley, capers, shallots, lemon zest, mustard, olive oil, and Worcestershire. Season with the sea salt and black pepper and gently stir to combine. Return to the refrigerator and let the flavors marry for at least 30 minutes.

Prior to serving, adjust the seasonings to taste. To serve, mold each serving of the meat mixture into a small ramekin and invert onto a serving plate. Make a well in the mound and break a quail egg yolk into it. Season with salt and pepper, and serve with toast points.

GARLIC AND FENNEL
VENISON SAUSAGE

There are many sources, both online and in books, that can tutor you in the craft of sausage making. I like Michael Ruhlman and Brian Polcyn's book *Charcuterie*, which gives great insight on sausage making as well as salting, curing, and smoking meat. One of my favorite websites for game recipes and techniques is honest-food.net, produced by Hank Snow. His blog on the site is Hunter Angler Gardener Cook. I adapted the following recipe from Hank.

Makes about 20 sausages

4 pounds lean venison meat

1 pound pork fatback or jowl fat

½ cup dry white wine

2 tablespoons kosher or sea salt

2 tablespoons very finely chopped garlic

1 tablespoon freshly ground black pepper

1 tablespoon crushed fennel seeds

2 teaspoons fennel pollen (optional)

10 feet of hog casings, soaked in cold water for at least 2 hours and well rinsed

Chop the venison and pork fat into relatively uniform cubes that will fit into your meat grinder. Alternatively, you can pulse the meat and fat in a food processor in 2-cup batches. Be careful not to overprocess. You want the mixture to have some texture. Add the wine, salt, garlic, pepper, fennel seeds, and fennel pollen, if using, and mix thoroughly with very clean hands. The most important thing to remember here is to keep everything very cold. In a sauté pan over medium heat, cook a tablespoon or so of the mixture, taste, and adjust the seasonings. Cover and refrigerate immediately for 8 hours or overnight.

Tie off one end of the casing and gently stuff the sausage into the casings. If you don't have a stuffer, a pastry bag fitted with a large, plain tip can be used (about an inch or 24 mm). Pull as much of the casing over the end of the stuffer or pastry bag as will comfortably fit. If you develop any air bubbles, prick them with a pin. The casing should be full but not tightly packed or it will burst when you form the links. Pinch the casing 5 inches from the knotted end and twist to make a link. Proceed down the casing repeating this twisting action every other pinch to make links. When you reach the end, tie another knot. Cut through the twisted casing to make individual sausages. You can also tie each with kitchen twine.

Since we're not using any curing salt in this recipe, be sure to refrigerate the sausages immediately and cook or use within 3 days. Otherwise, freeze in resealable plastic bags for up to 2 months.

GRILLED MEDALLIONS OF VENISON WITH BLACKBERRY-SAGE SAUCE

The most important point I can make about this recipe is to not overcook the venison. The meat should be rare to medium-rare. Because venison is so lean, cooking it beyond that leaves you with a dry, tough result. The sauce can be made ahead and reheated so this can be a pretty quick recipe to do. I love serving the medallions with some roasted wild mushrooms and a little polenta.

Serves 4

Marinade

¼ cup olive oil

2 tablespoons very finely chopped shallot

1 tablespoon very finely chopped fresh sage

1 teaspoon freshly ground black pepper

4 (5-ounce) venison medallions, cut from the loin

Sauce

¼ cup chopped shallots

1 tablespoon olive oil

5 cups beef or chicken stock

2 cups hearty red wine, such as zinfandel

2 cups fresh or frozen blackberries, plus more for garnish

¼ cup chopped fresh sage leaves

1 tablespoon wild honey, or more to taste

Salt and freshly ground pepper

Sage sprigs, for garnish

TO PREPARE THE MARINADE: In a shallow dish, whisk together the oil, shallot, sage, and black pepper. Add the venison, turn to coat, cover, and marinate in the refrigerator at least 6 hours and up to overnight. Turn at least twice to evenly marinate.

TO MAKE THE SAUCE: In a saucepan, sauté the shallots in the olive oil over medium heat until lightly brown. Add the stock, wine, blackberries, and sage, and reduce the mixture over high heat to a light sauce consistency. The sauce should coat the back of a spoon. If not, reduce further. This may take 45 minutes or more. Adjust the seasonings with drops of honey and salt and pepper to taste. (The addition of the honey is not to sweeten the sauce but to balance the acidity of the wine and enhance the blackberry flavor.) Strain through a fine-mesh strainer, pressing the solids to extract all the liquid. Keep warm. This sauce can be made up to 5 days ahead and stored covered in the refrigerator.

TO COOK: Prepare a charcoal grill or preheat a gas grill for high indirect heat.

Remove medallions from the marinade and grill, which will only take a couple of minutes on each side for medium-rare, depending on their thickness. You can also pan-broil.

TO SERVE: Place the medallions on warm plates and surround with the sauce. Garnish with blackberries and sage sprigs.

A Conversation with
Broken Arrow Ranch Owner Chris Hughes

THE TOPIC:

Wild Meats

Broken *Arrow Ranch* is both a working ranch and a purveyor of high-quality, sustainably raised meats. Under full inspection by the Texas Department of Health, Chris and his team harvest and process wild game meat, such as venison, antelope, and wild boar, from their ranch and other ranches in Texas. Their quail farm, Diamond H Ranch, in Bandera, Texas, raises top-quality quail for meat as well as for release on ranches. They have also partnered with a co-op of ranches nearby to provide Dorper lamb, an animal specifically bred for its meat.

CHEF: I understand your ranch humanely field-harvests only wild animals. What does this mean?

CHRIS: Here in Texas, there are tens of thousands of nonnative deer and antelope roaming freely on vast ranches and open ranges. They are descendants of animals brought to this area in the 1930s for their beauty and as livestock alternatives. These animals we harvest are not farmed or pen raised, but are truly wild and free ranging on ranches from five hundred to two hundred forty thousand acres. They subsist on natural vegetation, are self-sufficient, and do not interact with humans.

CHEF: Talk a little bit about your field-harvesting process.

CHRIS: In 1983, my father, Mike Hughes, pioneered the field-harvesting and processing techniques that allow us to harvest these wild animals in a humane, stress-free manner under full government inspection. The harvest begins by transporting a mobile trailer–mounted processing facility to a ranch, along with our harvest crew and a government meat inspector. Instead of taking the animals to a processing plant, we take the inspector and facilities to the animals. Our harvest crew then searches the ranch for appropriate animals to harvest. Each animal is individually harvested in its natural environment from long range using a sound-suppressed rifle. This technique eliminates stress on the animal that would negatively impact meat quality.

The harvested animal is then transported back to our portable processing facility that has been set up on the ranch. Within an hour of harvesting the animal, it is eviscerated, skinned by hand, and placed into the trailer's cooler for transportation back to our fixed facilities in Ingram. It should be noted that field-harvesting puts us at the mercy of Mother Nature, just like our ancestors. After fifteen hours in the field, we may have a successful harvest, or we may leave with nothing if the animals do not present themselves. There is a lot of uncertainty with this method, but it is what you must do to harvest truly wild animals while maintaining meat quality.

CHEF: What would you say is the main difference between wild, free-range meat and the meat today's consumers buy at the grocery store?

CHRIS: Over the last fifty years, meat production has become more and more industrialized. This is due, in part, to the efficiencies needed for a shrinking agricultural population to feed a growing urban population. Only a handful of people can produce a tremendous amount of meat, but it comes at a price. The result is commodity meats that are less flavorful than their ancestors, and the animals have often been exposed to medications. The good news is, consumers are becoming increasingly aware of the provenance of their food, and more options are becoming available. Meat from wild and free-ranging animals represents the most pure and primal option. No medications, no feeding regimen, no human intervention. Unfortunately, with wild meats come limited supply, higher cost to harvest, and more variation in sizes and flavor.

CHEF: What do your wild animals eat?

CHRIS: The wild animals we harvest forage on the wide variety of vegetation available to them in the natural landscape. Exactly what they eat varies from season to season and species to species. This variation gives the meat a more complex flavor profile compared to a farmed animal that may subsist on only few or a single source of nutrition.

CHEF: Do you think eating wild or exotic meat is a trend, like ostrich used to be, or do you look at this as an important agricultural resource consumers should incorporate into their diet?

CHRIS: Humans have been eating meat from wild animals since the Paleolithic era. In the scope of human history, I believe eating farmed animals is a trend. [Laughs.] In all seriousness, even though the popularity of wild-game meats may vary over time, in rural America wild-game meats are a staple and will continue to be so. Urban America is now showing an interest in hunting and wild meats, which is wonderful. I think many could benefit from eating pure wild-game meat, whether it's harvested personally, by a friend, or by me.

CHEF: Talk a little bit about your free-range antelope, venison, and wild boar.

CHRIS: We currently field harvest five species of deer and two species of antelope for venison. Each has their own unique flavor profile. For example, axis venison is light and mild in flavor, while sika venison has a deep, gamy flavor. Wild boar meat, on the other hand, is darker, leaner, and more flavorful than its domestic counterparts. Farmed pigs and wild boar are the same species, so the difference is primarily due to their free-ranging lifestyle. Wild boar are feral pigs. They are descendants of pigs brought to Texas by Spanish explorers in the 1500s, pioneers in the 1800s, and ranchers in the 1900s. Today, there are millions of wild boar in Texas, and they are considered an invasive species due to the destruction they cause to farmland and habitat. We capture them in the wild and transport them to a USDA facility for slaughter as required by law. Eating wild boar is an enjoyable and responsible way to help control their growing population.

CHEF: Talk about the nutrition found in your wild meat.

CHRIS: If the world's health experts formed a committee to seek out the perfect red meat, they would discover venison. It is naturally low in fat and calories, comparable to chicken breast. It's also an excellent source of protein and iron, comparable to beef. In addition, meat from wild animals isn't full of medications, antibiotics, or any other human-induced additives.

CHEF: Why is aging meat an important step in the preparation process?

CHRIS: The main benefit of aging is increased tenderness by allowing natural enzymes in the meat to break down connective tissue in the muscles. We put our meats through a double-aging, double-handling process, which is labor-intensive but essential to quality. Once transported from the field, whole carcasses are allowed to dry-age for three to five days, which allows flavor concentration from moisture loss and tenderization from the muscles' natural enzymes. The carcass is then cut into primals—large, bone-in cuts such as whole legs and saddles—vacuum packaged, and allowed to continue aging for another twenty-one to twenty-eight days, maximizing tenderness and flavor. Since venison is extremely lean, we use extended wet-aging to obtain the benefits of proper aging without overly drying the meat. A key distinction in our process is that the meat is left on the bone as it ages. When muscle is left attached to the bone, the natural tension it creates helps "relax" the muscle fibers further increasing its tenderness. After the meat is fully aged, we bring it back to the butchers to be cut into "steaks" and then frozen. The meat must be frozen at this point or it moves from being high-quality aged meat to being spoiled meat. There can be too much of a good thing.

CHEF: Any tips or words of advice you can share with consumers who are considering wild meat? Anything they should look for when buying?

CHRIS: Purchasing meat from wild animals can be difficult for some because there are very few legal sources. Any meat legally sold will bear a government inspection stamp on the meat itself or on the label. Alternatively, many people can source wild game meat from hunter friends or by hunting themselves. The best advice I can offer here is to be sure the animal is quickly harvested (no stress), cleaned as soon as possible after harvest, and allowed to hang at least forty-eight hours before butchering.

CHEF: I must ask, what is your favorite wild meat?

CHRIS: It really depends on my mood and the season. In the summer, it's hard to beat a wild boar rack simply seasoned and cooked over a wood fire. During winter, I enjoy the deep, rich flavors of venison osso buco. My father taught me to love that dish!

INSECTS

LTHOUGH INSECTS OF VARIOUS KINDS HAVE BEEN EATEN FOR FOOD IN SEVERAL
cultures over time, recently more interest has been paid to this food source. In 2013, the
Food and Agriculture Organization of the United Nations issued a report entitled *Edible Insects: Future Prospects for Food and Feed Security*. This report discusses the possibility of rapid population growth in this century and details the limits of the world's capability to feed its people in the decades to come. The solution? Eat more bugs! Despite the probable distaste of many Americans for this idea, other countries are beginning to raise insects commercially as a way to add to the human diet.

Raising insects for food is a far more economical task that raising mammals; it also takes a much lower toll on the environment. Many insects such as mealworms are high in protein, as are grasshoppers. And the number of edible insect species in the world may reach 2,000.

Grasshoppers, called *chapulines*, are a popular food in Oaxaca, Mexico, where they are gathered in the fields and sold as street food, served in tacos, and ground with dried chiles and salt into a condiment powder found on many restaurant tables in this Mexican state.

Mealworms, which are the larvae of a kind of beetle, are as rich in nutrition as fish or meat. They grow widely in temperate climates and can be farmed using less land, energy, and water than farm animals require. Already farmed for fish food, mealworms are now being grown in the Netherlands as a food additive for humans. It's said that they taste like nuts when roasted, but their basic taste is bland and thus they take on the flavor of other foods they're cooked with.

MEALWORM (OR CRICKET) FRIED RICE

You can add other vegetables to this, of course. Check out the Fried Wild Rice recipe on page 145 for some tips on making fried rice.

Serves 4

⅓ cup vegetable oil, divided

2 tablespoons finely chopped garlic

2 tablespoons peeled and finely chopped fresh ginger

Salt

4 cups day-old cooked rice (preferably jasmine rice), at room temperature

4 large eggs

¼ cup thinly sliced green onions (white and green parts), cut on the bias

2 tablespoons roughly chopped fresh cilantro

2 teaspoons toasted sesame oil

4 teaspoons soy sauce

1 cup crisp roasted mealworms, or crickets (see "Roasting Mealworms" below)

In a large skillet, heat half the oil over medium heat. Add the garlic and ginger and cook, stirring occasionally, until crisp and brown. Be careful not to burn or the garlic will become bitter. Transfer to paper towels with a slotted spoon and salt lightly.

Add the rice to the skillet and cook, stirring, until heated through. Season with salt to taste. Keep warm.

In a separate nonstick skillet, fry the eggs in the remaining oil until the edges are set and crispy, but the yolk is still runny.

Stir the green onions and cilantro into the rice, and divide among four warm plates. Top each with an egg and drizzle with ½ teaspoon of the sesame oil and 1 teaspoon of the soy sauce. Sprinkle the mealworms and the reserved garlic mixture over top, and serve immediately.

Roasting Mealworms

Rinse live mealworms in a fine-mesh strainer and pick out any dead ones or pupae. Pat the worms dry with paper towels, transfer them to a container or resealable plastic bag, and put them in the freezer for about fifteen minutes to kill them. Oil a sheet pan, spread out the mealworms in a single layer, and bake in a preheated 225°F oven until they are dry and crispy, one to two hours.

LIVE FIRE GRASSHOPPER GUACAMOLE

You can sometimes find dried or fried grasshoppers at a Mexican market
that features foods from Oaxaca.

Serves 4

2 garlic cloves

1 jalapeño pepper, or more as desired

1 ear yellow corn, husked

3 firm-ripe Roma tomatoes

3 medium avocados, halved and pitted

¼ cup diced red onion

¼ cup chopped fresh cilantro

Freshly squeezed juice of 1 lime,
  or more to taste

Salt and black pepper

1 cup dried grasshoppers

Grated Cotija cheese

Corn tortilla chips, for serving

Thread the garlic and jalapeño on a toothpick or skewer so that they won't fall through the grates of a charcoal or gas grill. Over a smoky wood fire, grill the garlic and jalapeño, corn, and tomatoes until just beginning to color. Chop the garlic and jalapeño, cut the corn kernels from the cob, seed and dice the tomatoes, and combine all in a large bowl.

Scoop the avocado flesh into the bowl along with the onion, cilantro, lime juice, and salt and pepper to taste. Gently mash the ingredients into a chunky consistency, and adjust the seasonings to taste. Top with the grasshoppers and cheese. Serve with chips.

WILD DUCKS AND GEESE

DUCKS CAN BE FOUND ALMOST ANYWHERE IN THE WORLD WHERE YOU CAN FIND A body of water, except Antarctica. Most are members of the *Anatidae* bird family, but there are many different species and some are closely related, which leads to confusion in classifying them. The confusion extends to their names, as some ducks are commonly called geese, which is one reason birders like to use the scientific names for birds.

Wild ducks provide a very different eating experience than do farm-raised ducks, as their meat is leaner, darker, and more intensely flavored. The biggest complaint about wild ducks and geese is that they are often tough and have a gamy or muddy taste. To understand why, we must examine a duck's life. A duck spends most of its time flying. In order to do this, the bird's body uses a process called reoxygenation, which results in twice the amount of capillary blood than a land animal possesses. This extra blood keeps the duck's heart and lungs supplied with the necessary oxygen for long flights. This is why the flesh of a just-harvested duck is a very dark purple or red.

The capillary blood in muscles is the broken-down by-product of what an animal eats. So, if you have a duck that has been eating plants out of a muddy swamp, it's going to taste like mud. The conventional techniques for getting rid of the muddy, often livery flavor of duck meat and tenderizing it is to brine it in beer, milk, or buttermilk and baking soda, but none of these work effectively. The only way to remove excess blood and break down the highly developed muscle structure of waterfowl is through a process called dry-aging. Most of us are aware how much better beef is when it has been dry-aged for twenty-one to twenty-eight days. But although aged meat tastes better and is more tender, aging isn't absolutely necessary, especially with tender steaks. However, it is a necessity with wild ducks and other birds that migrate.

The rules of harvesting an animal are the same across the board, whether you are dealing with waterfowl, big game, or domestic animals: a quick, clean kill, followed by immediate evisceration and the removal of any contamination or buckshot, followed by cooling and proper storage. Dry-aging is nothing more than the draining of the capillary blood and the evaporation of the internal moisture of the muscles. Without the blood, the taste becomes delicate and mild. Without the internal moisture, the fiber structure of the muscle tissue breaks down and becomes tender. In other words, you won't need outrageous glazes, rubs, and sauces to cover up the gamy flavor.

Dry-aging can be done right after a hunted bird is frozen. For a fresh-killed bird, cut out the breast meat and place it cut-side down on a wire rack set on a rimmed baking sheet and age, uncovered and uncrowded, in the refrigerator for three to six days; geese will take from seven to twelve days. For a frozen bird, leave it in its wrapping and put it on a rimmed baking sheet. Defrost in the refrigerator, which will take about two days, and then cut out the breast meat and age it as instructed for a fresh-killed bird. When aged, the flesh of a waterfowl changes from dark purple to pale pink. Squeeze the breast meat to see if it yields to pressure; if so, it means the meat is ready to cook. If not, age it a little longer.

Recommended Dry-Aging Time
for Red-Meat Birds

DOVES: 1 day

BAND-TAILED PIGEONS: 1 to 2 days

TEAL AND OTHER SMALL DUCKS: 1 to 2 days

MEDIUM-SIZE DUCKS, SUCH AS WIGEONS: 2 to 4 days

LARGE-SIZE DUCKS, SUCH AS SPRIGS/MALLARDS: 4 to 7 days

SPECKS/SNOW GEESE: 7 to 10 days

CANADA GEESE (HONKERS): 10 to 14 days

After dry-aging is the time to brine. If you were to brine before dry-aging and the removal of the capillary blood, the salt in the brine would penetrate the proteins, creating a matrix that locks in the moisture. This is okay for upland birds, such as quail, partridge, and doves, but not so much when locking in the capillary blood of a fresh duck or goose. Generally, the smaller upland (nonwaterfowl) birds don't need to be aged, although many hunters will do it anyway to develop more flavor.

A simple brine for all birds is a mixture of ⅓ cup kosher salt and ⅓ cup brown sugar to 4 cups cold water. Mix them together and stir until the salt and sugar have dissolved. Brine small birds for up to 6 hours and large birds up to 1½ days. If the bird tastes a little salty after cooking, simply cut down the brining time the next time. Incidentally, you can find many kinds of amazing brine mixtures online to add more complex flavors to the bird.

Typically, ducks are "breasted out," as duck breasts are better after dry-aging, while the legs and rest of the carcass are used for making stocks and soups, or the excess meat is removed to make sausages, meatballs, or chili. Breasts from your prepared bird are best cooked by high-heat methods, such as grilling, roasting, and sautéing. Be sure not to overcook. The meat should be medium-rare. The rest of the bird will be tougher and so is best cooked with "low and slow" cooking methods such as braising. One additional thought: I'd avoid fish-eating ducks like scaups or mergansers. The flesh tends to be fishy, and the fat can be very strong. My favorite ducks for eating are teals and mallards, followed by canvasbacks.

DUCK DUMPLINGS

These dumplings can be made with any of your favorite birds, but I believe duck is especially good. You can use either wild or domestic duck. This Chinese-inspired recipe no doubt has a long history because the Chinese were the first to domesticate duck and other birds.

Makes about 20 dumplings

Filling

2 cups loosely packed, finely shredded napa cabbage, plus more for garnish

4 ounces ground duck meat (about ½ cup; see note)

1 green onion, finely chopped, white and green parts

1¼ ounces fresh shiitake mushrooms (about 4 medium), stems discarded, caps finely chopped

¼ bunch chives, finely chopped

1 teaspoon peeled and grated fresh ginger

1½ teaspoons sesame oil

1½ teaspoons sake

½ teaspoon finely chopped garlic

½ teaspoon soy sauce

Dipping Sauce

½ cup soy sauce

2 tablespoons rice vinegar, or more to taste

½ teaspoon hot chile oil, or more to taste

Dumplings

20 round Asian dumpling wrappers (3-inch diameter)

Canola oil, for cooking

Sesame oil, for cooking

TO MAKE THE FILLING: In a bowl, combine the 2 cups cabbage, duck meat, green onion, mushrooms, chives, ginger, sesame oil, sake, garlic, and soy sauce. Gently mix until just combined. Do not overmix.

TO PREPARE THE DIPPING SAUCE: In a small bowl, mix together the soy sauce, vinegar, and hot chile oil. Set aside.

TO ASSEMBLE THE DUMPLINGS: Place the dumpling wrappers on a work surface and keep covered with a clean, slightly damp kitchen or paper towel. Line a sheet pan with waxed or parchment paper for the assembled dumplings, and place a small bowl with water next to the work surface.

(Continues on page 233)

Holding a wrapper on the palm of one hand, place about 1 teaspoon of the filling in the center of the wrapper. With a fingertip, swipe one half of the edge of the wrapper with a little water, then fold over the other edge to meet the dampened edge, enclosing the filling and pinching to seal securely. With your fingers, make three or four evenly placed pleats along the sealed edge and place the dumpling flat-side down (pleats facing upward) on the prepared pan. Repeat until all of the filling has been used.

TO COOK: Heat a large sauté pan with a lid over medium heat. Once hot, add enough canola and sesame oil (2 parts canola to 1 part sesame) to coat the bottom of the pan. Swirl to distribute and allow the oil to heat. Test the oil temperature by flicking just a drop of water into the pan. If it sizzles instantly, the pan is ready. You will need to work in batches of 10 dumplings in the pan at a time.

Place the dumplings in the pan flat-side down as they were on the sheet pan, lining them up neatly to prevent touching. Cook undisturbed, until the bottoms are lightly browned, about 3 minutes. You may need to adjust your heat, possibly turning it down, to attain the right color in 3 minutes, so keep your eye on them.

Move the pan off the heat to a cool part of your range for 1 minute. **NOTE:** If the oil is too hot when you add the water, it can ignite and splatter. Stand back and add about ⅛ inch of water, cover, and return the pan heat to medium heat. Cook for 5 minutes. Uncover and cook a few minutes longer to evaporate the water and crisp the bottom of the dumplings. The dumplings should be a deep golden brown. Carefully remove from the heat, being careful not to tear the wrappers. Repeat with the remaining dumplings until all are cooked.

TO SERVE: Arrange a little bit of shredded cabbage on a serving plate. Add the dumplings browned-side up. Serve with the dipping sauce.

DUCK AND SAUSAGE JAMBALAYA

There are countless variations on this Cajun-Creole dish. According to food historian and writer John Egerton, Gonzales, Louisiana, is the self-proclaimed Jambalaya Capital of the World. There you can find about as many recipes for this dish as there are households that make it. Every year on Memorial Day, Gonzales holds a famous annual jambalaya cooking contest (www.jambalayafestival.org). You may have to add this to your bucket list!

Serves 6

1 (4- to 5-pound) duck, trimmed of excess fat and cut into 8 pieces

1 teaspoon cayenne pepper

Kosher or sea salt, as needed

1 cup all-purpose flour

3 tablespoons vegetable oil

12 ounces andouille, or other spicy sausage, cut into large dice

1½ cups diced green bell peppers

1 cup finely chopped yellow onion

¾ cup diced celery

2 teaspoons finely chopped garlic

2 cups fresh or canned diced tomatoes

2 bay leaves

4 cups chicken stock

1½ cups long-grain white rice

1 tablespoon Worcestershire sauce, or more to taste

Hot sauce, as needed

1 cup thinly sliced green onions (white and green parts), cut on the bias

Pat the duck dry with paper towels, and season on all sides with the cayenne and salt as needed. (**NOTE:** If using wild duck, see the discussion on dry-aging on pages 228–229.)

Put the flour in a shallow dish. Dust the duck pieces with the flour and shake off excess. In a heavy Dutch oven or stockpot, heat the oil over medium heat, and, working in batches, if necessary, sear the duck pieces on all sides for several minutes, or until a rich brown. Transfer the duck to a large plate and set aside.

Pour off all but 3 tablespoons of fat from the pot, add the andouille, and brown lightly. Transfer to the plate with the duck. Stir in the bell peppers, onion, celery, and garlic, and cook until the onions are translucent and softened but not brown. Stir in the tomatoes, bay leaves, and 2 cups of the stock, and bring to a boil over high heat, scraping bottom of the pot to incorporate any browned bits.

Return the duck and andouille to the pot, along with any accumulated juices on the plate. Bring to a boil over high heat, then reduce the heat to a simmer. Partially cover, and cook until the duck is just tender, 1 hour and 15 minutes. Stir in the rice and the remaining 2 cups stock, and bring to a boil. Reduce the heat to low, cover, and simmer until the rice is tender and the grains have absorbed most of the liquid, about 20 minutes. Discard the bay leaves. Add the Worcestershire and season with salt and hot sauce to taste. Top with the green onions, and serve immediately.

ROASTED WILD MALLARD WITH A SIMPLE RED WINE SAUCE

This is a recipe from Jean-Pierre Moullé, a chef for more than thirty years at the acclaimed Chez Panisse in Berkeley, California. He notes: "Both my parents were passionate hunters. The fall and winter seasons provided a lot of different game on the table. . . . My mother had many different recipes for each one, and if we were getting tired of eating them, she would turn the birds or beasts into patés and terrines. . . . This recipe for wild duck is very easy but also very pure; you want to keep the full flavor of the wild."

Serves 4

1 mallard duck, trimmed of excess fat and prepared for roasting (pages 228–229)

Salt and freshly ground black pepper

2 bay leaves

1 sprig thyme

2 garlic cloves

6 juniper berries

1 tablespoon duck fat or olive oil

1 shallot, chopped

1 cup red wine

1 cup chicken stock or water

1 tablespoon unsalted butter (optional)

Preheat the oven to 450°F. Season the duck with salt and black pepper. Stuff the inside of the duck with the bay leaves, thyme, garlic, and juniper berries.

In a heavy skillet, heat the duck fat over medium heat, and sauté the duck until crisp on all sides, about 10 minutes. Place in the oven, and roast for 15 to 20 minutes for rare to medium-rare. The thickest part of the breast should register 135°F on an instant-read thermometer when you take it out of the oven.

Remove the duck from the oven, place on a large plate, cover, and let rest breast-side down for 5 minutes. Remove both legs at the base with a kitchen knife, and set the legs aside. Slice off both sides of the breast in two large pieces, and cover them with a clean kitchen towel along with the legs. Chop up the carcass bones, and add them to the skillet over medium heat. Brown the bones, turning often. Add the shallot, cook 5 more minutes, and deglaze the pan with the wine, scraping the bottom of the pan to incorporate any browned bits. Reduce the wine until almost dry, then add the chicken stock. Reduce the heat and let simmer until reduced by half, about 30 minutes. Strain and finish the sauce with the butter, if using. Keep warm.

Reheat the breasts and legs, slice the breast, and pour the hot sauce over the duck. I usually serve this duck with braised savoy cabbage and roasted potatoes in duck fat. This dish is also delicious without the sauce, just deglaze the skillet with a little water.

GOOSE RAGÙ WITH POLENTA

This is a traditional "hunter style" meat sauce, which can used for any large wild bird.
Start the polenta while the sauce simmers.

Serves 6

⅓ cup olive oil

12 ounces boneless, skinless goose breast,
 very finely chopped

6 ounces goose liver, very finely chopped

1 cup finely diced yellow onion

½ cup finely chopped celery

½ cup finely chopped carrot

1 tablespoon finely chopped garlic

1½ tablespoons finely chopped fresh rosemary

1 teaspoon fennel seeds

½ teaspoon red pepper flakes, or more to taste

1 cup dry white wine

1 (28-ounce) can whole peeled tomatoes
 (preferably San Marzano)

3 cups chicken stock

1 recipe Soft Polenta (page 237)

Freshly grated pecorino or Parmesan cheese,
 for serving

In a deep, heavy saucepan, heat 2 tablespoons of the olive oil over medium-high heat. Add the breast meat and cook until browned, about 5 minutes, and remove to a bowl. Add the liver to the pan, and cook until it is just browned, about 4 minutes. Transfer the liver to the bowl with the cooked breast meat. Add the remaining oil to the pan, and cook the onion, celery, carrot, and garlic until lightly browned, about 7 minutes.

Stir in the rosemary, fennel seeds, and red pepper flakes, and cook a couple more minutes. Add the wine, and cook until the liquid is nearly evaporated, about 5 minutes. Meanwhile, crush the tomatoes with your hands, and add them to the pan along with the stock, reserved goose breast and liver, and salt and pepper to taste. Cook over medium heat until thickened, about 20 minutes.

Adjust the seasonings to taste. Spoon the polenta into wide bowls, spoon the ragù on top, and garnish with a healthy sprinkling of cheese.

SOFT POLENTA

Serves 6

1 cup whole milk

1 cup yellow cornmeal

1 teaspoon salt, plus more to taste

Freshly ground black pepper

Unsalted butter, as needed

Freshly grated Parmesan or pecorino cheese,
  for serving

In a heavy saucepan, combine the milk and 4 cups water and bring to a boil over high heat. Add 1 teaspoon salt. Slowly pour in the cornmeal, stirring with a wire whisk or wooden spoon. Continue stirring as the mixture thickens, 2 to 3 minutes.

Reduce the heat to low so the mixture barely simmers. Cook for at least 20 minutes, stirring every few minutes to make sure the polenta isn't sticking to the bottom of the pan. If the polenta becomes very thick, thin with ½ cup water, stir well, and continue cooking. Add up to another cup of water, if necessary, to keep the polenta soft enough to stir.

Carefully taste, making sure the grains are tender. Season with salt and pepper to taste. Stir in a couple of tablespoons of butter, and serve immediately, or cover and set the saucepan in a pot of barely simmering water for up to 2 hours. Add more water or milk, if necessary, to keep the soft consistency. Stir in the cheese to taste just before serving.

WILD GOOSE HAM OR PASTRAMI

I'm using Canada goose breasts in this recipe because of their large size. You can also use domestic breasts. Be careful when smoking goose, as the internal temperature can skyrocket in such small pieces of meat. Typically, hot smoking is at 200°F. If you can maintain 180°F, you will be able to smoke longer and develop a more pronounced smoke flavor. Be sure to consume the ham within ten days. Otherwise, vacuum seal it and freeze.

Note: Pink salt, which is a curing salt, not Himalayan pink salt, is used in most smoking recipes. It's insurance against botulism, especially when smoking below 300°F.

Makes 2 cured breasts

Brine

¾ cup kosher salt

¾ cup packed brown sugar

3 teaspoons pink curing salt (sodium nitrite)

½ cup port or Madeira

1 bunch thyme

2 large bay leaves

1 tablespoon juniper berries

2 teaspoons whole black peppercorns

1 tablespoon chopped fresh sage

2 large goose breasts

In a large pot, combine the salt, sugar, pink salt, port, thyme, bay leaves, juniper berries, peppercorns, and sage with 2 quarts water. Bring to a simmer over low heat, stirring occasionally to dissolve the salt and sugar. Remove from heat, and allow to cool to room temperature, then refrigerate until completely chilled.

Add the goose breasts to the brine, and weight them down with a small plate to keep them submerged. Refrigerate for 8 hours or up to overnight.

Rinse the breasts under cold water and pat dry. Refrigerate on a wire rack set over a rimmed plate or baking sheet for at least 8 hours and up to 24 hours.

Hot smoke the breasts to an internal temperature of 160°F, about 2½ hours. Refrigerate until ready to use. When ready to serve, slice as part of a charcuterie plate, or use to top a salad or spicy greens.

SMALL UPLAND GAME BIRDS

U PLAND IS AN AMERICAN TERM REFERRING TO GAME BIRDS THAT ARE NOT WATER-fowl and are typically hunted with dogs to flush them out, point to, or retrieve them. This includes native birds, such as bobwhite quail, ruffed grouse, doves, prairie chickens, woodcocks, white-tailed ptarmigans, and wild turkeys. Hunting upland birds has been described as an intricate dance between dog, bird, and hunter. One website (www.ultimateupland.com) glowingly describes the sport as "a choreography that few understand and even fewer master. So many mistakenly believe upland hunting consists of one or two species of bird that virtually jump into a game pouch at the crack of the nearest shotgun. There are actually no less than 27 different upland species (not counting numerous sub species) distributed throughout all 50 states."

Pheasant may be the most popular upland bird. Although we often think of it as native, the pheasant is an introduced bird from China. Several attempts were made to introduce pheasant as far as 1733, but efforts were not successful until 1882 and again in 1884, when ring-necked pheasants were shipped from China and released into Oregon's Willamette Valley. (Historians disagree whether any pheasants from a shipment in 1881 survived in the wild.) Today, ring-necked pheasants thrive in forty states.

Upland birds exist in a wide variety of habitats, which is one reason why they are such a popular game. They can be found in deserts, forests, and in the mountains. Forest grouse are popular in the East/Northeast; bobwhite quail in the Southeast and South; pheasants and prairie grouse in the Midwest; forest grouse in the North; and partridge, sage grouse, and prairie grouse in the West.

Though they obviously vary in size, upland birds can be cooked in similar ways. Their flavor, like that of all wild things, is heavily influenced by age and what they eat. Some upland birds, like quail and pheasant, are farmed extensively, and their flavor is milder and more predictable.

KUNG PAO PHEASANT

Every Chinese restaurant has some version of kung pao on its menu. It's a quick wok-fried dish with heat from chiles and sweetness from sugar and hoisin sauce. I'm using pheasant here, but you can use the meat from any upland bird.

Serves 2 to 4

Marinade

1 tablespoon soy sauce

1 tablespoon rice wine or dry sherry

1 teaspoon cornstarch

½ teaspoon red pepper flakes, or more to taste

2 boneless, skinless pheasant breasts (about ¾ pound), cut into ½-inch cubes

Sauce

⅓ cup chicken stock

1 tablespoon Chinese black or balsamic vinegar

1 tablespoon soy sauce

2 teaspoons hoisin sauce

2 teaspoons chili-garlic sauce

1 teaspoon granulated sugar

Stir-Fry

Vegetable oil, such as peanut oil, for frying

⅔ cup roughly chopped (½-inch pieces) red bell pepper

⅔ cup roughly chopped (½-inch pieces) green bell pepper

2 teaspoons cornstarch dissolved in 2 tablespoons water

¼ cup dry-roasted, unsalted peanuts

Cooked white rice, for serving

TO PREPARE THE MARINADE: In a medium bowl, combine the soy sauce, rice wine, cornstarch, and red pepper flakes, and mix well to combine. Add the pheasant and stir to coat. Let sit for several minutes so the flavor can penetrate the bird.

TO MAKE THE SAUCE: In a small bowl, combine the chicken stock, vinegar, soy sauce, hoisin sauce, chili-garlic sauce, and sugar. Mix well, and set aside.

TO COOK THE STIR-FRY: In a wok or nonstick skillet, heat a tablespoon or two of oil over high heat and swirl to coat the sides. Add the marinated pheasant and stir-fry until just opaque, about 2 minutes. Add the bell peppers and cook for another minute or two or until they take on a little color. Add the reserved sauce mixture and bring to a boil. Stir in a bit of the dissolved cornstarch mixture and cook, stirring, until it thickens. You may not end up using all of the cornstarch mixture. The idea here is to have a nicely thickened sauce that isn't too gloppy.

Stir in the peanuts and serve immediately with white rice.

PHEASANT WITH APPLES

I received my early training in France, and the pheasant there was usually barded or wrapped in fat before cooking. This preparation recognized that pheasant is a very lean bird and can easily dry out. The technique remains useful. You can find thin sheets of pork fat at good butchers if you are lucky enough to have one nearby. Otherwise you can use bacon.

Serves 2 to 4

1 young pheasant, about 2 pounds

Salt and freshly ground black pepper

6 to 8 strips of bacon

2 tablespoons unsalted butter

1 pound sweet-tart apples, such as Golden Delicious or Jonathan, peeled, cored, and roughly chopped into ¾-inch pieces

¼ cup Calvados (French apple brandy) or dark rum

1 cup crème fraîche

Season the pheasant liberally with salt and pepper inside and out. Wrap the pheasant in the bacon and tie with cooking twine to hold it in place. In a deep, stovetop-safe casserole dish, melt the butter over medium-high heat and brown the bird on all sides, 8 to 10 minutes.

Reduce the heat, cover, and cook the bird gently for 25 minutes. Uncover, remove and discard the barding fat, and add the apples. Cover, and continue to cook until the apples are tender, about 20 minutes more. Check the internal temperature of the bird with an instant-read thermometer inserted into in the thickest part of the thigh. When it registers 160°F, remove the pheasant and transfer to a platter. Cover with foil and keep warm.

Skim off any excess fat from the dish, stir the Calvados and crème fraîche into the apples, and bring to a boil. Season to taste with salt and pepper. To serve, cut the bird into portions and top with some of the apple mixture.

DEEP-FRIED QUAIL WITH DRIED-FRUIT CHUTNEY

Deep-frying is a quick and delicious way to cook quail. The accompanying chutney for this recipe needs to be made ahead; it also makes much more than you'll need, which is a good thing. The chutney is delicious with most grilled and roasted meats and makes a lovely accompaniment for cheese. It also lasts almost indefinitely in the refrigerator.

Serves 4

2 tablespoons olive oil

3 tablespoons dry sherry

3 tablespoons chopped green onions, white part only

2 tablespoons freshly squeezed orange juice

2 tablespoons peeled and finely chopped fresh ginger

Salt and freshly ground black pepper

4 semiboned quail

⅓ cup cornstarch dissolved in ½ cup water

2 cups Dried-Fruit Chutney (page 243), at room temperature

In a mini food processor or blender, combine the olive oil, sherry, green onions, orange juice, ginger, and salt and pepper to taste. Process until relatively smooth. Rub the marinade all over the quail, inside and out, and marinate in the refrigerator at least 4 hours or up to overnight. Remove the quail from the marinade, and pat dry.

In a shallow dish, dip the quail in the cornstarch mixture until evenly coated. Set aside on a wire rack.

In a deep, heavy saucepan or wok, add the oil to a depth of at least 1 inch and heat to 375°F. Add the quail breast-side down and cook for 3 minutes. Turn and cook until the quail is cooked through, about 3 minutes longer. Check for doneness at the leg joint. The leg should move freely at the joint.

Remove the quail and drain on paper towels. Serve hot with about ¼ cup of room temperature chutney on the side.

DRIED-FRUIT CHUTNEY

This pairs well with smoked meats of all kinds. It's one of my favorite accompaniments, along with Peppered Maple Walnuts (page 193), to serve with cheeses.

Makes about 1 quart

1 (750 ml) bottle dry white wine, such as Sauvignon Blanc

¾ cup granulated sugar

2 whole star anise

2 bay leaves

1 tablespoon coriander seeds, crushed

1 tablespoon whole black peppercorns, crushed

1 cup raisins (preferably golden and unbleached)

12 ounces assorted dried fruits, such as apricots, cherries, mangoes, and/or figs, coarsely chopped

3 tablespoons finely chopped candied ginger

2 large tart-sweet apples or pears, peeled, cored, and cut into 1-inch chunks

3 tablespoons freshly squeezed lime or lemon juice

In a nonreactive pan, combine the wine, sugar, star anise, bay leaves, coriander seeds, and peppercorns, and simmer, uncovered, over medium heat for 10 minutes. Remove from the heat and let cool. Strain, discarding the spices. You should have about 2½ cups strained liquid. Return the liquid to the pan, and add the raisins, dried fruits, and candied ginger, cover, and simmer for 5 minutes. Add the apples, and simmer gently until they are just tender, about 3 minutes. Remove from the heat and let cool. Stir in the lime juice.

Store covered in the refrigerator for several weeks. Serve at room temperature for maximum flavor.

GRILLED QUAIL WITH PICKLED FIGS AND PROSCIUTTO

This is a recipe I first made during my stage (study) days in France. It was included in *Culinary Birds*, which won a James Beard Award in 2014. If you make the figs ahead, refrigerate them in their poaching liquid and return them to room temperature before serving. The bonus with this recipe is the leftover fig-poaching syrup. It's delicious on grilled meats or even ice cream. Be sure to strain the syrup before using. The figs are served at room temperature, but the quail should be hot, right off the grill.

Serves 4

8 semiboned quail

2 tablespoons olive oil

Kosher or sea salt and freshly ground
    black pepper

1 recipe Pickled Figs (page 246)

12 thin slices of prosciutto

Prepare a charcoal grill or preheat a gas grill for high indirect heat, or preheat the broiler.

Brush the quail with the oil and season with salt and pepper. Grill the quail, breast-side down, 3 to 4 minutes. Turn and continue cooking until nicely browned, about 4 minutes. Alternatively, place the quail breast-side up on a baking sheet and under a hot broiler, and broil until crisp on the outside, about 4 minutes. Turn and continue broiling for another 3 minutes or until done. The quail should be slightly pink and juicy inside. Be careful not to overcook.

Meanwhile, wrap each pickled fig with a slice of the prosciutto. Grill or broil until the prosciutto is lightly browned, about 3 minutes. Serve alongside the quail with a little drizzle of strained fig cooking liquid.

PICKLED FIGS

Makes about 3 cups
(use any leftovers to top that big bowl of vanilla bean ice cream)

1 cup granulated sugar

1½ cups red wine vinegar

½ cup balsamic vinegar

1 stick cinnamon (3 inches)

6 cardamom pods, slightly crushed

2 whole star anise

6 quarter-size slices peeled fresh ginger

4 lemon slices, seeds removed

6 whole black peppercorns

12 fresh firm-ripe figs, such as Black Mission

In a medium nonreactive pot, combine the sugar, vinegars, cinnamon, cardamom, star anise, ginger, lemon, and peppercorns. Simmer, uncovered, for 10 minutes. Add the figs, cover, and continue simmering for 3 minutes. Remove from the heat and let the figs cool in the syrup. The figs can be prepared up to this point and stored in their syrup in the refrigerator in an airtight container for up to 2 weeks. Using a slotted spoon, carefully remove the figs, reserving the poaching syrup for another use.

QUAIL BROILED WITH MUSTARD BUTTER WITH WILD RICE PANCAKES

This is another wonderful preparation for any small upland bird. Some quickly roasted wild mushrooms would be a nice addition.

Serves 4

1 head garlic

1½ teaspoons olive oil

Salt and freshly ground black pepper

½ cup (1 stick) unsalted butter, melted

¼ cup Dijon mustard

2 teaspoons wild honey

2 teaspoons freshly squeezed lemon juice

1 teaspoon finely chopped fresh savory
  or oregano

8 semiboned quail

⅓ cup dry white wine

⅔ cup rich quail or chicken stock

1 tablespoon cold butter

½ recipe Wild Rice Pancakes (page 143)

2 cups loosely packed watercress
  (preferably upland cress)

Preheat the oven to 325°F.

Cut off the top quarter of the garlic head, and drizzle with the olive oil, and season with salt and pepper. Wrap securely in aluminum foil and bake until the garlic is soft and creamy, 30 to 40 minutes. When cool enough to handle, measure out 1 tablespoon of the soft roasted garlic into a bowl, and save the rest for another use. (Be sure the garlic is stored in an airtight container or else everything in the refrigerator will take on a garlicky flavor. Wrapped tightly in the fridge, the roasted garlic should keep for up to 2 weeks.)

Add the melted butter, mustard, honey, lemon juice, and savory to the bowl with the roasted garlic and whisk to combine. Brush on the quail. Season lightly with salt and pepper. Cover and marinate in the refrigerator at least 2 hours.

Preheat the broiler.

Remove the quail from the marinade and place breast-side down in a broiler pan. Transfer the marinade to a small saucepan, bring to a boil, cook 1 minute, and set aside.

Broil the birds for 3 to 4 minutes. Turn over, brush with the boiled marinade, and broil until the quail are golden brown but still juicy, about 3 minutes more. Remove from the pan and keep warm.

Add the wine, stock, and the remaining marinade to the broiler pan juices, and set the pan over two burners on high heat. Reduce quickly to a light sauce consistency, whisking constantly. Remove from the heat, whisk in the cold butter, and season with salt and pepper to taste.

To serve, divide the pancakes among four serving plates, top with watercress, and arrange birds on top. Spoon the reduced pan juices over top, and serve immediately.

SMALL BIRDS SARDINIAN STYLE

This is a very old and traditional recipe from Sardinia, and it is similar to many preparations found around the Mediterranean. You can use partridges, quails, squabs, doves, or any other small bird.

Serves 6

1 small yellow onion, sliced

2 medium carrots, chopped

1 large stalk celery, sliced

6 anchovy fillets, packed in oil

2 large bay leaves

3 large quail, partridge, dove, or other meaty little bird

2 cups dry white wine

1 to 2 cups chicken stock, or as needed

1 cup extra-virgin olive oil

¼ cup white wine vinegar

3 tablespoons finely chopped fresh Italian parsley

2 tablespoons chopped drained capers

Salt and freshly ground black pepper

Combine the onion, carrots, celery, anchovies, and bay leaves in the bottom of a saucepan just large enough to hold the birds in a single layer. Rinse the birds and place in the pan, then add the wine and enough stock to cover. Bring to a simmer, cover, and cook gently until the birds are very tender, about 45 minutes.

Meanwhile, make the sauce: In a bowl, whisk together the olive oil, vinegar, parsley, and capers, and season to your taste with salt and pepper. Remove the birds from the pan, cut them in half lengthwise, and arrange them on a serving dish. Pour the sauce over top and allow to cool before serving.

NOTE: Strain and save the stewing liquid for other uses.

WILD TURKEY

WILD TURKEY (*MELEAGRIS GALLOPAVO*) IS A TRUE NATIVE AMERICAN BIRD AND also an upland (nonwaterfowl) bird. It gets its own special section because of its iconic American presence—and because these birds walk down my street and challenge cars, dogs, or anything else in their path. There are only two species of wild turkeys, and the other is native to the Yucatán. The American wild turkey ranges throughout the States from Canada and into Mexico.

When the Pilgrims arrived in this country, wild turkeys were abundant and said to be numbered in the millions. Uncontrolled hunting and loss of habitat over the years decimated the flocks to such an extent that by 1920, the hunting of this bird was restricted to a few states, mostly in the Southeast.

In response, many states formed conservation agencies in order to protect game. At the same time, the movement of people to the cities for work meant some previously farmed land became available again for habitat, as did the allocation of land for protected forests. Turkeys were raised in pens by some states and released into the wild; unfortunately, this failed to work, as turkeys raised in captivity have no self-protective mechanisms. A special trap developed in the 1950s, called the rocket net trap, was used to catch wild turkeys so they could be transplanted to other areas. This changed the course of the wild turkey's history, so much so that by the early 1980s, they were found in large numbers in every US state except Alaska. Wild turkeys are now the most popular game in the United States, with deer ranking first. The wild turkey is a wary and elusive bird (except in some neighborhoods like mine in Northern California, where they seem to know we won't hurt them and they aggressively take over fields and roadways). They are difficult to hunt because of their excellent eyesight, which is telescopic (with a wide field of view—more than 180 degrees!) and clearer than that of humans or any other kind of game. If hunting from an open stand, turkey hunters have to wear camouflage, and even face nets, as the birds can detect the smallest movement, such the blink of an eye, from a distance of one-hundred yards.

Male turkeys can weigh as much as forty pounds. Females are much smaller, only around fifteen pounds. Wild turkeys can move quickly if necessary, up to twenty-five miles per hour on the ground and up to fifty-five miles per hour in flight. The young broods are able to move freely from birth or after hatching and require little parental care, which means they can leave the nest almost immediately. They can fly to roost in trees at about two weeks old. Wild turkeys move in flocks led by a dominant polygamous male. Male wild turkeys provide no parental care. Newly hatched chicks follow the female, who feeds them for a few days until they learn to find food on their own. As the chicks grow, they band into groups composed of several hens and their broods. Winter groups sometimes exceed two hundred turkeys.

Wild turkey meat is quite different from domestic. The breasts are much smaller, and the meat is dark and flavorful, even gamy, depending on the age of the animal. Wild turkeys are very lean and require special care in cooking to make sure they don't become dry and tough. Lower temperatures are key, and, as with ducks, I tend to make two meals out of the bird, cooking the more tender breast for one and the legs for another. Breasts can be roasted or grilled, while the legs are best slowly braised to tenderize them.

Roasting a Whole Wild Turkey

The best method is to slow-roast the turkey after brining for up to 8 hours. (See page 229 for a discussion on brining.) Preheat the oven to 275°F. Place the brined bird in a pan breast-side down with no liquid added and cover with aluminum foil. Use an oven thermometer to check the temperature, as the roasting temperature is critical. Cook by weight as follows:

8 to 10 pounds: 3 to 3½ hours

10 to 14 pounds: 3½ to 4 hours

14 to 18 pounds: 4 to 4½ hours

Do not constantly check the oven, as this will cool the oven and extend the cooking time. The turkey is done cooking when the internal temperature, measured with an instant-read thermometer in the thickest part of a thigh and not touching bone, reaches at least 165°F.

BUTTERMILK FRIED TURKEY

This is *Outdoor Life*'s Best Wild Turkey recipe from 2012. Celebrity chef Charlie Palmer
was the judge and said: "I chose John MacDonald's Buttermilk Fried Turkey for several reasons.
For one, wild turkey meat tends to be a little on the drier side compared to your regular Thanksgiving
dinner turkey. By soaking the turkey in buttermilk overnight, you are locking in the moisture and enriching
the flavor of the meat. Secondly, pan-frying is a good way to go. John's recipe has us filleting off
the turkey breasts and pan-frying them, which will continue to keep the meat moist. Finally, the cayenne
pepper and seasonings used in his flour will give you some great flavor with just the right amount of kick.
Nice work, John!" Personally, I think this recipe can use a little sauce, so I've included a simple
tarragon butter sauce (beurre blanc) to serve with the dish.

Serves 4

1 wild turkey breast half, about 2½ pounds

1 quart buttermilk

2 cups all-purpose flour

2 tablespoons salt

1 tablespoon freshly ground black pepper

1 tablespoon granulated garlic

1 tablespoon granulated onion

2 teaspoons dried sage

1 teaspoon cayenne pepper, or more to taste

1 teaspoon ground white pepper

Vegetable oil, for frying

1 recipe Tarragon Butter Sauce (page 252),
optional

Cut the wild turkey breast into ½- to ¾-inch-thick cutlets and place in a shallow baking dish. Add the buttermilk and turn to coat. Cover and refrigerate overnight.

Whisk together the flour, salt, black pepper, granulated garlic, granulated onion, sage, cayenne, and white pepper. Remove the turkey pieces from the buttermilk and place directly into the seasoned flour. Dredge thoroughly and gently shake off any excess.

In a deep, heavy skillet, heat ¼ inch vegetable oil over medium heat. Cook, turning once, after 4 to 5 minutes, until golden brown. Alternatively, you can deep-fry in 350°F oil until golden brown, about 6 minutes.

Serve with Tarragon Butter Sauce, if desired.

TARRAGON BUTTER SAUCE

Makes about ²/₃ cup

½ cup dry vermouth or dry white wine

½ cup shellfish or chicken stock

2 tablespoons finely chopped shallot

1 tablespoon chopped fresh tarragon leaves

⅓ cup heavy whipping cream

4 tablespoons cold unsalted butter

Salt

Freshly ground white pepper or hot sauce

Freshly squeezed lemon juice,
    as needed

In a small, deep saucepan, combine the wine, stock, shallot, and tarragon, and bring to a boil over high heat. Boil until the liquid is reduced to about ⅓ cup. Add the cream, and continue to boil until the mixture is again reduced to about ½ cup or has a light sauce consistency. Reduce the heat to low, and whisk in 1 tablespoon of the butter until it's completely incorporated. As you whisk, you can move the saucepan back and forth from low heat to no heat; the trick is to melt the butter into a cream sauce without breaking (which is when the butter separates and the sauce turns oily). Repeat with the remaining butter 1 tablespoon at a time. Strain through a fine-mesh strainer into a clean saucepan, and season with salt, pepper, and lemon juice to taste. Keep warm until ready to serve.

WILD TURKEY CARNITAS

This is an easy dish that takes advantage of the turkey legs, which often get thrown away.
If using lard, seek out leaf lard (from around the pig's loin and kidneys) as opposed to shelf-stable
hydrogenated lard. Leaf lard can be found at butcher shops and online.

Serves 4

2 bone-in turkey legs and thighs (3½ pounds)

⅓ cup freshly squeezed orange juice

2 tablespoons freshly squeezed lime juice

2 tablespoons packed brown sugar

1 tablespoon dried Mexican oregano

1 tablespoon kosher salt

1 tablespoon cracked black peppercorns

1 tablespoon cracked coriander seeds

2 teaspoons cumin seeds

1 small stick cinnamon, broken into pieces

3 small dried hot chiles, such as chile de árbol, or ½ teaspoon finely crushed dried chiltepín chiles (page 17)

2 large bay leaves

4 tablespoons lard or olive oil

Corn tortillas, warmed, for serving

Finely shredded green cabbage, finely sliced radishes, and finely diced white onion, for garnish

Cilantro sprigs and lime wedges, for garnish

1 large avocado peeled, pitted, and diced, for garnish

Remove the skin from the turkey parts and discard. In a large Dutch oven or lidded pot, combine the turkey, orange juice, lime juice, brown sugar, oregano, salt, peppercorns, coriander seeds, cumin seeds, cinnamon, chiles, and bay leaves. Add enough water to just barely cover the turkey in the pot. Cover and simmer until the meat is falling off the bone, 2 to 2½ hours. When tender, remove the turkey from the pot and let cool. Shred with two forks or your fingers. Discard the bones and any tendons. You can refrigerate the meat for up to 1 week at this point.

To finish this dish, use a sauté pan or skillet to heat the lard over high heat and brown the meat so it has nice crispy edges. Serve on tortillas with accompaniments.

Chapter 5

FISH, SHELLFISH, AND AQUATICS

Many people in this country, especially those not living on a coast, prefer to cook meat and poultry as their main sources of animal protein rather than fish. Some reasons for this include not knowing what kind of fish to buy or how to prepare it, or the belief that cooking fish can make a house smell fishy, or because the cook simply doesn't like fish. Yet fish is so nutritious and heart-healthy that some health professionals advise eating it twice a week, and, of course, it adds variety and interest to anyone's regular diet. Following is some information to make buying and cooking fish and shellfish easier and more pleasant for the home cook.

Fish and shellfish should always be purchased fresh or fresh-frozen. Although this may sound like an obvious statement, sometimes the supply chain takes too long to get fresh seafood to our local stores, shortening its shelf life so that it appears unappetizing to the consumer. Frozen finned fish is a great alternative. I spend a lot of time fishing in Alaska, and the fish I catch there are immediately filleted, vacuum packed, and frozen. This same process is used commercially and makes fish available to all of us that is every bit as "fresh," if not fresher, than its unfrozen cousin. Many times I've cooked a frozen-and-thawed fillet alongside its never-frozen but older counterpart and served them both in a blind taste test. More often than not, the previously frozen fish has won the taste and texture contest.

Any cook who wants to learn to prepare fish needs to learn how to determine whether a fish is fresh. Seafood should never smell fishy. In fact, fresh fish should never have any usual or offensive odor whatsoever. Always smell the fish before you buy it. If the head is intact, take a moment and inspect the eyes, which should be clear. A cloudy eye is a sign the fish is not fresh or has been previously frozen. The same holds true with the gills. They should be bright red. Pink or brown gills indicate a mishandled fish or one that has already spoiled. Also inspect the flesh or meat. Fresh fish should be firm and not soft, while the skin should be clean and any protruding fins crisp and moist and not discolored or dry, particularly around the edges. For shellfish like clams, always try and buy them live. Clams should be tightly closed. If they are open, they should close when you touch them. The best are clams housed in circulating seawater. If they are displayed on ice, make sure they are very cold—and alive.

The other consideration is that some fish and shellfish are sustainable. It used to be that we were at the mercy of the supply chain and had no idea whether a particular seafood was being overfished, was contaminated with metals like mercury or antibiotics in a fish-farming operation, was losing ground to habitat destruction, was being caught in ways that damage the seafloor such as dredging, or was creating significant loss of other species known as bycatch as a result of purse seining or longline trolling. Fortunately, today there are two nonprofit organizations that can help you make good, sustainable choices. The Seafood Watch program of the Monterey Bay Aquarium (www.seafoodwatch.org) is probably the gold standard for guiding us on what seafood to buy and avoid. If you have a smartphone, you can download the Seafood Watch app and have the best recommendations at your fingertips, whether you are buying seafood to cook or are dining at a restaurant. The other organization is the Marine Stewardship Council (MSC) (www.msc.org). Look for the MSC label on wild fish to see whether they have been caught by eco-friendly methods.

Adding fish and shellfish makes your diet not only more varied but also more nutritious, as fish is more healthful than red meat and even poultry. Salmon, mackerel, bluefish, herring, and sardines, all oily fish, are rich in omega-3 fatty acids that are believed to be both heart healthy and brain healthy. The benefits of eating seafood have been proved by studies of fish-eating populations, especially those in Scandinavia and Japan.

A comment on fish farming, or aquaculture: Unfortunately, our oceans are being overfished. The future is in fish farming, and we need to learn to do this sustainably. For years, farmed salmon have been on the "avoid" list due to a variety of problems with the method. But in 2014, Seafood Watch gave their "good alternative" designation to a couple of salmon farmers who are proving that salmon can be farmed can be without harming the environment and the quality of the fish.

I've picked a few of my favorite recipes for this chapter, including some that feature unusual species, for you to improve your skills if you are a little timid about cooking seafood. Sprinkled throughout are techniques that can be universally applied to finned fish and also shellfish. If I had one caveat for cooking fish it would be: "Don't overcook!"

CLAMS

CLAMS HAVE BEEN ENJOYED AS A FOOD SOURCE SINCE PREHISTORIC TIMES. There are over two thousand varieties of clams in the world, and they can be found in both saltwater and freshwater, though saltwater clams are considered superior for eating. They range in adult size from nearly microscopic to the giant clam of the South Pacific, which can weigh more than four hundred pounds.

Clams of all types are still wild harvested, but the vast majority we see in the market are from farming operations where the clams are constantly monitored for signs of contamination, which can result from land-based sources as well as red tides.

As with many types of seafood, clams have a lot of names that can be confusing. For example, the same species can have different names depending on size, and, as in the case of steamers (so-called because people like to steam them), a name can represent various species of bivalves. The following is a quick guide to clams.

Hard-shell clams (*Mercenaria mercenaria*) go by many names. Littlenecks, top necks, cherry-stones, chowders—they are all the same clam, just different sizes (listed here from smallest to largest). Littlenecks are often eaten raw, as are top necks, which are a little larger. Cherrystones, a little larger still, are often grilled and used for chowder. Large chowder clams are used to make the famed red or white clam chowder. They all live burrowed in the sand of intertidal areas along the eastern coast of the United States and Canada. They are harvested by simply digging them up.

Soft-shell clams, commonly called steamers or Ipswich clams, are the species *Mya arenaria*. You can tell them from hard-shell clams by their lighter-colored, more oblong shells, which are also quite brittle and thus require some care when handling. They live in tidal flats on the eastern shore of Canada and the States as well as across the Atlantic in the United Kingdom, where they are also known as Essex clams. Because they live in the sand, these clams are famously gritty! In New England, they are often steamed and served with the resulting broth. To eat, you pull the clam from its shell, dip it in the broth to rinse away any sand or grit, and then dunk it in melted butter before popping it in your mouth. They're also delicious fried or used in chowders. Although hard-shell clams can be served raw on the half-shell, soft-shell clams are rarely served this way.

Manila clams (*Venerupis philippinarum*) are, like Atlantic soft-shell clams, often called steamers, since steaming and pulling them from their shells is a popular way to eat them. Originally from the shores of China and up to Siberia, Manila clams now grow on the western coast of North America, where they are farmed along with other bivalves like mussels and oysters.

Razor clams (*Siliqua patula*), also called Pacific clams, are popular in Oregon and Washington. They have long, thin shells and plant themselves in the sand vertically. Razors need proper cleaning to make sure they aren't sandy or gritty when cooked. How to cook them? The most popular way is to coat them in breadcrumbs and give them a quick dunk in the fryer. They can also be sautéed or broiled with great success.

Surf clams (*Spisula solida*), which are also known as bar clams or skimmers, live on the eastern coast of the United States and Canada, from South Carolina up to Nova Scotia. Beachgoers along the Atlantic know the shells well; the surf tends to bring them to shore. These clams are delicious sliced, fried, and served as "clam strips." This is also a great clam for chowder.

Atlantic jackknife clams (*Ensis directus*), which are sometimes also referred to as razor clams, are long and skinny, and burrow vertically into intertidal beach areas on the East Coast.

Geoducks (*Panopea abrupta* or *Panopea generosa*) are massive clams. To give you an idea of how big, the Chinese name for them translates to "elephant trunk clam." They burrow deep into the sand in tidal flats along the northwest coast of the United States and Canada, but they have become very popular in different Asian cuisines. They are prized for their flavor and chewy texture, as well as their rumored aphrodisiac properties. They are delicious raw in sushi, used in ceviche, cut up and fried, or simmered in broth or chowder.

Ocean quahogs (*Arctica islandica*) are distinct from the common hard-shell clams often called quahogs on the East Coast. They are also known as black clams, mahogany clams, or black quahogs. As their various names suggest, their shells are an extremely dark purple, verging on black. They are also much rounder than hard-shell clams. They are known as ocean quahogs because they live on the ocean floor, not burrowed in the sand in intertidal areas.

CLAM DIP

Make this wonderful, easy-to-do nosh for picnics, barbecues,
and watching football on TV.

Serves 8

2 teaspoons olive oil

3 ounces thinly sliced prosciutto, chopped

2 teaspoons finely chopped garlic

3 tablespoons dry white wine

8 ounces chopped fresh steamed clams
of your choice

4 ounces cream cheese

4 ounces Boursin or fresh herb goat cheese

2 tablespoons chopped fresh chives

1 teaspoon Worcestershire sauce

⅛ teaspoon cayenne pepper, or more to taste

Salt and freshly ground black pepper

Thick potato chips or crackers, for dipping

In a small sauté pan, heat the oil over medium heat, and fry the prosciutto until crisp. Transfer to a paper towel–lined plate and set aside. Add the garlic to the pan, and cook until fragrant and soft but not brown. Deglaze the pan with the wine, scraping the bottom to incorporate any browned bits. Add the clams, and simmer until most of the liquid has evaporated. Add the cream cheese, Boursin, chives, Worcestershire, and cayenne, and season with salt and pepper to taste. Cook over medium heat, stirring thoroughly, just until the cheeses have softened. Top with the reserved crisp prosciutto, and serve with potato chips or crackers for dipping.

MANHATTAN CLAM CHOWDER

There are many recipes for this red chowder, which James Beard famously described as "horrendous" compared with classic white New England chowder. I love him, but I don't agree with him this time.

Serves 6

1 cup dry white wine

10 pounds large chowder clams, well scrubbed

3 tablespoons olive oil

4 ounces thick-cut bacon, diced

1 tablespoon thinly sliced garlic

2 cups diced white onions

1 cup diced celery

1 cup diced red bell pepper

1 cup diced carrots

2 teaspoons fennel seeds

2 teaspoons dried oregano

2 medium bay leaves

¼ teaspoon red pepper flakes, or more to taste

1 large (about 12 ounces) Yukon Gold potato, scrubbed and diced

Fish or chicken stock, as needed

1 can (28-ounce) petite diced tomatoes

Salt and freshly ground black pepper

12 ounces bay scallops

3 tablespoons chopped fresh Italian parsley

2 teaspoons lemon zest

In a large heavy-bottomed pot, combine the wine with 1 cup water and bring to a boil over high heat. Add the clams, cover, and cook until they open, about 5 minutes. Discard any unopened or cracked clams, and transfer the others to a bowl. Strain the liquid through a fine-mesh strainer into a bowl and set aside. When the clams are cool enough to handle, remove from the shells and chop the meat into ¼-inch pieces. Set aside.

In a stockpot, heat the olive oil over medium heat. Add the bacon and sauté until golden brown, about 4 minutes. Transfer to a paper towel–lined plate and set aside. Stir in the garlic, then add the onion, celery, bell pepper, carrot, fennel seeds, oregano, bay leaves, and red pepper flakes. Sauté until softened, about 8 minutes.

Add the potato, the reserved clam broth, and enough stock to cover the vegetables. Bring to a boil, lower the heat, and simmer until the potatoes are tender, 8 to 10 minutes. Stir in the tomatoes, and season with salt and black pepper to taste. Add the scallops and simmer until they are barely cooked through, about 2 minutes. Stir in the chopped clams. Discard the bay leaves before serving.

Ladle the chowder into soup plates, sprinkle with the reserved bacon, top with the parsley and lemon zest, and serve immediately.

CLAM FRITTERS WITH SMOKED PAPRIKA AIOLI

This dish is based on a recipe from Craig Claiborne, longtime food editor of the *New York Times*. He was a great believer in authentic American cooking, and in 1976 he called this dish "Americana, pure and simple."

Makes about 16 fritters

4 dozen cherrystone clams

1 cup all-purpose flour

2 teaspoons baking powder

1 teaspoon baking soda

2 large eggs

¼ cup milk

1 tablespoon freshly squeezed lemon juice

1 tablespoon melted unsalted butter

Pinch of cayenne pepper

2 tablespoons finely chopped fresh Italian parsley

Salt and freshly ground black pepper

Vegetable oil, for frying

1 recipe Smoked Paprika Aioli (below)

Shuck the clams, draining and reserving ⅓ cup of the juice. Chop the meat coarsely and set aside.

In a mixing bowl, sift together the flour, baking powder, and baking soda. Whisk in the eggs, milk, lemon juice, butter, cayenne, and the reserved clam juice, whisking until the batter is smooth. Mix in the parsley and the chopped clams, then season with salt and pepper.

In a deep, heavy skillet, heat ⅛ inch of vegetable oil over medium heat. When the oil is hot (350°F) but not smoking, spoon about 2 tablespoons of the clam batter for each fritter into the hot oil. Work in batches and avoid crowding the pan. Fry the fritters until golden on one side, then turn the fritters and continue frying about 2 minutes longer. Drain on paper towels, and serve immediately with the aioli.

SMOKED PAPRIKA AIOLI

Makes about ¾ cup

⅔ cup mayonnaise

4 large poached garlic cloves (page 117)

1 tablespoon olive oil

2 teaspoons smoked paprika, or more to taste

Salt and freshly ground black pepper

Freshly squeezed lemon juice, as needed

In a mini food processor, combine the mayonnaise, garlic, olive oil, smoked paprika, and salt, pepper, and lemon juice to taste, and pulse until smooth. Cover and refrigerate for at least 1 hour to allow flavors to blend before using.

SAIGON CLAMS

This is a Southeast Asian riff on traditional steamed clams.
To be historically correct, I guess I should call them Ho Chi Minh City clams!

Serves 4

2 tablespoons vegetable oil

½ cup sliced yellow onion

⅓ cup rice wine, such as sake

2 teaspoons chili-garlic sauce

2 teaspoons palm or light brown sugar

3 pounds cherrystone or Manila clams

3 tablespoons freshly squeezed lime juice,
  or more to taste

2 tablespoons unsalted butter

1 tablespoon Asian fish sauce, or more to taste

4 generous sprigs Thai basil or cilantro

In a stockpot, heat the oil over medium-high heat. Add the onion, and sauté for a couple of minutes. Stir in the wine, chili-garlic sauce, and sugar, and then add the clams. Cover and steam until the clams have opened, about 4 minutes. Discard any unopened or cracked clams. Add the lime juice, butter, and fish sauce, adjusting the seasonings to taste. Serve immediately topped with basil or cilantro.

CLAMS CASINO

This is a classic recipe for clams. Try to get smaller ones, since they are more tender.
You can also use oysters in this recipe.

Makes 30 clams

Olive oil, as needed

8 ounces thick-cut bacon, finely chopped

1 cup finely chopped red bell pepper

½ cup finely chopped fresh poblano chile

1 tablespoon finely chopped garlic

Sea salt and freshly ground black pepper

⅓ cup chopped green onions
(white and green parts)

1 tablespoon freshly squeezed lemon juice

⅔ cup panko breadcrumbs

Coarse salt, as needed

30 littleneck clams, well scrubbed

Preheat the oven to 450°F.

In a medium sauté pan, heat a little olive oil over medium heat. Add the bacon and cook, stirring, until brown and nearly crisp, about 4 minutes. Transfer to a paper towel–lined plate and set aside. Add the bell pepper, poblano, and garlic to the pan, and season lightly with sea salt and black pepper. Cook until the vegetables have softened a bit. Transfer the mixture to a bowl, and add the green onions, lemon juice, the reserved bacon, and ⅓ cup of the panko. Toss the remaining panko with a few drops of olive oil in the pan and set aside.

Pour enough coarse salt onto a baking sheet to make a base for the clams. This will prevent the clams from tipping over and losing their juices.

Shuck the clams, leaving them in the bottom shells but running your knife under the clams to release the meat. Top each clam with about 1 teaspoon of the bacon mixture and then some of the oiled breadcrumbs. Nestle them into the salt on the baking sheet.

Bake until the breadcrumbs are lightly browned and juices are bubbling, about 10 minutes. Let cool for about 1 minute before serving. Caution: The clams will be hot!

MISO SOUP WITH CLAMS AND SPINACH

The clams here are cooked in a dashi broth. Dashi is the fundamental, basic cooking stock of Japanese cuisine and is made from kelp and a specially dried and smoked fish, usually bonito tuna. It can be made from scratch (refer to a good Japanese cookbook), but it's easiest to dissolve instant dashi granules (called *hon dashi*) in hot water. A passionate Japanese cook probably wouldn't approve of this, but I think the granules are fine used here. Look for *hon dashi* wherever Japanese ingredients are sold or you can buy them online.

Serves 4

3 cups dashi made from instant granules

16 littleneck clams or 24 smaller clams, such as Manila, well scrubbed

2 tablespoons white miso paste (known as shiro miso)

2 cups loosely packed baby spinach leaves

Toasted or hot-pepper sesame oil, as needed

3 tablespoons thinly sliced green onions (white and green parts), cut on the bias

In a heavy, deep saucepan, bring the dashi to a boil over high heat. Add the clams, cover, and cook until the clams open. Discard any unopened or cracked clams, and transfer the others to a bowl. Strain the broth through a fine-mesh strainer or cheesecloth into another bowl. When the clams are cool enough to handle, remove from the shells and set aside and keep warm.

Return to the broth to the pan and bring to a simmer over low heat. In a small bowl, combine the miso with about 3 tablespoons of the broth, and stir to form a smooth paste. Whisk into the broth. Add the spinach and cook until wilted, about 1 minute.

Divide the clams among four warm bowls, and sprinkle with a couple of drops of sesame oil. Ladle the hot broth and spinach over and top with the green onions. Serve immediately.

Purging Clams

If you harvest clams yourself, it is necessary to purge them to get rid of the sand in their bellies. If you purchased your clams at the market, they probably have already been purged. The simplest way to purge clams is to soak them for a couple of hours in cold water that is salted enough so that it tastes like the sea. During the soaking period, the clams should expel any remaining sand.

MULLET

MULLET ARE FOUND WORLDWIDE IN TROPICAL AND SUBTROPICAL WATERS. RED mullet is one of the most sought-after fish in the Mediterranean because it likes to eat crustaceans, and this diet flavors the flesh of the fish. In the United States, Florida is ground zero for mullet. The Florida Department of Agriculture and Consumer Services and its "Fresh from Florida" website notes that "mullet are especially plentiful in the bays and estuaries of Florida's Atlantic and Gulf Coasts. Striped mullet (*Mugil cephalus*) and white mullet (*Mugil curema*) are the two varieties of mullet commercially fished in Florida. Striped mullet are commonly called black mullet, grey mullet, or jumping mullet. White mullet are often called silver mullet. Their average weight is 2 to 3 pounds, but they can grow as large as 6 pounds. The mullet's habit of jumping makes them easy for fishermen to spot, even in the dark." This site also offers lots of interesting facts about mullet including some great recipes, so it's worth checking out if you find yourself in mullet territory (www.freshfromflorida.com). Mullet are firm-textured and relatively oily fish similar to Spanish mackerel and amberjack, so they tend to retain their moisture when cooked, especially if cooked in hobo packs (page 273).

Fishermen catch mullet for their delicious flesh but also for their roe, or eggs, which are highly prized both in Europe and Asia. The roe sacks can be eaten fresh by gently poaching them for a couple of minutes to tighten them up (be sure to poke each lobe a couple of times with a toothpick) and then sautéing them in butter, which is similar to the way shad roe are cooked in the Northeast. In southern Italy, the roe sacks are salt cured and sun dried to become the intensely flavored food known as bottarga. One of the classic dishes in Sicily is spaghetti with bottarga (page 274). In America, the Anna Maria Fish Company in Florida (www.annamariafishcompany.com) is famous for its bottarga, which it produces using traditional methods. They note on their website that the history of bottarga production in America is very old: "The writings of De La Vaca during the Narvez expedition of the Gulf of Mexico in the 1530s mentions that explorers encountered Native Americans around Cortez Florida drying golden mullet roe in the sun." Bottarga is also delicious with scrambled eggs or shaved into risottos and salads.

MULLET HOBO PACKS

Hobo packs and their fancier French cousin, *en papillote*, is a very simple way of infusing fish with delicious flavor. It can be done using parchment paper (the French method) and cooking in an oven, or using aluminum foil and cooking on a grill or in the coals of a campfire. It's a versatile technique that works well for a variety of fishes; I've shared this recipe approach many times over the years through my cooking classes and my work with Alaska Seafood Marketing Institute, among others. The term hobo pack goes back to the Great Depression when those knights of the road, or hobos, cooked a whole meal in a single container, usually a coffee can over an open fire.

Serves 4

3 tablespoons extra-virgin olive oil, divided

4 (5-ounce) mullet fillets (about 1 inch thick), scaled and preferably with skin on

Salt and freshly ground black pepper

8 thin lemon slices (from 1 large lemon)

8 sprigs thyme

12 cherry or grape tomatoes, halved

3 tablespoons roughly chopped fresh basil or parsley, or a combination

2 tablespoons drained capers

2 large garlic cloves, very thinly sliced

Prepare a charcoal grill or preheat a gas grill for medium indirect heat. On a work surface, lay four 12-inch sheets of aluminum foil out in a single layer and brush with 1 tablespoon of the olive oil.

Pat the fish dry, and sprinkle both sides with salt and pepper. Arrange the fillets, skin-side down, on the bottom half of each foil sheet, and slide 1 lemon slice under each fillet and place another other on top of each fillet. Arrange 2 thyme sprigs on top of each fillet.

In a small bowl, combine the tomatoes, basil, capers, and garlic, and season to taste with salt and pepper. Spoon the tomato mixture over fish, then fold the foil over the fish, tenting it slightly. Crimp the edges together tightly to firmly seal. Transfer the packets to the grill (or oven), cover, and cook until the fish is just cooked through, 8 to 10 minutes (depending on thickness of fish). Though it's a little tricky to check, you can remove one packet and carefully open, taking care not to lose any of the wonderful juices while checking for doneness of the fish. Remember the fish will continue to cook as it sits off the heat.

To serve, carefully open each pack and discard the thyme before eating.

SPAGHETTI WITH BOTTARGA

This couldn't be simpler once you've purchased the bottarga.

Serves 4

1 pound spaghetti

⅓ cup extra-virgin olive oil

2 large garlic cloves, thinly sliced

Large pinch of red pepper flakes

Zest and freshly squeezed juice of 1 large lemon

2 ounces bottarga, divided

½ cup chopped fresh Italian parsley

Sea salt

In a large pot, bring 8 cups of well-salted water to a boil, add the spaghetti, and cook until al dente, or just done.

While the pasta is cooking, in a large sauté pan, heat the olive oil over medium heat. Add the garlic and cook until it just begins to color and is fragrant, about 2 minutes. Be careful not to burn or the garlic will be bitter. Remove from the heat, and ladle a little of the spaghetti cooking water into the pan to stop the garlic from cooking further. Add the red pepper flakes.

When the pasta is done cooking, drain, and add to the garlic mixture along with the lemon zest and juice. Grate half of the bottarga over top, add the parsley, season with salt to taste, and toss the spaghetti to combine. Divide among four bowls, and grate the remaining bottarga over the spaghetti at the table.

ROCKFISH

ONE OF THE PROBLEMS PLAGUING THE SEAFOOD INDUSTRY IS THE MISIDENTIFI-cation of finned fishes. In a recent study on the West Coast, more than 65 percent of the fish in restaurants and markets were mislabeled. This isn't necessarily a case of retailers and chefs being dishonest; instead, it's often due to the fact that fish go by different names in different places. Rockfish is a great example. On the East Coast, if you call a fish "rockfish," then you are referring to a striped bass. Even on the West Coast, the home of the rockfish, you'll find all kinds of names being used for this fish, including "snapper" and "rock cod." These are entirely different species. Other names that often surface are yellow-eye, vermillion rockfish, bocaccio, chili-pepper, red stripe, shortbelly rockfish, canary rockfish, quillback, and more.

Pacific rockfish (*Sebastes* genus in the family *Sebastidae*) is the most common nearshore fish on North America's west coast, and it is a favorite of sport fishermen. Rockfish come in many different shapes, sizes, and beautiful color patterns. Most of the names have something to do with either the color or specific parts of the fish.

Rockfish have bony plates on their heads and bodies and range in color from black to red. They live in many different habitats, from reefs to depths of three hundred feet. They can float under kelp forests or rest on the ocean floor. These long-living fish (one estimate is two hundred years) don't breed until late in their life span and then not prolifically, so they can be harmed by overfishing, which was the case for several populations in the later part of the past century. Thanks to emergency fishing closures on the West Coast in 2002, rockfish have returned to sustainable levels, and they are now on the Seafood Watch "best choice" list (see page 257).

Rockfish are an excellent fish for eating and work well for most whole-fish preparations as well as those for fillets. If you've caught or bought a whole rockfish but prefer to fillet it before cooking, be sure to keep the head and bones. They make fantastic fish stock because they are lean and clean tasting. Asian communities on the West Coast love steaming or frying rockfish whole. Try this fish battered and deep-fried, in ceviche or for sushi, as crudo, or chopped in a tartare (always be sure to freeze any fish first before eating raw to kill any parasites that might be lurking—this is standard practice in sushi restaurants).

GRILLED ROCKFISH SOFT TACOS

Fish tacos originated in Baja California in Mexico, and they are now ubiquitous in America.
All of the components can be made ahead of time and the fish grilled at the last moment.
You can use salmon, halibut, sea bass, or tilapia in place of the rockfish.
Crema is a Mexican sour cream available in many supermarkets.

Serves 4

¼ cup olive oil

1 tablespoon ancho or New Mexico chile powder

1 tablespoon freshly squeezed lime juice

4 (4-ounce) fresh rockfish fillets

Kosher salt and freshly ground black pepper

8 (6-inch) corn or flour tortillas

1 recipe Cabbage Slaw (below)

1 recipe Citrus Salsa (page 277)

1 recipe Cilantro Cream (page 277)

Prepare a charcoal grill or preheat a gas grill for medium indirect heat.

In a small bowl, combine the olive oil, chile powder, and lime juice. Brush the mixture liberally on the fillets and season generously with salt and pepper. Grill the fish until it is cooked through and flakes easily.

To serve, stack two of the tortillas on each of four plates. Top with one-quarter of the slaw, a portion of the grilled fish, a heaping tablespoon or two of the salsa, and a tablespoon or so of the crema. Fold over and eat with gusto!

CABBAGE SLAW

Serves 4

2 cups finely shredded green cabbage

½ cup thinly sliced red bell pepper

⅓ cup thinly sliced red onion

2 tablespoons seasoned rice vinegar

2 tablespoons olive oil

Kosher salt and freshly ground black pepper

In a bowl, combine the cabbage, bell pepper, onion, vinegar, and olive oil. Gently toss, and season with salt and pepper to taste. This slaw can be prepared an hour in advance and stored covered in the refrigerator.

CITRUS SALSA

Serves 4

3 large navel oranges, peeled and segmented

2 large limes, peeled and segmented

2 teaspoons seasoned rice vinegar

2 teaspoons olive oil

1 teaspoon chopped fresh cilantro

1 teaspoon seeded and finely chopped
serrano chile

Kosher salt and freshly ground black pepper

Combine the citrus segments in a bowl. Add the vinegar, olive oil, cilantro, and serrano, and gently toss to combine. Season with salt and pepper to taste. This can be prepared in advance and stored covered in the refrigerator until ready to serve.

CILANTRO CREMA

Serves 4

½ cup Mexican crema or sour cream

3 tablespoons chopped fresh cilantro

1 tablespoon finely chopped green onion
(green part only)

1 teaspoon seeded and finely chopped
serrano chile

Kosher salt and freshly ground black pepper

In a bowl, combine the crema, cilantro, green onion, and serrano, and season with salt and pepper to taste. This crema can be prepared 1 day in advance and stored covered in the refrigerator.

NOTE: The crema should be the consistency of heavy pancake batter.

ROCKFISH CAKES WITH HOMEMADE TARTAR SAUCE

I often serve these cakes on a bed of salad greens. You'll note that I call for the fish to be both diced and finely chopped. This gives a nice texture to the finished cake. Any firm fish can be used here.

Serves 8 as an appetizer, or 4 as a main course

4 ounces fresh rockfish, finely diced

4 ounces fresh rockfish, very finely chopped

2 ounces fresh uncooked shrimp, finely diced

1 large egg white, beaten

2 tablespoons finely diced red or yellow bell pepper, or a combination

1 tablespoon finely chopped green onion (white and green parts)

2 teaspoons lemon zest

2 teaspoons mayonnaise, or more as needed

2 teaspoons drained and chopped capers

½ teaspoon seeded and finely chopped jalapeño pepper, or more to taste

Kosher or sea salt and freshly ground black pepper

⅓ cup to ½ cup panko, or other coarse dry breadcrumbs, plus more for dredging

Olive oil, for sautéing

1 recipe Homemade Tartar Sauce (below)

In a medium bowl, combine the rockfish, shrimp, egg white, bell peppers, green onion, lemon zest, mayonnaise, capers, and jalapeño. Season with salt and black pepper, and stir in the panko breadcrumbs. The mixture should just hold together and at the same time not be too dense and heavy. Add more breadcrumbs or mayonnaise if needed. Divide the mixture and pat to form into eight cakes no thicker than 1-inch. **NOTE:** The cakes may be prepared in advance to this point. Store uncovered in the refrigerator for up to 4 hours. To finish, place more panko in a shallow dish and season with salt and black pepper, and dredge the cakes, patting gently to adhere panko. In a large sauté pan, heat ⅛ inch of oil over medium heat. Sauté the cakes, turning once, until golden brown, about 3 minutes per side. Serve immediately with a dollop of tartar sauce.

HOMEMADE TARTAR SAUCE

Serves 8 to accompany an appetizer, or 4 with a main course

½ cup good-quality mayonnaise

1 small hard-cooked egg, roughly chopped

2 tablespoons finely chopped pickles or cornichons

1 tablespoon white wine vinegar

1 tablespoon drained capers

1 teaspoon grainy mustard

Pinch of kosher salt

Pinch of freshly ground black pepper

In a mini food processor or chopper, combine the mayonnaise, egg, pickles, vinegar, capers, mustard, salt, and pepper. Pulse several times until all the ingredients are well mixed but not puréed. Refrigerate until ready to use.

BEER-BATTERED FRIED ROCKFISH WITH SPICY CARIBBEAN PICKLE

According to *Scientific American*, beer is great in batters because it simultaneously adds three ingredients: carbon dioxide, natural and added foaming agents, and alcohol. Each of these brings to bear different aspects of physics and chemistry to make the crust light and crisp.

Serves 2

1 cup dark Mexican beer, such as Negra Modelo

1 teaspoon kosher salt, plus more for seasoning

⅛ teaspoon cayenne pepper

2 cups all-purpose flour, divided

4 cups canola or vegetable oil

1 (12-ounce) fresh rockfish fillet,
    cut into six 1-inch cubes or slices

2 tablespoons freshly squeezed lime juice

Freshly ground black pepper, for seasoning

Spicy Caribbean Pickle (page 281), for serving

In a medium bowl, whisk together the beer, 1 teaspoon salt, cayenne, and 1 cup of the flour until smooth. The batter should be the consistency of pancake batter. Add a bit more beer if the batter seems too thick. Cover and let sit at room temperature for 30 minutes.

In a deep, heavy saucepan or Dutch oven, heat the oil to 365°F. Spread the remaining cup of flour in a large, shallow dish. Place the fish on a plate, toss with the lime juice, and season generously with salt and pepper.

Dredge the fish pieces in the flour, and tap off the excess. Dip the fish in the batter, one piece at a time, and let the excess run off. Fry in the oil until golden brown on both sides and just cooked through, about 4 minutes. Remove to a paper towel–lined plate to drain, and season with salt and pepper to taste. Divide fish between two plates, and serve with a generous tablespoon or two of the pickle.

SPICY CARIBBEAN PICKLE

In Haiti, this spicy slaw/pickle is traditionally served with rich meats and fried foods. It's also a wonderful condiment to serve with rice and beans, noodles, roast chicken, and anything else that needs a little zip.

Makes 1 quart

2 cups thinly sliced green cabbage

1 cup halved and thinly sliced yellow onion

1 cup julienned or coarsely grated carrots

1 cup thinly sliced red bell pepper

2 tablespoons seeded and thinly sliced serrano chiles, or more to taste

1 tablespoon thinly sliced garlic

1½ teaspoons kosher salt

12 whole black peppercorns

3 whole cloves

1½ cups cider or cane vinegar

1 tablespoon granulated sugar

1 tablespoon freshly squeezed lime juice

In a large bowl, combine the cabbage, onion, carrots, bell pepper, chiles, garlic, salt, peppercorns, and cloves. Toss well.

Pack the vegetables into a 1-quart jar with a tight-fitting lid. In a measuring cup, combine the vinegar, sugar, and lime juice and mix until the sugar dissolves, then pour over the vegetables. Press down on the vegetables, if necessary, until they are completely submerged in the liquid. Cover with the lid and refrigerate for at least 3 days before eating. Stored covered in refrigerator for up to 1 month.

ROCKFISH CIOPPINO

This is a traditional fish stew from San Francisco. Its origins are thought to go back to Genoa. Early immigrants who came to San Francisco from Italy improvised on a recipe they called *guippin*. Basically, any leftover fish and/or shellfish went into the pot. Rockfish, of course, is an important component.

Serves 8

¼ cup olive oil

3 cups chopped yellow onions

1 cup chopped carrots

⅔ cup chopped celery or fennel

3 tablespoons chopped garlic

5 cups fish or chicken stock flavored with shrimp shells (see note page 307)

3 cups canned whole peeled or diced tomatoes

2½ cups hearty red wine, such as cabernet

¼ cup chopped fresh basil leaves

1 tablespoon chopped fresh oregano

2 teaspoons fennel seeds

½ teaspoon red pepper flakes, or more to taste

3 large bay leaves

Salt and freshly ground black pepper

1 whole (2- to 3-pound) Dungeness crab, cleaned and chopped into sections

18 to 24 fresh mussels in shells (about 1½ pounds), well scrubbed

2 pounds rockfish fillets, cut into 2-inch cubes

16 medium shrimp, peeled and deveined

8 thick slices of sourdough brushed with garlic olive oil and toasted

¼ cup chopped fresh Italian parsley or basil

In a stockpot, heat the olive oil over medium heat. Add the onions, carrots, celery, and garlic, and sauté until the vegetables are lightly browned. Add the stock, tomatoes, wine, basil, oregano, fennel seeds, red pepper flakes, and bay leaves. Bring to a boil over high heat, then reduce the heat to low and simmer. Partially cover, and cook, for 25 minutes. Strain, discarding the solids, and return the broth to the pot. Season with salt and pepper to taste.

Add the crab and mussels to the broth, and cook over medium heat until the mussels open (discard any that do not open). Add the fish and shrimp and cook until fish is just cooked through, 3 to 4 minutes longer. Place a piece of toasted sourdough in the bottom of eight warm bowls and ladle the soup over top. Sprinkle with the parsley, and serve immediately.

SABLEFISH

SABLEFISH (*ANOPLOPOMA FIMBRIA*) IS ALSO KNOWN AS BUTTERFISH, BLACK COD (though it's not a member of the cod family), and gindara. This richly flavored fish has a high oil content and satiny texture. If I am forced to eat only one fish for the rest of my life, this is my fish! They are highly valued for their buttery texture and are frequently sold to Japan before the US market. Sablefish inhabit shelf and deep-sea waters (up to 5,000 feet) from central Baja California to Japan and the Bering Sea. They are extremely long-lived, some reaching more than ninety years of age. For this species, life begins with winter spawning along the continental shelf at depths greater than 3,300 feet. Sablefish are a favorite sportfish in Alaska. They average eight to ten pounds, but big lunkers can weigh as much as forty pounds.

The Monterey Bay Aquarium rates sablefish as a "best choice" or "good alternative" fish for the table. One of its great virtues is that this fish is nearly impossible to overcook. Even if you have left the fish in the pan or oven a little too long, it will still be moist and tender because of its high fat content. For those who love Chilean sea bass (a misnomer; it's actually Patagonian toothfish, which the Monterey Bay Aquarium encourages us to avoid because of overfishing), sablefish is a great substitute. It takes well to many cooking techniques, including pan sautéing, baking/roasting, grilling, and steaming, and it is superb smoked. It's also a delicious fish for sushi, replacing the endangered yellowfin and bluefin tuna.

STEAMED SABLEFISH WITH GARLIC AND GINGER

Salmon or other oily fish can also be used here. Avoid halibut or swordfish, which can dry out and/or toughen when steamed. Serve with steamed rice and baby bok choy to catch all of the sauce.

Serves 4

3 green onions

2 tablespoons oyster sauce

2 tablespoons soy sauce

1¼ teaspoons brown or palm sugar

¼ teaspoon freshly ground black pepper

2½ tablespoons canola or other vegetable oil

2½ teaspoons finely chopped garlic

2 tablespoons peeled and finely julienned fresh ginger

2 (8-ounce) deboned sablefish fillets

2 teaspoons sesame seeds, toasted

1 teaspoon lime or lemon zest

Cilantro sprigs, for garnish

Chop the green parts of the green onions, cut the white parts lengthwise into thin strips, and set aside.

In a bowl, combine the oyster sauce, soy sauce, sugar, and pepper, and stir to dissolve the sugar. In a small skillet, heat the oil over medium heat. Sauté the garlic for about 15 seconds, then add the ginger and cook until fragrant, about 1 minute. Add the oyster sauce mixture and bring to a boil. Stir to combine, remove from the heat, and stir in the chopped green onions (save the strips for later). Set aside at room temperature. This sauce can be made a couple of hours ahead. Cover with plastic wrap to prevent it from drying out.

Select a heatproof plate or nonreactive cake pan 1 inch smaller in diameter than your steamer tray. Set aside some of the green onion strips for garnish and scatter the rest on the plate. Arrange the fish on top and pour the reserved sauce over top. Place the dish in the steamer tray.

Fill the steamer pan (or wok) half full with water and bring to a boil. Place the tray with the plate in the pan, cover, and steam fish until cooked through, 6 to 8 minutes.

Carefully remove the plate from the steamer and place on a platter. Sprinkle the sesame seeds and lime zest over the dish. Top with the reserved green onion strips, garnish with cilantro, and serve immediately.

SABLEFISH WITH TOMATOES, PINE NUTS, AND OLIVES

This recipe can be used with any firm-fleshed white fish.

Serves 4

2 tablespoons extra-virgin olive oil

4 (4-ounce) skinless sablefish fillets

Sea salt and freshly ground black pepper

2 medium garlic cloves, thinly sliced

½ cup dry white wine, such as pinot grigio

2 cups grape tomatoes, halved
(quartered if large)

1¼ cups shrimp or chicken stock

½ cup pitted and slivered niçoise olives

½ teaspoon chopped fresh rosemary

½ cup pine nuts, lightly toasted

1 tablespoon chopped fresh chives

In a large nonstick skillet, heat the oil over medium-high heat. Add the fish, season with salt and pepper, and cook until lightly browned crust forms. Remove the fish to a plate and set aside. Add the garlic and cook, stirring, until fragrant, about 1 minute. Add the wine and let simmer until reduced by half, about 2 minutes. Add the tomatoes, stock, and olives. Bring to a simmer and cook, stirring occasionally, until the tomatoes begin to soften, about 3 minutes. Stir in the rosemary.

Nestle the fish in the sauce, browned-side up. Return to a simmer, cover, and reduce the heat to low. Cook until the fish is cooked through and is just starting to flake. Divide the fish among four shallow soup bowls. Add the pine nuts and chives to the sauce and adjust the seasoning to taste. Spoon the sauce over the fish, and serve immediately.

MISO-GLAZED SABLEFISH

This is a famous recipe that was introduced to most of us by master chef Nobu Matsuhisa.
The fish can be grilled, but it's a little tricky because of the sugar in the marinade,
which can easily burn and stick to the grill. Instead, I suggest starting in a sauté pan and
finishing in a hot oven, which only takes a few minutes.

Serves 4

½ cup white miso paste
  (also known as shiro miso)

3 tablespoons mirin

3 tablespoons sake

¼ cup granulated sugar

4 (6-ounce) skinless sablefish fillets
  (at least ¾ inch thick)

Vegetable oil, for sautéing

Pickled ginger, for serving

In a small saucepan, combine the miso, mirin, and sake. Whisk over medium heat until the mixture is smooth. Add the sugar, bring to a boil, and whisk until the sugar is dissolved. You can thin with a little water, if needed. Transfer the marinade to a large dish and let cool. Add the fish and turn to coat. Cover and refrigerate for at least 6 hours or up to overnight. If you can remember, turn the fish once or twice during that time to evenly coat.

Preheat the oven to 400°F.

In an ovenproof sauté pan large enough to hold the fish in a single layer, heat just enough oil to film the bottom over medium-high heat. Scrape the marinade off the fish before adding to the pan. Cook over medium-high heat until browned, about 2 minutes. Turn the fish over, place the pan in the oven, and roast until just cooked through, 6 to 8 minutes, depending on thickness of the fish. Transfer to plates, and serve with pickled ginger.

SEA URCHIN (UNI)

THE SEA URCHIN, SOMETIMES CALLED A SEA HEDGEHOG BECAUSE OF ITS LONG, spiny exoskeleton, is part of a large group of organisms called echinoderms. Urchins and their relatives, starfish and sea cucumbers, have been with us for eons. There are many species—at least seven hundred—found in shallow to deep saltwater around the globe. They feed primarily on algae and other seaweeds, such as giant kelp. Sea urchins can destroy kelp beds in the absence of predators, but they are kept in check along the West Coast of this country by three dominant ones: humans, sea otters, and starfish. Seagulls also take their share. Urchins are also susceptible to tiny parasites and bacteria infestations, which our stomach acids can easily destroy if present.

California, where I live, is a big producer of sea urchins, which are gathered wild. Urchins are also collected up and down the Pacific coast. They are a special feature in Japanese cuisine and a popular food in the Mediterranean, particularly in Italy, Spain, and France. The edible part of the sea urchin is its creamy "roe" (which is misnamed, as it's actually the gonads).

The Japanese have a fondness for urchin roe, better known as "uni." Uni has been consumed in Japan for hundreds if not thousands of years, in part because it is thought to be an aphrodisiac. Though urchins grow in Japan, overconsumption has wiped out local stocks, so the American West Coast provides an abundant supply. Uni is simply scooped out of the five custard-like golden sections of the opened spiny shell. Each section is small and offers an intense flavor of the sea. For many, it's an acquired taste, as well as being relatively expensive. In Japan, uni is generally eaten fresh and raw as part of a sushi presentation or made into delicious sauces. In the Mediterranean, uni is incorporated into cooked dishes, especially pasta.

SEA URCHIN AND
ROAST BEEF

This is more of a method than a detailed recipe and arguably the best "surf and turf"
I've ever had during a Japanese *kaiseki* meal. *Kaiseki ryori* is a traditional Japanese multicourse repast
that originated many centuries ago in the simple meals served at tea ceremonies. Later, it evolved
into an elaborate dining style popular among aristocratic circles.

Here, you simply wrap a fresh piece of sea urchin uni in a paper-thin slice of premium beef such as Kobe.
Alternatively, you can use rare cooked beef that has been chilled and thinly sliced. Next, wrap the uni and
beef in a large fresh shiso leaf and serve it with ponzu and wasabi (preferably freshly grated). Delicious!

UNI DRESSING FOR
A COLD VEGETABLE SALAD

This very simple Japanese dressing is used for composed salads called *aemono*.
The thick dressing can also be poured over vegetables, fish, and poultry. Note: This dressing
must be used the same day and must be kept refrigerated. Also, the consumption of raw
or undercooked eggs may increase your risk of food-borne illness.

Makes about ⅔ cup

2 large egg yolks

½ cup fresh uni, or more as desired

4 teaspoons mirin

1 tablespoon sake

In a bowl, beat the egg yolks lightly. Using the back of a spoon or spatula, rub the uni through a fine-mesh
strainer to purée. Add the uni, mirin, and sake to the yolks and stir until smooth.

How to Open a Sea Urchin

All you need are gloves to protect you from the sharp spines, good kitchen shears, a towel, and a spoon to remove the roe (uni), which are aligned in a star-shape pattern inside the outer shell (or exoskeleton).

Wearing gloves, turn the sea urchin upside down to expose the mouth. Using a towel for stability, take the kitchen shears and pierce a hole near the perimeter of the outer shell. Then cut a three-inch-diameter round out of the shell.

Use the spoon to lift up the cut round, removing it and the entire chewing organ known as Aristotle's lantern, which looks like a white, star-shaped flower.

Discard the liquid and "black stuff," which is made up of partially digested food such as seaweed and other organic matter. Or, if you are feeling particularly adventurous, drink the sea urchin "liquor." The gonads of both male and female sea urchins are the prized roe, or uni, also referred to as "corals."

Use a spoon to carefully scoop out each piece of roe. Gently rinse the roe in a bowl of cool water and, with your fingers, remove any sediment still clinging to the roe.

Enjoy with a squeeze of lemon juice, a drizzle of good olive oil, and a touch of flaky sea salt.

UNI TEMPURA

Shichimi togarashi is a blend of dried red peppers, roasted orange peel, sesame seeds, seaweed flakes, and dried ginger. The blend comes in the familiar little bottle with the red top you see on the table in sushi restaurants. It's wonderful in miso soup, and it is my go-to pepper at home.

Makes 4

½ sheet dried nori

8 shiso leaves

4 lobes fresh uni

1 recipe Tempura Batter (below)

All-purpose flour, for coating

Vegetable oil, for deep-frying

Sea salt

Shichimi togarashi pepper blend

1 lime, cut into 8 wedges

Cut the nori into four narrow strips of equal size. Place one strip of nori on a clean work surface. Place two shiso leaves at one end. Top the leaves with one piece of uni, and roll up in the nori to enclose. Dab the end of the nori with a drop of tempura batter to seal. Repeat the process with the remaining three strips of nori. Coat each roll lightly with flour.

In a deep, heavy pot, heat 2 inches of oil to 350°F. Dip the rolls in the tempura batter to completely coat. Drain off any excess for a couple of seconds, and then fry until crisp, about 3 minutes.

Serve immediately with salt, *shichimi,* and lime wedges on the side.

TEMPURA BATTER

½ cup all-purpose flour

½ cup cornstarch

1 cup ice-cold seltzer, club soda, or sparkling water

1 large egg

Pinch of salt

In a bowl, whisk together the flour, cornstarch, seltzer, egg, and salt, just before you are going to fry. Do not overmix or you will develop the gluten in the flour, which makes the batter heavy. A few lumps in the batter are okay.

SEA URCHIN WITH LINGUINE

In Italian, this dish is called *linguine ai ricci di mare*.
Feel free to add a little chopped fresh tomato.

Serves 4

12 ounces dried linguine

½ cup fresh uni, or more as desired

2 tablespoons unsalted butter,
  at room temperature

1 tablespoon olive oil

1 teaspoon finely chopped garlic

3 tablespoons heavy whipping cream

Large pinch of red pepper flakes,
  plus more to taste

Sea salt

2 tablespoons chopped fresh Italian parsley

In a large pot, bring salted water to a boil, add the pasta, and cook per the package directions, or until al dente, or just done. Reserve ½ cup pasta water.

In a mini food processor, combine the uni and butter, and process until smooth. Set aside.

In a small saucepan, combine the olive oil and garlic. Cook over medium heat, stirring, until lightly golden brown and aromatic, about 3 minutes. Be careful not to burn. Add the cream, red pepper flakes, and the reserved sea urchin mixture to the pan. Stir until smooth. Slowly whisk in the reserved pasta water 1 tablespoon at a time until the sauce thins out but is still slightly thick. Season with salt and more red pepper flakes to taste, and then stir in the parsley. Toss with the pasta and enjoy!

TROUT

TROUT BELONG TO THE VERY LARGE *SALMONIDAE* FAMILY, AS DO SALMON. THESE family members are called salmonids and are found in bodies of water around the globe, although they prefer cold water.

"True" trout is a category including rainbow, brown, and golden trout. Some fish may be called trout but aren't, such as lakes, brooks, and Dolly Vardens. Whitefish, ciscos, and graylings are also salmonids. Salmon include chinook (king), coho (silver), chum (dog), pink (humpy), sockeye (red), Atlantic, and kokanee.

Some salmonids, such as salmon, brown trout, brook trout, and striped bass, are anadromous, which means they are born upstream in a river or stream, mature downstream in lakes or oceans, then return to their place of birth to spawn. The steelhead is a large, anadromous strain of rainbow trout.

Trout, in whatever form or name, are one of the premier game fishes in America. They are often hatchery reared to seed dwindling populations in the wild, which helps continue their appeal for anglers. Trout are also successfully farm raised. According to the Monterey Bay Aquarium's Seafood Watch program, freshwater rainbow trout farmed in ponds, raceways, and recirculating systems are considered a "best choice" option. Most of the farmed trout in America comes from the Magic Valley region of Idaho near Twin Falls, with the largest producer in the world being Clear Springs Trout Company (www.clearsprings.com). If you cannot catch your own trout in the wild, the farmed variety is a good second choice.

When buying trout, look for clear, firm eyes and moist, slippery skin. Trout scales are so small and delicate there is no need for scaling. If you catch your own, gut the trout immediately and keep them well chilled and moist, preferably on ice or in the refrigerator for a day or two, although fresh fish are best eaten the day they're caught.

As with most wild food, a trout's flavor will depend on what it's been eating and where it's been swimming. Trout is a delicate meat, so try not to overpower it with bold sauces and strong seasonings.

GRILLED TROUT
WITH HERBS AND PANCETTA

Other herbs may be used in this recipe; you could substitute rosemary for the sage and parsley for the mint. The sweet-and-sour onions are a nice counterpoint to the mild-flavored fish.

Serves 1 or 2

Olive oil, as needed

2 teaspoons finely chopped mint leaves

2 teaspoons finely chopped sage leaves

½ teaspoon lemon zest

1 whole trout (8 to 10 ounces),
   cleaned and deboned

Kosher or sea salt and freshly ground
   black pepper

4 thin slices of pancetta or strips of bacon

Onions Agrodolce (page 298), for serving

Prepare the grill for direct heat. If using a gas grill, preheat to medium (350°F). If using a charcoal grill, light the charcoal or wood briquettes. When the briquettes are ready, distribute them evenly under the cooking area. For a medium-hot fire, you should be able to hold your hand about 6 inches above the coals for about 6 or 7 seconds. Have a spray water bottle on hand for taming any flames. Lightly coat the grill rack with oil.

Meanwhile, in a small bowl, combine the mint, sage, and lemon zest. Open the trout like a book; lay the fish flat on a cutting board, flesh-side up. Brush with olive oil and season generously with salt and pepper. Sprinkle the herb mixture inside of the trout. Fold the trout over to close.

Wrap the trout with the pancetta and brush lightly with more olive oil. Gently place the fish, with the open side away from you, on the hot grill. Close the grill lid, and cook until the flesh is opaque, about 8 minutes. Carefully slide a large spatula underneath the fish to transfer it to a plate. Top with a spoonful or two of the onions and serve warm or at room temperature.

ONIONS AGRODOLCE

Agrodolce in Italian means "sour" (*agro*) and "sweet" (*dolce*). Recipes such as this have a long history. The mixture will keep almost indefinitely covered in the refrigerator, and it is a delicious accompaniment to a wide variety of dishes including cheese. Frozen pearl onions make this an easy dish to prepare.

Makes about 2 cups

3 tablespoons extra-virgin olive oil

1 (10-ounce) package frozen pearl onions, thawed

1 large garlic clove, thinly sliced

1 small bay leaf

¼ teaspoon whole black peppercorns

⅓ cup white wine vinegar

2 tablespoons freshly squeezed orange juice

1 tablespoon golden raisins

1 tablespoon pine nuts, toasted

1 teaspoon fragrant honey, or more to taste

Kosher or sea salt and freshly ground pepper

In a large skillet, heat the olive oil over medium heat. Add the onions and cook, stirring until they are lightly browned, about 6 minutes. Add the garlic, bay leaf, and peppercorns, and cook until garlic has softened but is not browned, about 2 minutes.

Stir in the vinegar, orange juice, raisins, pine nuts, and honey. Reduce the heat to low and simmer until the mixture has thickened a bit, about 3 minutes. Season with salt, pepper, and more honey to taste. Store covered in the refrigerator for up to 4 weeks. Bring back to room temperature to serve.

TROUT WITH BALSAMIC VINEGAR–BUTTER SAUCE

Fresh trout are generally available in most markets and represent one of the success stories with regard to sustainable aquaculture. The sauce used here is one I serve with a variety of fish and is also delicious on poultry. Note that white or golden balsamic vinegar is used, which won't "stain" the sauce as regular balsamic would.

Serves 4

2 tablespoons unsalted butter

2 tablespoons olive oil

4 (8-ounce) deboned fresh trout, trimmed into 8 fillets

Salt and freshly ground black pepper

1 cup fine cornmeal

1 recipe Balsamic Butter Sauce (below)

1 tablespoon chopped fresh herbs of your choice, such as chives, for garnish

In a large sauté pan, melt the butter with the oil over medium heat. Season the trout liberally with salt and pepper. Spread the cornmeal on a plate. Dredge the trout in the cornmeal and shake to remove any excess. Carefully add the trout to the pan and cook, turning once, until golden brown on both sides, about 4 minutes total. The fish should be completely cooked and opaque at this point but still very moist. Place two fillets attractively on four warm plates. Spoon the sauce over top and around the fish, garnish with a sprinkling of herbs, and serve immediately.

BALSAMIC BUTTER SAUCE

Makes about ½ cup

1 tablespoon olive oil

2 teaspoons finely chopped shallot

⅓ cup dry white wine or dry white vermouth

⅓ cup chicken or fish stock

3 tablespoons white or golden balsamic vinegar

½ cup heavy whipping cream

2 tablespoons unsalted butter

Salt and freshly ground white pepper

In a medium saucepan, heat the oil over medium heat. Add the shallot, and cook, stirring, until softened but not brown, 1 to 2 minutes. Add the wine, stock, and vinegar, increase the heat to medium-high, and cook until the mixture has thickened and is reduced by half, 5 to 7 minutes.

Add the cream, and reduce again, stirring occasionally, until the sauce has thickened, 4 to 5 minutes. Strain through a fine mesh-strainer, return the sauce to the pan, and reduce the heat to low. Whisk in the butter 1 tablespoon at a time. The sauce will thicken and take on a satiny sheen. Season with salt and white pepper to taste, and keep warm until ready to serve. This can be done be placing it in a small thermos or setting it over a pan of warm water for up to 2 hours.

SALT-BAKED WHOLE TROUT
WITH SALSA VERDE

This dish calls for a large trout of at least two pounds. Alternatively, you can use
two 1-pound trout. This recipe also works well with any whole fish, such as striped bass,
grouper, ocean perch, rockfish, and branzino.

Serves 4

1 (2-pound) gutted whole trout

4 cups kosher salt

4 large egg whites

Extra-virgin olive oil, as needed

1 small lemon, halved and cut into thin slices

1 garlic clove, thinly sliced

5 or 6 fresh basil leaves

1 recipe Salsa Verde (page 303)

Preheat the oven to 400°F. Let the fish stand at room temperature for 20 minutes. Meanwhile, in a bowl, mix the salt with the egg whites until the texture resembles moist sand.

Spread a large piece of aluminum foil on a baking sheet and brush with oil. Sprinkle a layer of the salt mixture (using about half of it) onto the foil. Brush the entire trout with oil, and lay on the salted foil. Stuff the trout with the lemon, garlic, and basil. Mound the remaining salt mixture over the trout, gently packing the fish. Using a skewer, poke a hole through the salt at the thickest part of the trout near the head.

Bake the fish for 20 minutes and check for doneness, removing the fish from the oven when an instant-read thermometer inserted into the fish through the hole registers 135°F. Bring the trout to the table on the baking sheet or a large platter. Crack the salt with a mallet or hammer, and, using a fork, peel off the salt with the skin and discard the salt. Brush any excess salt off the trout. Portion the trout, and serve on warm plates with a spoonful or two of the salsa.

SALSA VERDE

This salsa appears in my 2004 book, *Cooking One on One* (Clarkson Potter),
and has been used in many of my recipes.

This simple Spanish sauce is delicious on many kinds of grilled, pan-seared, or
roasted meats, fish, and vegetables. Blanched garlic works better in this sauce than raw,
especially if the sauce is made ahead. Raw garlic can give a harsh taste to a sauce
that sits for awhile, but blanched garlic will retain its sweet flavor.

Makes about 1 cup

2 cups coarsely chopped fresh Italian parsley

½ cup chopped fresh basil or mint leaves

4 anchovy fillets in oil, or more to taste

2 tablespoons drained capers

2 tablespoons poached or roasted garlic
(see note on page 117)

1 tablespoon lemon zest

⅔ cup extra-virgin olive oil, or more as needed

Salt and freshly ground black pepper

In a food processor or blender, combine the parsley, basil, anchovies, capers, garlic, and lemon zest. With the machine running, slowly add the oil until just blended. The sauce should still have some texture. Season with salt and pepper to taste. This sauce can be stored covered in the refrigerator for up to 1 day.

WALLEYE

WILD WALLEYE (*STIZOSTEDION VITREUM*) ARE A FAVORITE TARGET OF RECRE-
ational fishermen, and many say they are the best-tasting freshwater fish. Walleyes
are known by other names, such as pike perch and walleyed pike. They are the largest
member of the perch family, with a primordial-looking large mouth filled with razor-sharp teeth
and a spiny dorsal fin. Gloves are a necessity when handling walleye. The walleye gets its name from
its strangely glassy eyes, which have a special reflective pigment that allows them to see at night in
order to feed; during the day, they stay toward the bottom of the water, as they are sensitive to light.

Walleye are found throughout most of the interior of the United States and Canada. They are
active year-round, making them especially appealing to ice fishermen. On average, walleye measure ten to eighteen inches long and weigh one to three pounds, but they can grow to be well over
this size. Although there is some argument about the largest walleye ever caught, the International
Game Fish Association (IGFA) credits Mabry Harper with a record twenty-five-pounder landed in
Tennessee in 1960. Walleye tournaments are popular on waters where the fish grow bigger. Walleye
are also farm raised, but it's a difficult species to cultivate given its predator proclivities. They'll eat
their siblings, other fish, and most everything else that swims, flies, or crawls. In cultivation, walleye are reluctant to grow to large, consumer-preferred sizes.

In recent years, walleyes have been threatened by the introduction of a hybrid fish called the
saugeye. These fish are popular with fishermen, as they are easier to catch than walleye. Unfortunately, they sometimes escape waters where they have been stocked, which leads to more hybridization with walleye. This constitutes a threat to wild-walleye fisheries, which are considered a
sustainable, well-managed fishery in the Western Hemisphere.

Most recipes for walleye usually call for the fish to be either floured or breaded and pan- or
deep-fried. Alternatively, walleye can be baked. Really, almost any preparation or method that you
like for cooking mild, fine-textured white fish (whether fresh- or saltwater) will work, including
chowder (page 307), tacos (page 276), pan roasting (page 310), hobo packs (page 273), and baking in
salt (page 302). The three classic French preparations—meunière, amandine, and *grenobloise*—are
also excellent to use with walleye.

I also recommend serving classic and time-honored sauces to accompany simply prepared
fish. My two favorites are tartar sauce (page 278) and the following cocktail sauce.

CLASSIC COCKTAIL SAUCE

I can't prove it, but I'll bet the H. J. Heinz Company had something to do with this recipe, which has been widely circulated. I love its simplicity and taste.

Makes about 1½ cups

½ cup chili sauce, such as Heinz

½ cup ketchup

3 tablespoons prepared horseradish

2 teaspoons freshly squeezed lemon juice

½ teaspoon Worcestershire sauce

¼ teaspoon hot sauce

In a bowl, combine the chili sauce, ketchup, horseradish, lemon juice, Worcestershire, and hot sauce. Stir until well incorporated and smooth. Store covered in the refrigerator for up to 1 week.

WALLEYE MEUNIÈRE

Cooking fish *à la meunière* refers to both the sauce and the method of preparation. The name means "in the style of the miller's wife," and to cook fish *à la meunière* is to cook by first dredging it in flour. A meunière sauce is simple: butter, chopped parsley, and lemon. Here it is with walleye fillets.

Serves 4

½ cup all-purpose flour

2 teaspoons sea salt, plus more to taste

1 teaspoon freshly ground black pepper,
  plus more to taste

4 (6-ounce) deboned, skinless walleye fillets

6 tablespoons unsalted butter

½ cup freshly squeezed lemon juice

2 teaspoons lemon zest

1 tablespoon finely chopped fresh Italian parsley

1 tablespoon finely chopped fresh chives

On a large, shallow plate, combine the flour, 2 teaspoons salt, and 1 teaspoon pepper. Pat the walleye fillets dry with paper towels and sprinkle one side with salt.

In a sauté pan large enough to hold the fish in a single layer, melt the butter over medium heat until it starts to brown. Dredge the walleye fillets in the seasoned flour, coating both sides and shaking off excess, and place them in the hot butter. Reduce the heat to medium-low and cook for about 3 minutes. Turn carefully with a spatula (using a fish spatula if you have one), and cook until the fish is just cooked through, 2 to 3 minutes longer.

While the second side cooks, add the lemon juice and lemon zest to the pan. Carefully place the fish fillets on warm plates. Increase the heat to high, and cook the sauce for a minute or two to slightly reduce and thicken. Pour the sauce over the fish. Sprinkle with the parsley, chives, and salt and pepper to taste, and serve immediately.

MEUNIÈRE VARIATIONS: The two classics are amandine and *grenobloise*. You can add anything that strikes your fancy, like finely chopped shallots or other herbs, such as tarragon or dill, at the end to the butter. For amandine, simply heat slivered almonds in the frothing butter before you pour over the fish. For *grenobloise*, add drained capers to the butter sauce.

WALLEYE FISH CHOWDER

This cream-based New England chowder is a counterpoint to
the tomato-based Manhattan chowder on page 264.

Serves 6

4 strips of thick-cut smoked bacon, chopped

1 tablespoon olive oil

3 cups chopped yellow onions

1 cup chopped carrots

1 cup chopped celery
  (reserve the leaves for garnish)

6 cups shrimp stock (see note) or chicken stock

1 cup dry white vermouth or dry white wine

4 cups peeled and diced Yukon gold potatoes

2 cups heavy whipping cream

2 teaspoons dried dill or other dried herb
  of your choice

2 pounds deboned, skinless walleye fillet,
  cut into 1-inch pieces

2 tablespoons dry sherry (optional)

Sea salt and freshly ground pepper
  (preferably white)

2 tablespoons chopped fresh chives
  or green onions

In a stockpot, combine the bacon and olive oil. Cook over medium heat until the bacon is crispy, then remove with a slotted spoon and set aside on a paper towel–lined plate. Pour off all but 2 tablespoons of fat from the pot, and add the onions, carrots, and celery. Cook until the vegetables have softened but not browned, about 5 minutes.

Pour in the stock and wine, then add the potatoes and cook until they are just done and are pierced easily with a fork. Add the cream and dill, and cook until the mixture just begins to simmer. Carefully add the fish and sherry, if using, and cook until the fish begins to flake apart. Season with salt and pepper to taste. Ladle into warm bowls, sprinkle the reserved bacon and the chives over the top, and serve immediately.

NOTE: Shrimp shells make a simple, wonderful stock. Next time you buy shrimp, save their uncooked shells in a resealable plastic bag and freeze them. I know, this means you have to buy shrimp with the shells on, but this is a bonus. To make homemade shrimp stock, heat your favorite homemade or canned/boxed chicken stock, and add as many shrimp shells as you can to the stock. Simmer for about 5 minutes and strain, discarding the shells—and now you have a richly flavored shellfish stock for this soup.

THE TOPIC:

Incidental Catches and Sustainable Seafood

A conversation with commercial fisherman Jason Chin from the F/V Silver Fin in Monterey, California, and Michael Leviton, owner of Lumière restaurant in West Newton, Massachusetts, and board member of Chefs Collaborative, an inspiring organization that is working to help change the way America eats.

CHEF: What comes to mind when you hear the word incidental catches, often referred to as bycatch?

CHIN: I think of fish being discarded or released because they have no market value.

LEVITON: In a perfect world, there shouldn't be any bycatch. We need to fish smarter, and pay better attention to the entire ocean ecosystem.

CHEF: What if fishermen didn't throw back such fish?

CHIN: They would make their day more profitable if they could sell their catch. Because most bycatch is thrown back dead or barely alive, keeping and selling bycatch would help eliminate unwanted waste.

LEVITON: We cannot continue to do the same thing and expect the same results. Like Jason says, we need to create new markets, which would help eliminate waste while building for the future.

CHEF: What are you doing with your incidental catches?

CHIN: I'm selling them to fishmongers who are stewards of the environment. This is important because consumers and home cooks today are much more aware of where their food is coming from. They want to know how their seafood is obtained. Other effective methods like food television programming and the Internet are encouraging people to be more adventurous on what they will try and eat. This creates a growing interest in new species.

LEVITON: It's about trying to get folks to see beyond the usual four or five fish, and to understand we need to be using what is plentiful and sustainable in our local waters if we want to continue to have a local fishing industry for generations to come.

CHEF: You mentioned sustainable, Michael. What does this mean to you?

LEVITON: Every day when I speak to my fish purveyors, I am engaging in a very fungible, complex multivariable calculus where I try to balance environmental, economic, social welfare, and health concerns with what is in season, best and freshest, and that I think my customers will enjoy. Truly sustainable seafood will do a good job of answering all of these competing concerns.

CHEF: What are some of the interesting incidental or sustainable fish you're bringing back to the dock?

CHIN: I'm catching mackerel, sand dabs, starry flounder, barracuda, sea perch, Humboldt squid, even octopus. All of these species are caught when I'm targeting other species. But all are edible—and all are delicious.

LEVITON: At the restaurant, we're having a lot of success with porgy, Acadian redfish, pollock, and hake.

CHEF: Do you feel it's important to educate consumers and home cooks about the topic of incidental and sustainable seafood?

CHIN: Absolutely. It takes the pressure off heavily targeted species like tuna and swordfish. Sometimes I can't consistently catch my target species. Offering new species allows consumers to still enjoy fresh and obtainable seafood while knowing they're contributing to a greater cause.

LEVITON: If we want to have healthy oceans, healthy economies, and healthy children now and for generations to come, we have to do a better job of paying attention to where our seafood comes from, the health of that ecosystem, how particular fish are caught, and how it gets to us.

PAN-ROASTED FISH FILLETS WITH HERB BUTTER

Cooking fish often intimidates people, which it shouldn't. If I have to stick with one preparation for cooking fish fillets, pan roasting is my choice. You can use any fish fillet, preferably skin on, as long as the fillet is not too thick. If the butter is browning too fast, simply reduce the heat and add a nut of cold butter to prevent burning, or squeeze in a little lemon juice.

Serves 2

2 (6-ounce) fish fillets, such as black bass, haddock, fluke, striped bass, tilefish, snapper, or salmon (no more than ¾ inch thick)

Salt and freshly ground black pepper

2 tablespoons olive or canola oil

2 tablespoons unsalted butter

2 teaspoons chopped fresh herb of your choice, such as thyme, tarragon, or chives

2 teaspoons drained capers

1 tablespoon chopped fresh Italian parsley, for serving

Lemon wedges, for serving

Pat the fish fillets dry with a paper towel. Season on both sides with salt and pepper.

Heat a heavy 10-inch nonstick or cast-iron skillet over high heat. When the pan is hot, add the oil. Place the fillets in the pan, skin-side down.

Lower the heat to medium, and let sizzle until the fish is golden and caramelized around the edges, 2 to 3 minutes. Carefully turn the fillets and add the butter, chopped herb, and capers to the pan. Tilt the pan slightly to let the melted butter pool at one end. Use a spoon to baste the fish with the pooled butter. Continue basting until golden throughout and cooked through, 45 to 90 seconds more, depending on the thickness of the fish. Serve immediately topped with chopped parsley and lemon wedges.

FROG LEGS

THE CHINESE WERE APPARENTLY THE FIRST PEOPLE TO EAT THE LEGS OF FROGS (AS well as the rest of the body) during the first century AD. It is believed that the Aztecs also dined on frogs. The California gold miners nearly ate the California red-legged frog (*Rana draytonii*) to extinction in the nineteenth century, and the species has yet to recover.

The Catholic Church in France is believed to be responsible for adding frog legs to French cuisine. Apparently, French Catholic monks began the tradition of eating the leg part of the frog as food. The story goes that an increasing number of monks were becoming obese. To halt this trend, the Church issued orders for the monks to stay clear from meat on certain days. (If you were raised Catholic a few decades ago, you'll remember that Fridays were meatless days.) The monks started eating frog legs by disguising them as fish. The peasants followed the tradition and thus frog legs became a national delicacy in France.

Frog legs are eaten today in many parts of the world. Once caught in the wild as a sport and a local source of food, frogs were eventually so overharvested they almost became extinct. Today, they are farmed, mainly in Indonesia and China. The two frogs most farmed are the American bullfrog (*Rana catesbeiana*) and the Southern leopard frog (*Rana sphenocephala*).

In Louisiana and other parts of the South, frogs are still hunted by gigging. A frog gigger is a miniature harpoon, and the frogs are hunted usually at night from a boat, by shining a light that stuns or dazes the frog. The hind legs of large bullfrogs are big and meaty and are usually deep-fried or sautéed.

To prepare a frog (go straight to the recipes if you are squeamish), first make sure the frog is dead. It's important to note that frogs and amphibians in general are tough critters and don't die easily. Once the frog is pronounced deceased, remove the tough and slippery skin.

You'll need kitchen shears, a small, sharp knife, a set of pliers, and water to wash the frog legs. Start by snipping off the feet. Slice the skin around the frog's "waist." This isn't difficult, but the skin is very loose and very tough. Use either kitchen shears or a sharp knife. Take the pliers and grab the loose skin on the frog's back. Anchor the frog with one hand and pull the skin off with the other. It's like pulling the frog's pants down. Using the shears, cut the pair of legs off at the waist. Trim off any excess material, and you should end up with beautiful shiny white legs. Cut them into single legs if they are too large.

Frog legs are rich in protein, omega-3 fatty acids, vitamin A, and potassium. The texture is often referred to as like that of chicken wings. The taste of frog meat is somewhere between chicken and fish. Frog muscles do not enter rigor mortis as quickly as the muscles of warm-blooded creatures like chickens, so be aware that the heat from cooking may cause fresh frog legs to twitch!

CONGEE WITH FROG LEGS

Anyone who has traveled to China will recognize this dish. Congee, or *jook*, is generally served as the morning meal and is believed to be an important restorative. Big bowls of this are dished up along with an array of accompaniments, including soy sauce, chopped green onions, cilantro leaves, finely shredded cabbage, crisp fried slices of garlic or shallot, roasted peanuts, Chinese (Sichuan) pickled vegetables, pickled ginger, poached or roasted chicken or other meats, cooked and dried shrimp, and on and on, depending on where you're dining. For this recipe, I'm adding quickly cooked frog legs.

Serves 4

6 cups chicken stock or water,
　or more as needed

⅔ cup short-grain or broken white rice

Salt and freshly ground white pepper

1 recipe Wok-Fried Frog Legs (page 316)

2 teaspoons sesame oil, for serving

2 green onions (white and green parts),
　sliced on the bias, for serving

Cilantro sprigs, for serving

In a deep saucepan, bring the stock to a boil over high heat. Rinse the rice two or three times in cold water, drain, and stir into the stock. Return to a boil, then reduce the heat to a simmer, cover, and gently simmer, stirring occasionally to prevent the rice from sticking to the bottom, until the rice is soft, porridge-like, and almost smooth, about 1½ hours. (**NOTE:** Chinese tradition calls for 3 hours, during which time the soup gets "ricier" in taste, thicker in texture, and, according to Chinese medicine, easier to digest because 3 hours brings the yin and yang into harmony.) You can adjust the cooking time and/or add hot water or additional stock to create the desired texture. Season with salt and pepper to taste.

Ladle into four bowls, top with a set of fried frog legs, a drizzle of sesame oil, green onions, and cilantro sprigs.

FRIED FROG LEGS

This simple recipe is an adaptation from Ada Boni's seminal book *Italian Regional Cooking*, and comes from the Piedmont region. The dish is called *rane fritte* in Italian.

Serves 12 as an appetizer

24 prepared frogs legs (pairs if small)

Fresh milk, as needed

3 cups dry white wine

1 small yellow onion, sliced

4 sprigs fresh Italian parsley

Large pinch of ground nutmeg

Sea salt and freshly ground pepper (preferably white)

1 cup all-purpose flour (preferably Wondra)

Vegetable oil, for frying

2 tablespoons chopped fresh Italian parsley, for serving

Lemon wedges, for serving

In a bowl, soak the frog legs in milk to cover for at least 1 hour. This will help draw out any impurities and whiten and swell the legs. Drain the legs, wash well, and pat dry.

In a large bowl, combine the wine, onion, parsley sprigs, nutmeg, and salt and pepper to taste. Add the frog legs, cover, and marinate in the refrigerator for 1 hour, turning two or three times. Drain and dry the legs, then dust them with flour, shaking off any excess.

In a deep, heavy saucepan, heat 1 inch of oil to 350°F. Fry the legs until nicely browned, working in batches if necessary. Sprinkle with chopped parsley and salt and pepper to taste, and serve with lemon wedges to squeeze over top.

WOK-FRIED FROG LEGS

4 sets prepared frog legs

2 teaspoons light soy sauce

2 teaspoons cornstarch

1 teaspoon Shaoxing wine or dry sherry

½ teaspoon salt

Vegetable oil, for stir-frying

1 tablespoon fine strips of peeled
   fresh ginger

Rinse the frog legs and pat dry. In a large bowl, whisk together the soy sauce, cornstarch, wine, salt, and 1 tablespoon water. Add the frog legs and turn to coat. Cover and marinate in the refrigerator at least 1 hour or until ready to use. Heat a wok over medium-high heat, and add a couple of teaspoons of oil. Add the frog legs and cook, turning, until nicely browned and just cooked through. Add the ginger, and cook for a few seconds more.

BIBLIOGRAPHY

Aidells, Bruce. *The Great Meat Cookbook*. Boston: Houghton Mifflin Harcourt, 2012.

Arora, David. *All That the Rain Promises and More . . . A Hip Pocket Guide to Western Mushrooms*. Berkeley, CA: Ten Speed Press, 1991.

Ash, John, and Sid Goldstein. *American Game Cooking: A Contemporary Guide to Preparing Farm-Raised Game Birds and Meats*. Reading, MA: Addison-Wesley, 1991.

Barash, Cathy Wilkinson. *Edible Flowers: From Garden to Palate*. Golden, CO: Fulcrum, 1993.

Bay Area Mycological Society. "*Lactarius rubidus* and *Lactarius rufulus*, the 'Candy Cap.'" Accessed July 2015. www.bayareamushrooms.org/mushroommonth/candy_cap.html.

Berry, Wendell. *What Are People For? Essays*. San Francisco: North Point Press, 1990.

Bison Producers of Alberta. "I Love Bison Consumer Website." Accessed June 2015, www.ilovebison.com (site discontinued).

Boni, Ada. *Italian Regional Cooking*. New York: Crescent Books, 1989.

Chin, Ava. *Eating Wildly: Foraging for Life, Love and the Perfect Meal*. New York: Simon and Schuster, 2014.

Cox, Jeff. *The Organic Cook's Bible: How to Select and Cook the Best Ingredients on the Market*. Hoboken, NJ: Wiley, 2006.

D'Artagnan LLC. D'Artagnan . . . the Blog. Accessed July 2015. blog.dartagnan.com.

Deane, Green. "Mesquite." Eat the Weeds and Other Things, Too (blog). Accessed July 2015. www.eattheweeds.com/mesquites-more-than-flavoring-its-food-2.

Duke, James A. *Handbook of Edible Weeds*. Boca Raton, FL: CRC Press, 2001.

Egerton, John. *Southern Food: At Home, on the Road*, in History. Chapel Hill: University of North Carolina Press, 1993.

Fisher, M. F. K. *An Alphabet for Gourmets*. San Francisco: North Point Press, 1989.

Forest Preserve District of Cook County. "Cattail Chemurgy." *Nature Bulletin* No. 416-A April 24, 1971. Open Source Ecology Wiki. Accessed July 2015. http://opensourceecology.org/wiki/Cattail_Chemurgy.

Foster, Sara, and Carolynn Carreño. *Fresh Every Day: More Great Recipes from Foster's Market*. New York: Clarkson Potter, 2005

Gibbons, Euell. *Stalking the Wild Asparagus*. 50th anniversary ed. Chambersburg: A. C. Hood, 2012. First published 1962 by D. McKay.

Gibbons, Euell, and the RuralVermont.com Development Team. "Did You Ever Eat a Pine Tree?" Accessed July 2015. www.ruralvermont.com/vermontweathervane/issues/winter/97012/eatpine.shtml.

Gladstar, Rosemary. *Rosemary Gladstar's Medicinal Herbs: A Beginner's Guide*. North Adams, MA: Storey, 2012.

Goldstein, Darra, ed. *The Oxford Companion to Sugar and Sweets*. New York: Oxford University Press, 2015.

Green, Connie, and Sarah Scott. *The Wild Table: Seasonal Foraged Food and Recipes*. New York: Viking Studio, 2010.

Hesser, Amanda. *The Essential New York Times Cookbook: Classic Recipes for a New Century*. New York: W. W. Norton, 2010.

Hormaza, José I. "The Pawpaw, a Forgotten North American Fruit Tree." *Arnoldia* 72, no. 1 (2014): 13-23.

Iowa Department of Natural Resources. "Wild Turkey." Accessed July 2015. www.iowadnr.gov.

Jackson, C. J., ed. *Seafood: How to Buy, Prepare, and Cook the Best Sustainable Fish and Seafood from Around the World*. 1st American ed. New York: DK Publishing, 2011.

Johnson, Paul. *Fish Forever: The Definitive Guide to Understanding, Selecting, and Preparing Healthy, Delicious, and Environmentally Sustainable Seafood*. Hoboken, NJ: Wiley, 2007.

Jung, Jim. "A Short Social History of the Wild Turkey." *The Waterman and Hill-Traveller's Companion*. Accessed July 2015. www.naturealmanac.com/archive/wild_turkey/wild_turkey.html.

Lincoff, Gary. *The Audubon Society Field Guide to North American Mushrooms*. New York: Knopf, 1981.

MacFarlane, Bill and MacFarlane Pheasants Inc. "MacFarlane Pheasants." Accessed July 2015. www.gamebirdexpert.com.

Mayes, Frances, and Edward Mayes. *The Tuscan Sun Cookbook: Recipes from Our Italian Kitchen*. New York: Clarkson Potter, 2012.

Mayor, John J., I. Lehr Brisbin, Jr., and Texas A&M AgriLife Research and Extension Center. "Distinguishing Feral Hogs from Introduced Wild Boar." Accessed July 2015. texnat.tamu.edu.

Meredith, Leda. *Northeast Foraging: 120 Wild and Flavorful Edibles from Beach Plums to Wineberries*. Portland, OR: Timber Press, 2014.

Moose Lake Wild Rice. "About Wild Rice." Accessed July 2015. www.mooselakewildrice.com/aboutwildrice.html.

Moullé, Jean-Pierre, and Denise Lurton Moullé. *French Roots: Two Cooks, Two Countries, and the Beautiful Food along the Way*. Berkeley, CA: Ten Speed Press, 2014.

Native Seeds/SEARCH. "Get Seeds, Get Educated, Get Involved." Accessed July 2015. www.nativeseeds.org.

New Mexico Piñon Nut Company. "FAQ & About Pinon Nuts." Accessed July 2015. www.pinonnuts.com.

North American Truffle Society. "The Truffle." Accessed July 2015. www.natruffling.org.

Oldways Preservation Trust Whole Grains Council. "Amaranth." Accessed July 2015. www.wholegrainscouncil.org.

Peterson, James. *Fish and Shellfish*. New York: William Morrow, 1996.

Rathbone, Olivia. *The Occidental Arts & Ecology Center Cookbook Fresh-from-the-Garden Recipes for Gatherings Large and Small*. White River Junction, VT: Chelsea Green, 2015.

Ruhlman, Michael, and Brian Polcyn. *Charcuterie: The Craft of Salting, Smoking, and Curing*. Rev. ed. New York: W. W. Norton, 2013.

Selengut, Becky. *Shroom: Mind-Bendingly Good Recipes for Cultivated and Wild Mushrooms*. Kansas City, MO: Andrews McMeel, 2014.

Shaw, Hank. *Hunt, Gather, Cook: Finding the Forgotten Feast*. Emmaus, PA: Rodale Press, 2011.

Slow Food USA. "Chiltepin Pepper." Accessed July 2015. www.slowfoodusa.org/ark-item/chiltepin-pepper.

Stein, Rick. *Rick Stein's Complete Seafood*. Berkeley, CA: Ten Speed Press, 2004.

Swanson, Heidi. *Super Natural Cooking: Five Ways to Incorporate Whole and Natural Foods into Your Cooking*. Berkeley, CA: Celestial Arts, 2007.

Taranto, John. "Best Wild Turkey Recipe Contest Winner: And the Winner Is . . . " Strut Zone (blog). November 20, 2012. Accessed June 2015. www.outdoorlife.com/blogs/newshound/2012/11/wild-turkey-recipe-contest-and-winner- . . . "

Tatum, Billy Joe. *Billy Joe Tatum's Wild Foods Cookbook and Field Guide*. Edited by Helen Witty. New York: Workman, 1976.

Thayer, Samuel. *Nature's Garden: A Guide to Identifying, Harvesting, and Preparing Edible Wild Plants*. Birchwood, WI: Forager's Harvest, 2010.

———. *The Forager's Harvest: A Guide to Identifying, Harvesting, and Preparing Edible Wild Plants*. Ogema, WI: Forager's Harvest, 2006.

"The Boar Hunter," Greg. "Javelina Verses Wild Boar." Accessed July 2015. www.huntwildpig.com/javelina-verses-wild-boar.

Wood, Rebecca Theurer. *The Splendid Grain: Robust, Inspired Recipes for Grains with Vegetables, Fish, Poultry, Meat, and Fruit*. New York: W. Morrow, 1997.

INDEX

Note: Page references in *italics* indicate photographs.